Competence in Social Work Practice

**Handbook of Theory for Practice Teachers
in Social Work**
Edited by Joyce Lishman
ISBN 1 85302 098 2

Community Care Practice and the Law
Michael Mandelstam with Belinda Schwehr
ISBN 1 85302 273 X

Learning and Teaching in Social Work
Edited by Margret Yelloly and Mary Henkel
ISBN 1 85302 237 3

Learning Through Child Observation
Mary Fawcett
ISBN 1 85302 288 8

Good Practice in Risk Assessment and Management 1
Edited by Jacki Pritchard and Hazel Kemshall
ISBN 1 85302 338 8

Good Practice in Risk Assessment and Management 2
Edited by Jacki Pritchard and Hazel Kemshall
ISBN 1 85302 441 4

Staff Supervision in a Turbulent Environment
Managing Process and Task in Front-line Services
Lynette Hughes and Paul Pengelly
ISBN 1 85302 327 2

Competence in Social Work Practice

A Practical Guide for Professionals

Edited by Kieran O'Hagan

Jessica Kingsley Publishers
London and Bristol, Pennsylvania

First published in the United Kingdom in 1996 by
Jessica Kingsley Publishers Ltd
116 Pentonville Road
London N1 9JB, England
and
1900 Frost Road, Suite 101
Bristol, PA 19007, U S A

Second impression 1997

Library of Congress Cataloging in Publication Data
Competence in Social Work Practice: A Practical Guide for Professionals/edited by
Kieran O'Hagan
p.cm.
Includes bibliogroaphical references and index
ISBN 1 85302 332 9 (alk. paper)
1. Social work education – Great Britian. 2. Social service – Great Britian. 3. Competency
based education – Great Britain.
I. O'Hagan, Kieran.
HV11.S5873 1996
361.3'2'0941–dc20
9541378
CIP

British Library Cataloguing in Publication Data
Competence in Social Work Practice: A Practical Guide for Professionals
I. O'Hagan, Kieran
361.32

ISBN 1 85302 332 9

Printed and Bound in Great Britain by
Athenaeum Press, Gateshead, Tyne and Wear

Contents

List of Tables

List of Figures

CHAPTER 1

Social Work Competence
An Historical Perspective

Kieran O'Hagan

'robbed of competence and her obsequious shadow, peace of mind'
(Wordsworth, *Excursions*)

Introduction

In September 1991 I joined the social work department of a UK university after more than twenty years' frontline social work practice in statutory agencies. My social work career had begun in an NSPCC office in Hackney in the early 1970s, and had ended in a principal case worker post in Leeds. During this long period in practice, I wrote a number of books and many articles for social work journals; I accepted numerous invitations to provide workshops and training courses throughout the UK and abroad; and I frequently contributed to in-service training in whichever authority I was working. All these experiences seemed a reasonable basis for confidence in becoming a full-time trainer.

Within weeks that confidence was severely dented. Social work training in the UK as a whole, was in turmoil. The reason: CCETSW's Paper 30 (1989 1991), a publication which heralded the new two-year Diploma in Social Work, replacing its predecessor, the much criticised Certificate of Qualification in Social Work. Paper 30 required all social work training programmes for the new Diploma to be designed, organised, implemented and resourced by Partnerships. These partnerships would consist of academic institutions (which previously had been mainly responsible for social work training) and many of the statutory and voluntary social services agencies in which those attaining the new Diploma would ultimately serve. Creating and establishing these Partnerships proved to be a monumental task.

No less formidable was the perception that *'competence'* was a major goal: social work training was to be competence-led, competence-dominated, and always competence-seeking. This term competence had never been adequately defined, yet it emerged as the most frequently used term in Paper 30 and in the Diploma course literature of the fledgling Partnerships. Whereas the emergence of Partnerships between academic institutions and social service agencies seemed a logical and necessary development and was widely supported (despite the predictable chaos and uncertainty in establishing those Partnerships), the increasing prominence of 'competence' as both a concept and an all consuming goal in social work training was a much more controversial matter. If the Government or CCETSW believed that Partnerships and the consequential agency influence on course development would facilitate understanding and acceptance of competence-led training, they were mistaken. The fact is that most practice teachers located in the agencies could no more easily assimilate the competence stipulations into their working practice and supervision of students than could their college-based Partnership colleagues. Nor did they feel any more enthusiastic about attempting to do so. Resistance to competence-led training was not simply a matter of resisting a lot more work revolving around a concept and goal which wasn't clearly understood; resistance was more firmly rooted in the conviction that competence-led and competence-dominated training was the antithesis of much social work practice and principles.

Had anything changed?
The first intake of the new Diploma students qualified in 1992 (there was much variation throughout the UK on programme accreditation and getting the Diploma course started). Despite the immensity of the change and the accompanying doubts and scepticism, the Diploma course eventually took root. The term 'competence' was, according to Kemshall (1993) to become the 'Social Work Training "watchword" of the nineties'. But there were rumblings of criticism in the air. This criticism had many sources: the primacy of the concept of competence has remained a subject of fierce criticism (Timms 1991; Jordon 1991); Paper 30s pervasive references to stipulations on anti-discriminatory and anti-racist practice became a subject of ridicule and of critical Government scrutiny (Amiel 1993; Phillips 1993); some writers still condemn CCETSW for its earlier reforms replacing 'specialism' with 'genericism' – regarding the revised Paper 30, therefore, as an irrelevance (Pinker 1994); and, not least, competence-led social work training made no impact upon the press's perceived level of incompetence in social work practice (Aldridge 1994). 'Had anything changed?' they might well have asked.

Since 1991, there has actually been an increase in the number of 'newsworthy' tragedies in which blame has once again been levelled against 'incompetent' social workers; these include a number of cases in which, (1) elderly people died in their own homes and were not found for weeks after; (2) mentally ill patients were prematurely discharged to a non existent Community Care where they assaulted (and sometimes murdered) innocent bystanders; (3) adolescents convicted for numerous offences were taken on Safari and other expeditions, an effort and expense failing lamentably (or laughably) to deter them from re-offending; and of course (4) the inexplicable actions of some child protection workers, seemingly continuing unrelentingly, and contributing to fatal and tragic outcomes (Bridge 1991; Brown 1991; Clyde 1993; Kirkwood 1993; Levy and Kahan 1991; Miller 1995; NCB 1993). How competence-led training so recently implemented was supposed to prevent such tragedies is not a question the media is likely to be concerned about; nor would they be interested in the multiplicity of complex underlying causes beyond the actions of individual workers. But it is important to acknowledge that the press's continuing criticism of social work and social workers did influence the course of events culminating in the publication of CCETSW's revised Paper 30 (1995).

The debate, debased

During the period between the final draft of the revised Paper 30 (Nov 1994) and publication, CCETSW reaped a harvest of praise and condemnation (not in equal measure, of course: the latter far outweighed the former). Two conspicuous features of the debate are motivating factors in writing this book. First, the debate has not been enlightening; many of those who oppose competence-led training and the revised Paper 30 have indulged in sweeping generalizations, unsubstantiated allegations, and blatant insults (e.g., Letters to *Community Care* regularly referred to CCETSW's efforts as 'monumental shambles' 'tortuous and torturing exercise'; 'spurious competencies' etc.). The interests of social work students, their wishes, convictions, and aspirations, were seemingly forgotten in this 'debate'. Timms (1986), in an inaugural lecture on the values and value of social work, cautioned: 'in considering any necessary criticism I hope we can avoid that temptation whereby the making of points is rendered delicious by the scoring thereof'. Timms (1991) later wrote what he himself referred to as a 'trenchant' satire on the original Paper 30. Such crticisms encourage students on the competence-led road on which so many had already commenced.

Second, the vast majority of trainers (including this author) have been trained and have practiced in an entirely different ethos; we have instinctively, intellectually, and morally resisted competence-led training; many of us have watched the debate from the sidelines, approving of the criticism of CCETSW and competences on the one hand, yet compelled to implement CCETSW's stipulations and competence-led training on the other. Little wonder students were puzzled at best and, at worst, realised that their enthusiasm and idealism were not being reciprocated by those whose hearts and minds were far distant from the new order of things. The charade has not ceased. No sooner was the finalised Paper 30 published (Spring, 1995) than a national conference was convened by a core of social worker educators who announced that:

Professional social work education... has reached the end of the road: stuck in a cul-de-sac of regulation and conformity that stifles innovation and change. (Committee for Social Work Education and Policy)

This book is written by a team of practitioners and college-based tutors who endorse the revised Paper 30, who believe that it is an improvement on the original, and that its *Practice Requirements and Evidence Indicators* are accessible, and applicable in practice. Yet considerable opposition to the concept of competence, and to competence-led social work training, remains. This chapter will later explore some of the major criticisms within that opposition, and respond. Before that, however, it will (1) briefly consider the origins of the word 'competence', (2) look at available definitions, (3) trace the development of competence-based education and training in general and (4) explore the meaning and emphasis given to the KNOWLEDGE VALUES AND SKILLS upon which competence is based.

Word origin

The word 'competence' and 'competent' derive from the Latin word *'competens'*, meaning 'be fit, proper or qualified' (*Oxford Library of Words and Phrases, Vol.III, Word Origins*). This meaning has been sustained more or less intact throughout the centuries. There are, however, two developments worth noting: first, from the fifteenth century, the words were increasingly used in a legal context; the 'fitness, properness and sufficiency of qualification' in the original definitions, referred to necessary standards in legal matters and legal processes. Second, in contrast, it was commonly used in a far more personal sense by poets and writers of the eighteenth and nineteenth century. Clarendon wrote of 'a competency of discretion and foresight'; Charlotte Bronte spoke of 'References as to character and competency'; Samuel Smiles advised one 'to retire upon a competency', and Wordsworth, in one of seven uses of the word in a mere 60 lines of his *Excursions*, added a spiritual dimension with his line: 'Heights which the soul is competent to gain'. More recently, Hodkinson and Issitt's (1995) collection of highly critical papers nevertheless concludes on competence: 'the resounding message is that it [competence] is a holistic concept, and any assessment framework which is developed needs to recognise this' (p.149). Those who believe that the word 'competence' is a newly invented, impersonal, value-less jargon, foisted upon social workers, and which is anathema to social work, need to think again.

Definition

Many may respond to the question: 'What is competence?' with: 'Doing a job well'. While this may be acceptable generally, and is not incompatible with its historical meanings, a little more precision is necessary. Hyland (1995) writes about the 'plethora of opinions about competence and its definitions' leading to 'considerable confusion and equivocation' (p.47). Available definitions of competence in American, UK, and Australian literature range from the unhelpful (e.g., 'it could be just about anything', Woodruffe, 1991) to the slightly more helpful (e.g., 'an underlying characteristic of a person in that it may be a motive, trait, skill, aspect of one's self-image, or social role or a body of knowledge which he or she uses', Boyatzis 1982) or, to the more assertive: 'Professional competence is the demonstration of knowledge, skills and values in the workplace to agreed standards' (NIPQETP 1992). Woodruffe (1991) mirrors the two contrasting developments in the evolution of the term, mentioned above, by differentiating between 'job-related areas of competence' and 'personal competence' (person related). Both of these developments are subsumed within the broader categories of 'managerial competence' and 'competence in vocational work'. The NCVQ (National Council for Vocational Qualifications), was instrumental in the development of competence-led training, and has produced a definition more comprehensive than most:

> Competence is a wide concept which embodies the ability to transfer skills and knowledge to new situations within the occupational area. It encompasses the organisation and planning of work, innovation and coping with non-routine activities. It includes those qualities of personal effectiveness that are required in the workplace to deal with co-workers, managers and customers. (NCVQ 1988)

The revised Paper 30 adds an entirely different perspective on competence; rather than explanatory definitions as in the above, i.e., *competence is a wide concept embodying... etc. a demonstration of knowledge values and skills... etc.*, it designates six very common social work tasks as core competences in themselves. These are:

- communicate and engage
- promote and enable
- assess and plan
- intervene and provide services
- work in organisations
- develop professional competence.

These tasks have such wide applicability that it may have been more intelligent to refer to them as 'areas of competence'. Paper 30 further stipulates that in the unique context of social work practice, these core competences stem from, and can only be validated by an application of KNOWLEDGE VALUES AND SKILLS. What precisely does this mean in social work training?

Everyone can *communicate and engage* to some extent in everyday life. In social work practice, the task of communicating and engaging is often more complex and hazardous than it is in everyday life. The student on practice placement attempting to *communicate and engage* with particular clients presenting particular problems should be informed by relevant literature and research about both client and problem (KNOWLEDGE); she must be aware of, and be sensitive and responsive to the ethical issues arising (VALUES); and, she must demonstrate reason and discernment in whatever responses and actions she takes (SKILLS). Similarly, with each of the remaining five competences. Hodkinson and Issitt (1995) write:

> The first conceptualization of holism concerns the integration of knowledge and understanding, values and skills, that reside within the practitioner. (p.149)

Origins of competence-based education and training
THEORETICAL ORIGINS
Competence-based education and training (CBET) has its origins in behaviourism and functional analysis, two theoretical orientations which were popular in the 1960s and 1970s. Melton (1994) traces the development of competency-based teacher education in the USA, from the 1960s onwards. He links this development with the 'behaviorable objectives' movement, the central goal of which was to 'identify what individuals should ultimately be able to do' (p.286). Functional analysis has an identical goal, and was adopted by the department of employment in 1991 in standardising all NCVQ qualifications (Burton and Goudge 1992). Jeffrey Greenwood, Chair of CCETSW, and Daphne Statham, Director of the National Institute of Social Work, have both publicly acknowledged that the revised Paper 30 derives in large measure from functional analysis (Letters, *Community Care* 1994). An earlier social worker advocate of functional analysis (Smalley 1967) wrote: 'The use of agency function and function in professional role gives focus, content, and direction to social work processes' and, 'assures accountability to society and agency' (p.151). The competence-based approach (whatever its debt to functional analysis) specifically addressed the task of assessing and/or measuring what individuals do in a variety of workplaces. It identified areas of competence and established performance criteria.

ORGANISATIONAL ORIGINS
The National Council for Vocational Qualifications (NCVQ) was set up 1986, with a mandate to develop a competence-based system for defining and assessing standards for all occupations. This was partly in response to the realisation that Britain desperately lagged behind in the quality and usefulness of further education and training generally, and partly because of the 'qualifications jungle' then in existence (Hodkinson 1995). It is important to remember at this point that NCVQ set out to establish an employer-led, workplace-located system, physically and psychologically distant from the traditional academic

training centres. But its rapid growth and establishment, due in the main to enthusiastic Government support and encouragement, has ensured its increasing influence over all kinds of training bodies, including CCETSW (Hyland 1995).

NCVQ created Industrial Lead Bodies (ILB) for each occupational area. Each ILB had representatives from employers and employees. The ILB for the caring professions became known as the Care Sector Consortium (1992). CCETSW is a member of the Care Sector Consortium. This consortium monitors the development of competence-based occupational standards in Health and Personal Social Services, including statutory, voluntary and private care agencies. All occupational standards development programmes in any of the care agencies must be approved by the Care Sector Consortium. Key jobs and tasks have been identified within care provision generally, for example, the job of providing hands-on care to patients, residents, or clients; the task of enabling and promoting clients' independence. Each task has been divided into units (of competence). Each unit is further divided into elements which describe precisely what care workers should be doing. Examples (i.e., performance criteria) are usually provided. Ethics are crucial in care provision, and this is reflected in the fact that 'values' has been given the status of a separate unit of competence (another indication of the considerable licence taken in the use of the word 'competence'). The important point, however, is that assessors of all care training programmes expect to see evidence that the maintenance of values (such as upholding individual rights, personal beliefs and identity, promoting anti-discriminatory practice, etc.) has been manifest throughout the demonstration of each unit of competence; nowhere is this more obvious than in the professional training of social workers, based upon CCETSW's revised Paper 30.

POLITICAL AND IDEOLOGICAL ORIGINS

All these developments towards competence-based education and training were fuelled in a political and ideological context in which a significant shift occurred in the public service industries, namely, away from a predominantly 'role' culture to that of task/performance (and performance-monitoring) culture. Personal responsibility and accountability emerged as central tenets underpinning competence-led training. A new breed of 'manager' was necessary to implement this training (writers unanimously believe that CBET is primarily in the interests of managers and employers, e.g., Field 1995; Hodkinson 1995; Hyland 1995; Melton 1994). Margaret Thatcher perceived the welfare state and the professionals and administrators who ran it as unenterprising and incompetent. She believed the higher education system (including and in particular social work education and training) sustained this incompetence; it became a prime target in an overall strategy aimed towards drastically increasing the influence of a new, highly competitive, enterprising workplace, upon the exclusive academic locations from which educational and welfare professionals emerged. Cannan (1994) wrote:

School teachers' and social workers' theories and practices have been
repeatedly scorned by Government ministers – because they apparently
do not promote enterprising qualities in their pupils and clients or
demonstrate them in their own professional practice or politics. (p.11)

Knowledge Values and Skills

In the available definitions of competence it is interesting to note the location
and emphasis given to knowledge, skills and in particular, values. The importance of these varies enormously throughout commerce, industry, and vocational work. 'Values' may not be as significant in training, qualifying, and
practicing in, for example, bricklaying, as they are in training, qualifying and
practicing in nursing care for people with learning difficulties (thus the
importance attached to Values by the Care Sector Consortium [1992] and by
CCETSW in the original and revised Paper 30). Knowledge and skills may vary
in importance too; many employers are not likely to demand to know the
knowledge and skills base of a workforce which (however it may do so) always
produces sufficient quantity and quality of the desired goods. This is not the
case in social work, in which knowledge values and skills are a crucial goal in
training, and remain so in practice. They are the foundation from which
competences arise, a constant reference point (see Figure 1.1) helping to
determine the appropriateness of chosen competences, and enabling those
chosen competences to be verified. In CCETSW's own words:

> It is only practice which is founded on values, carried out in a skilled
> manner and informed by knowledge, critical analysis and reflection,
> which is competent practice. (CCETSW Paper 30, revised edition,
> 1995, p.3)

There are many reasons why knowledge values and skills are of paramount
importance, but at this stage we may concern ourselves only with the most
obvious: social work is complex and hazardous, and part of the origin of tragic
outcome of so much social work action of the past is nearly always traceable
to a lack of knowledge values and skills, or, an inability to apply them. The
knowledge base, in particular, is worthy of further comment.

Knowledge

The knowledge underpinning social work practice derives from many different
sources. Competent practice will depend upon knowledge of law, social policy,
philosophy (ethics), sociology, social administration, organisational policies
procedures and guidelines, numerous theories, differing social work methods
(or disciplines as they may sometimes be called; e.g., behaviourism, family
therapy, psychodynamics, mediation, groupwork therapy). All of these compo-

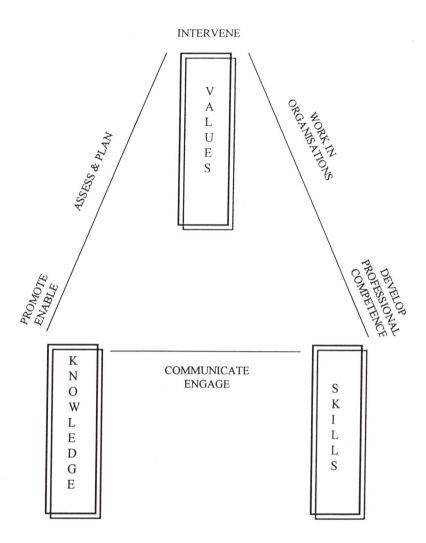

Figure 1.1 Pillars of social work competence

nents of knowledge are self-explanatory, with the exception of theory; Mitchell (1975) says it is:

> one of the most misused and misleading terms… There is a very loose use of the term *theory* to mean that part of the study of a subject which is not practical. In the training of social workers *theory* is often contrasted with *practical work*, but what is meant here is merely the more academic aspects of a course of instruction. (p.211)

Understanding theory

Thus, students are led to believe that convenient academic tools such as 'definitions' 'concepts' 'frameworks' 'categorizations' 'tables' 'grids' and 'figures' are all theories, and they studiously label them as such in written assignments and practice portfolios. A 'definition' is the descriptive, explanatory and most precise meaning given to any subject. A 'concept' is nothing more or less than an idea or general notion about something; the idea may be original or not; concepts can, however, be used as building blocks in the construction of meaning. A 'framework' is a boundary within which one can impose order and sense upon something which otherwise may appear chaotic and unmanageable. Categorizations, tables and grids and figures are all frameworks; they appear regularly throughout this text, performing the same function as frameworks in differing ways. None of these common academic tools, of themselves, constitute theory, yet the exposition and application of theory may depend upon the use of any of them. Figure 1.1 above may justifiably be referred to both as a framework and a concept, illustrating and emphasising the paramountcy of KNOWLEDGE, VALUES AND SKILLS in social work. But it is not a theory.

The two most important and necessary functions of theory are enhancing understanding and enabling one to predict process and/or outcome. Psychoanalysis, crisis intervention, behaviourism, systemic and structural family therapy, are all methods or disciplines dependent upon theories, which, for those who use them, enhance understanding of the problem they encounter, and enable the users to predict outcome of the various processes within that problem (e.g., deteriorating relationships, intensifying neurosis, the social and psychological impact of poverty and stigma). Theory also enables its advocates to formulate strategies of intervention and articulate goals. It is obvious therefore, that theory is not (as some practitioners may believe) divorced from reality; rather, it consists of concepts and propositions about reality. Theory is not rigid or inhibiting; rather, it demands vision and imagination. In approaching the complexities and dilemmas of social work within the framework of a theory, social workers add a dimension to their work which observation, rules and guidelines, policies and procedures cannot themselves provide. Theory often leads to greater insights. It is an instrument by which social workers can construct more comprehensive and effective intervention stratergies, and predict outcome with more confidence.

Types and uses of knowledge

The boundless nature of the social work knowledge base has compelled social work writers (e.g. Timms 1991) to attempt to categorize it. Rosen (1994) concentrates upon the purpose for which knowledge is to be used, emphasising the necessity of continuously testing all social work knowledge. He carried out research on the use of knowledge in social work practice. There was almost no use made of research-based knowledge. Only 24 per cent of practice decisions made were based upon theoretical rationales. The most common form of knowledge which *was* used was that of (1) agency policy and procedure, invariably used for (justifying or rationalising) intervention; (2) value-based normative assertions (i.e., based upon common assumptions or convictions as distinct from social work values). Examples of these value-based assertions may be that children should always be placed in a family; or, elderly people should never be exposed to any risk. Rosen refers to these assertions as 'instrumental values' and writes:

> By valuating a preposition [i.e., making it sound like an expression of inherently desirable, unquestionably ethical, social work values] one transforms it from the realm of a hypothesis into a categorical assertion, inherently and universally correct and not subject to empirical validation or limitation on generalizability. (p.563)

Using these value-based assertions is much easier and a great deal more common than embarking upon the more 'deliberate and difficult process of applying scientific knowledge prepositions' (p.564). A similar conclusion was reached by Sommerfield and Hughes (1987) in their research into health professionals' assessment of the parenting potential of pregnant mothers: professional criteria and all the knowledge upon which it was based was largely discarded in favour of 'subjective judgements' and personal experiences. Nissim and Simm (1994) is a rare example of research findings (on the subject of fostering) being fully implemented in practice with (predictable) satisfactory results.

The extent to which crucial components of the knowledge base are often forgotten by professionals, makes CCETSW's statement particularly welcome:

> Qualifying social workers and probation officers must take a rigorous approach to the acquisition of knowledge, and be able to select and apply it to practice. They must be able to conceptualise, reflect, analyse and critically evaluate both underpinning knowledge and their own practice. They must be strategic thinkers, able to weigh up the advantages and disadvantages of proposals, and to anticipate the possible consequences of decisions or actions. (Revised Paper 30, 1995)

Values

Perceptions of the ethical base have advanced significantly from the time when students were led to believe that the issue of values was uncomplicated and conflict-free. There is in fact no more contentious issue in social work than values, a fact implicitly acknowledged in CCETSW's statement on the subject, in which it emphasises 'the complexities of competing rights and demands'.

This whole statement (p.4, to be read and reflected upon in its entirety) is a significant improvement on the stipulations on values in the original Paper 30, which provoked a scathing criticism in Timms (1989). Rosen (1994) makes an interesting distinction between values and knowledge:

> Values delineate a profession's conception of the preferred human conditions and serve as a basis and a reference point for the profession's agenda and service goals. Values are formulated and evolve through social and political thought, ideologies, and dialectic processes. Knowledge consists of those statements, assertions, or principles that contribute to the profession's understanding of its subject matter. (p.562)

The point made in the previous section about professionals sometimes confusing values with value laden assumptions cannot be over-emphasised. Abuses in child protection work, and abuses against women in particular, often stem from convictions, or assumptions, or traditional beliefs mistakenly interpreted as values (O'Hagan and Dillenburger 1995). Braye and Preston-Shoot (1995) link value assumptions with 'workers' own personal histories and characteristics' which can lead to 'very negative attitudes, judgementalism and discriminatory behaviour' amongst care staff working with Aids sufferers and elderly people.

Skills

The words 'skills' 'competence' 'practice' and 'techniques' are often wrongly used synonymously. Skills is commonly used to describe some type of action. The word is derived from the Old Norse term *skil* meaning 'distinction, discernment and knowledge'; the verb *skila* means: 'give reason for, expound, decide'. The Middle English word *skilful* meant: 'endowed with reason'. In the seventeenth century the word *skill* meant 'to have discrimination or knowledge especially in a specified manner'. This intellectual quality is still evident in the present-day dictionary meaning, though the complete definition is far more diffuse: *practical knowledge in combination with ability... cleverness, expertise... knowledge or understanding of something...* We will assume that whoever decided that skills should be one of the three foundational pillars of social work competences was well aware of the more precise definition given to the original word. In which case it was a sound decision.

Criticisms of competence-based education and training

Before considering criticisms of competence-led social work training, it is instructive to look at some of the criticisms of competence-based education and training (CBET) in general, and the NVQ system from which it derives. Hyland's (1995) criticism is perhaps the most severe, referring to CBET as 'viciously reductionist' in its implementation. He lauds Collins (1991) who calls for a 'concerted and vigorous resistance to this destructive approach to education and training' (p.44). Collins later specifies on CBET: 'a narrow technicist approach to education which defines knowledge in the light of bureaucratic and corporate needs' (p.45). Hyland's primary object of criticism however, is the behavioural base of CBET. He sees behaviourism as an out-dated 'minimalist and impoverished conception of human thought and action' which fails to 'account adequately for key aspects of human reasoning, understanding and learning' (p.50). He seeks a return to experiential learning theory, with its 'distinctive emphases upon learning as a continuous process... learning as the creation of knowledge' (p.52). This contrasts starkly with CBET which Hyland and others see as nothing more than a production line. Hodkinson (1995) identifies the underlying problem: 'For NCVQ...' knowledge and understanding 'are clearly subservient' to performance.

Melton (1994) emphasises that CBET is a development devised primarily in the interests of employers and their organisations and companies. Hodkinson (1995) writes about 'the current rampant managerialism upon which NCVQ conceptions of competence are based' and reminds us that the Government's 'insistence that funded courses must use the NCVQ competence structure reinforces the managerial approach' (p.61). Hodkinson and Issitt (1995) quote from Gibson (1986): 'Instrumental rationality [a core tenet of the new managerialism] is concerned with method and efficiency rather than with purposes... it is the divorce of fact from value and the preference in that divorce for fact' (Gibson 1986, p.7). Output, the quality of output, and, the measurement of output, are primary goals in managerial technical rationality.

CBET is perceived as a mechanistic, compartmentalised system incompatible with the altruism and sense of values of students entering health, welfare and education professions. Hodkinson (1995) interprets professional growth and independence as 'empowerment' a holistic concept consisting of personal effectiveness, critical autonomy, and community. The latter two components are distinctly lacking in much CBET, and in its parent, NVQ. 'Critical autonomy' refers to the worker's capacity for critical thinking about the context in which the work takes place, its purpose, and the values underpinning it: 'It is this dimension of empowerment which distinguishes the professional from the technician' (p.64). The 'community' component of professional empowerment refers to the collaborative and collective aspects of work. Health, welfare and educational professionals are permanently collaborating within their own team collectives and within multi-disciplinary systems necessary for serving clients. Nowhere is this more important than in child protection work (Jones 1995). But NVQs distinctly focus on individual performance. Responsibility for all professional activity rests with the 'isolated teacher or social worker'; power inequalities and micro political struggles which impact upon the quality of service, are ignored. Hodkinson (1995) believes this 'deflects from problems of context and makes it easy to blame the individual professional for any short-comings in the system' (p.61).

Commentary on criticisms of CBET

Some of these opinions reappear in specific criticisms of competence-led social work training (see below); others simply do not apply. For example, it would be difficult to imagine a social work student undergoing training without a strong sense of 'community', a realisation that social work fundamentally depends upon team cohesion and harmony, multi-disciplinary collaboration, and a pervasive consciousness of the societal and political contexts in which work is carried out. Most social work students have acquired this before they commence training. Social work trainers continually strive to heighten aware-ness of this reality, and no training partnership could afford to interpret or implement competence-led social work training in a way which didn't facilitate them doing so. Trainers are well aware of the behavioural origins of CBET. Behaviourism has never been widely endorsed in social work training, and trainers are alert to and critical of its more extreme manifestations in the competence-led social work training being imposed upon them. We will now address the more specific criticisms of that training, and provide a response to each of them.

Competence-led social-work training: the main criticisms

1.   Competence-led social work training has narrowed the assessment process to a 'tick-box' exercise. Students become obsessed with finding work enabling them to produce evidence for each unit of competence; in other words it is a 'reductionist' approach which ignores the holistic and dynamic complexity of social work and assumes that overall competence is the sum total of achieved competences (Cannon 1994; Hodkinson 1995; Hyland 1995, Timms 1991).

Response: The revised Paper 30 should ensure that Partnerships do not once again recreate the impression of a tick-box system. Its emphasis upon the necessity of knowledge, values and skills underpinning competence is pervasive and unmistakable. It demands an 'holistic approach...' and a depth of knowl-edge, values and skills which enable students to cope with novel situations and problems. Hodkinson (1995) is one of the critics referred to above; yet he also sees benefit in 'some deconstruction of the role by competence attributes' for 'getting to grips with the complexity of teaching or social work' (p.66).

2.   Platt (1994) expresses concern about the dilution of social work values in competence-led training. Cannon (1994) argues *values* will also be subjected to the same reductionist tendencies, and

'appropriate', simplistic, one-dimensional value statements will be imposed upon students, demanding that they see and express values strictly in measurable, behavioural terms: 'Ideals – promoting justice, helping and empowering individuals, families and communities, and a belief in personal and professional effectiveness in so doing, seem remote to students assessed in narrow, job-focused competences' (Cannon 1994, p.13). More specifically, the real interests and needs of the client are relegated to a level of importance below the all-consuming preoccupation with providing evidence of competence; the client becomes a mere object of potential gain along the competence route to qualification.

Response: The last point in this criticism is a potential danger in any social work training assessment system, but there is no evidence to suggest that it is a prevalent outcome in competence-led social work training. On the contrary, it is such an obvious and blatant abuse of training principles and goals that it would be quickly exposed and eradicated. Most students, tutors and practice teachers (PTs), for example, saw the danger of an unyielding demand to provide evidence of competence in anti-racist practice in geographical or work settings where it was simply impossible to do so. Many students posed the rhetorical question: 'Do we invent black clients then... do we just wait, hoping some black client will come along enabling me to demonstrate a competence...?'

There is nothing 'one dimensional' or 'simplistic' about the revised Paper 30s statements on the purpose and values of social work. They are both challenging and realistic. Anyone involved in teaching social work will know that the ethical–philosophical debate is alive and well, in class discussion, practice placements, portfolios and written assignments. If anything, the debate has intensified, partly as a consequence of heightened awareness, on the part of students, of ethical issues, and partly as a result of the ceaseless flow of new social welfare and criminal justice legislation (much of it oppressive) and the dramatic increase in poverty, homelessness, child abuse referrals, mental illness, divorce, one parent families, and reconstituted families. Issues such as abortion, sexuality, and euthanasia also ensure lively debate stemming from the diverse value systems amongst each yearly intake of students.

3.   Kemshall (1993) casts doubt on the objectivity of assessment in competence led social work training: 'Assessment is overladen with values, and attempts to ground it in direct evidence, namely observation, can be problematic. Direct evidence is neither very direct, or evidence in any secure objective sense' (p.42).

Response: The importance of observation in social work cannot be overstated (i.e., *observation* in its widest sense, seeing, hearing, perceiving). It is the most basic, necessary, and valuable asset of trainers, students, and qualified workers alike. If in training the student's observations are unduly subjective, it is the responsibility of the practice teacher and tutor to enlighten the student. If the PT's assessment of the student appears to be unduly subjective, there are a number of safeguards within training programmes: the tripartite meetings between student, PT and tutor; the Practice Assessment panel's review of the PT's validation of the evidence; the Examination Board, including external examiners.

There is another potentially advantageous feature of competence-led training, not usually recognised, yet most pertinent to the issue of subjective influences: placements seldom run smoothly; personalities sometimes conflict and values bases may be incompatible. In previous training systems, PTs had enormous discretion and power; they could respond in an authoritarian, challenging, even threatening way. Assessment of the student, their success or failure, depended wholly upon the PT's report. Whatever challenges competence-led training poses, its concentration on evidence certainly minimises the possibilities of the abuse of power within the tutor, student, and PT relationship. Finally, despite highlighting the risk of atomising and fragmenting the assessment process in competence led training, Hodkinson (1995) concludes 'it is possible that careful use of competence attributes might inform a more holistic assessment judgement'.

4.   'the notion of competency as translated into performance indicators inadequately describe what occurs in an encounter either between service users and workers, or between workers and those assessing their competence' (Braye and Preston-Shoot 1995, p.66). A similar point is made by Jones (1995) who provides a brilliant example of the 'whole person in action' in a complex child protection case (albeit a post-qualifying student). How can the breaking down of this impressive work into constituent parts 'accurately demonstrate the interaction of skills, abilities, experience, intuition and knowledge'? (p.88).

Response: This may be true: a performance indicator (or *Evidence indicator* as it is referred to in Paper 30) may describe nothing at all. But the workers' evidence may be written in such a way (better still, it may be an actual transcript) that it graphically and unmistakably conveys precisely what occurs in the encounter between worker and client. Jones (1995) actually provides the student's written evidence for the case in question. It is an excellent piece of writing, aptly conveying the nature and 'wholeness' of her achievement. Similarly with what occurs between workers and those assessing them; if 'encounters' between them are pertinent to the workers' professional development (Core competence: *Develop professional competence*) then the language can be found to describe it. Competence-led social work training and practice should not be perceived as something inhibiting artistry and expertise; nor should criticism of such training and practice conveniently conceal an inability to evidence artistry and expertise. Throughout this book there are examples of Paper 30 *Evidence Indicators* being presented in such a way as to capture the 'tensions and complexities' arising from the worker–clients interactions and relationships.

5.   Kemshall's critique concentrates upon the effects of subjective inference and interpretation in 'observing' competences (see No. 3 above) with particular reference to anti-racist and anti discriminatory practice. This critique is based on Berger and Luckmann's (1967) concept of a 'commonsense knowledge world of typifications', shaped by our own values and perceptions. Kemshall contends that within social work agencies, the predominent commonsense typifications upon which assessment of competences is based have been formulated and consolidated by the values and perceptions of white males. Assessors are likely to be white males. Their expectations of the professional worker are restricted to that of white middle class professional workers. Qualities such as confidence, innovation, initiative-taking, reflective analysis, articulation, etc. will be perceived highly in performance criteria; differing yet unique qualities of black people may be misinterpreted, undervalued, reclassed under a 'white assessment scheme which may value the virtues of authority and assertion above those of humility and self-effacement... at present the competences are intrinsically bound up with white values and as such they are white competences' (p.42). Kemshall's paper is often quoted by critics who perceive competence-led training as lacking an anti-discriminatory, anti-racist, equal opportunities perspective. Issitt (1995) asks: 'does the inevitably individualistic, technically rational response perpetuate structural inequalities while giving an illusion of tackling oppression?' (p.83).

Response: Representatives of ethnic communities, within the social work profession, have expressed much dissatisfaction and apprehension with the revision of Paper 30. It is generally acknowledged that requirements in respect of racist and anti-discriminatory practice are not as pervasive and emphatic as they were in the original. A significant body of opinion within social work suggests that they were too emphatic and pervasive, and ultimately self-defeating. Whether this is the case or not, Statham and Carroll's (1994) response to the allegation that race issues were ignored in the consultations preceding publication of the revised Paper 30 is impressive (as two of the architects of revised Paper 30, it would need to be). As for the above critique, it is seriously outdated, without supportive research, and possibly condescending if not insulting to many aspiring black students. Issitt's criticism is more difficult to refute. But it was obviously written before publication of the revised Paper 30.

She believes, rightly, that the promotion of equal opportunity necessitates 'group' rather than individual competence. The core competence of *Work in Organisations* is accompanied by many examples of evidence indicators: most of these necessitate not just working in groups, but attempting to influence the organisational collective of which the student is a part towards upholding clients' rights, and combating discriminatory and oppressive practice.

The challenge of competence

Literally thousands of social work publications have been produced in the last three decades, the vast majority of them aimed towards equipping social workers with knowledge, values and skills. Most social work students today, however, will testify that the acquisition of knowledge, values and skills is not their main difficulty. Rather, it is identifying opportunities on placement in which the tasks of fulfilling CCETSW's new *Practice Requirements* and pinpointing the *Evidence Indicators* can be accomplished. These are somewhat more complex tasks, often the source of acute anxiety and frustration in student and practice teacher alike. 'Doing the job' is no longer the sole prerequisite for qualification; how one thinks about the job, prepares for it, applies and integrates the knowledge, values and skills normally required for it, demonstrates it, accumulates and displays the evidence for it – these are the essential tasks students are now expected to carry out.

At first sight, this looks a daunting task. Many students welcome the challenge of action and shrivel at the prospect of proving their actions in a practice portfolio. The plethora of social work literature available to them is of little comfort. Thus the principal purpose in writing this book: to give direction and example in responding to the new Paper 30. This is not a textbook aiming to give comprehensive exploration of any particular social work field of activity; its focus is narrower: recreating social work practice to enable students to fulfill the *Practice requirements* and provide the *Evidence Indicators* of each of the six core competences. Such language (i.e., 'practice requirements', 'evidence indicators', 'competences', etc.) is not likely to inspire students, but they will discover very quickly that it is a language with which they must become knowledgeable and confident. This book should make the task easier, not because such terminology is used frequently, but, more interestingly, it is frequently used and applied to actual cases.

Social work students seldom lack enthusiasm for practice, and the amount of practice they carry out often goes far beyond what is expected of them. But they still carry a burdensome legacy: the *tendency to act* far more than to *think about their actions*. It is surprising how many social workers and aspiring students who engage in so much sound practice, are stumped when asked to recount the detail and the benefits of that practice. Too much of what they do is taken for granted, goes unrecorded, is quickly forgotten about. The most encouraging consequence of CCETSW's new paper is that it compels students to think positively: it facilitates their realisation and acknowledgement that even the smallest action or gesture (should it stem from or be compatible with the appropriate knowledge, values and skills) will probably constitute an evidence indicator, another step towards fulfilling the practice requirement of a particular competence.

Each chapter of the book revolves around a particular case within a particular field of practice. In most of the chapters a practice teacher delegates responsibility for each case (or, an appropriate section of it) to a student. The cases and students have all been heavily anonymised. Each chapter charts the progress of the student in responding to some of the challenges in the case. In some chapters, the student's work is longterm, necessitating numerous face-to-face contacts with clients and other professionals; in other chapters, the work is relatively brief, and or reflective, based upon minimum encounter with client. This underscores the scope for diversity in choosing work which will provide evidence of competence, and the potential for finding evidence in a whole array of work experiences. Some of the cases enable the worker to fulfil requirements partially and provide evidence indicators for *all* the six core competences; other cases do not. It is worth emphasising that no single piece of work in any of these chapters would, of itself, constitute a successful practice portfolio; but each certainly can make a contribution to the contents of a practice portfolio. To the experienced, competent and confident practitioner, some of these students may appear slow of action, too cautious, too contemplative, their achievement limited; and, their commentary and provision of evidence may appear too detailed; the clients they are serving, and the students and newly qualified practitioners who may follow in their footsteps, probably will not think so.

In Chapter 2, Fawcett and Lewis present a formidable yet common challenge to the student: mediation between parents in conflict. A soaring divorce rate and the consequential trauma endured by countless individual parents and children, ensure even greater demand for competence in *conciliation*. The experiences of the student are meticulously recorded from the time of referral, through preparation, introductions, difficult and problematic interviews with both parents, to resolution.

In Chapter 3, Gibson and Turtle provide insight into student competence in an adolescent residential setting. Their introduction includes a comprehensive review of the development of residential care, particularly in the aftermath of recent highly publicised scandals. They demonstrate not just the need and the value of residential care for particular children, but also the abundant opportunities for students to considerably enhance the lives of those children through competent and imaginative residential practice.

Campbell develops a broad knowledge base in his analysis of competence in mental health social work in Chapter 4. He guides the reader and student given the responsibility of providing a social work service to a woman diagnosed as schizophrenic. The case is complex and longterm, and provides the opportunity to fulfil some of the practice requirements for all the core competences.

Chapters 5 and 6 focus on child protection. Given the limitations which many agencies impose on students with regard to the amount of responsibility they may carry in child protection work, these two chapters cover only the first and second phase of a particular child protection case. O'Hagan demonstrates that even in the very common, seemingly uncomplicated task of referral taking, the achievement of competence necessitates the integration and application of substantial knowledge, values and skills. Kelly takes the same case beyond the referral phase, and provides a contrasting, mainly reflective piece of work in which the student, relying upon current literature and research, seeks to establish the degree of risk to which the children may be exposed.

In Chapter 7 McLaughlin tackles some of the challenges arising within health care social work; more specifically, he details a case in which an elderly man suffers a stroke, and the hospital-based student attempts to provide a competent service to both patient and family.

Chapter 8 contains Heery's detailed account of a probation student attempting to bring about change in the life of a petty offender. Here, as always, competence stems from the integration and application of specialized knowledge, values and skills; but it is also obvious in this case that competence could not have been achieved without the student's faith in the essential goodness and potential for betterment in her client.

Waring, in Chapter 9, concentrates on a student's efforts in helping the parents of a child with learning difficulty face up to the consequences of the father's serious illness; respite care is an obvious possibility in alleviating the parents of some of their burden, but resistance is strong. In this situation competence is mainly manifest through patience, empathy and sensitivity; but attention is also given to the organisational, legal, and ethical imperatives.

In Chapter 10 Iwaniec's student is given the responsibility of *assessment* in a case of a child failing to thrive. Naturally, much of the work centres upon the parents. The achievement of competence in this case is located primarily in the method of assessment; comprehensive assessment frameworks ensure that the treatment plan will be soundly based.

Pinkerton and Houston provide an imaginary case in Chapter 11, to demonstrate that CCETSW's new requirements are compatible with many of the key principles and regulations of the 1989 Children Act. Their student is based in a community work placement. He seeks to implement some of the Act's principles regarding partnership and empowerment amongst a group of parents who have been involved with social services departments over a long period of time. Imaginary the case may be, but the challenges and obstacles the student confronts are highly realistic.

Conclusion

I began this chapter by reflecting on the impact of competence-led social work training on students, tutors and practice teachers, and ended it by addressing criticisms which have accumulated along the way. It is quite evident now that some of the criticisms are unjustified, and are based upon (1) unawareness of the meaning and origins of the concept of competence; (2) a long-standing antipathy towards CCETSW; (3) a knee-jerk reaction to some of the jargon associated with competence-based education and training (CBET): (4) a failure to differentiate between competence-led social work training and CBET in general; (5) perceiving competence-led training as nothing more than another manifestation of Thatcherite ideology. Thatcherism produced a social, economic, and educational revolution, much of which has been very painful (and much of which is already proving to be disastrously costly in terms of social cohesion, and the body politic as a whole); but some writers have perceived competence-led social work training only in the context of that pain and cost, seeing it as little more than a parallel action alongside (or as a consequence of) the dismantling of the educational system and the health service, the decimation of trade unions; the reorientation of a whole society around the threat-laden demand to justify one's job, one's existence, purely in monetary terms.

Cannon (1994) suggests that some critics see even more: that all these developments in competence-led training are a manifestation of the Thatcherite goal of socialising and controlling social workers and social work. It is precisely perceptions like these which have significantly impeded social work training since the original Paper 30 was published. Social work has *not* been subjected to the imposition of a singularly ruthless stipulation that 'competence' is the be all and end all of training (as may be the case for many other occupations); on the contrary, social work training, and the revised Paper 30 upon which it is based, repeatedly stress that social work competence can only stem from certain KNOWLEDGE, VALUES AND SKILLS, and that the application of such must be demonstrated. It is the KNOWLEDGE VALUES AND SKILLS underpinning competence, rather than the achievement of competence itself, which will be the focal point of assessment. And yet, as the extracts from Paper 30 clearly imply, underpinning competence is not the only purpose of knowledge and understanding: social workers must be able to:

> conceptualise, reflect, analyse and critically evaluate both underpinning knowledge and practice. They must be strategic thinkers, able to weigh up the advantages and disadvantages of proposals, and to anticipate the possible consequences of decisions or actions.

The point has already been made that many of the criticisms were written before the revised Paper 30 was published; and indeed, some of the criticisms were made in a context other than social work training. For these reasons alone, the revised Paper, with all its imperfections, should be carefully read, and those involved in social work training should at least attempt to make it work, disregarding the often heated, largely ill-informed, debate which has preceded it. It is revealing that this newly adopted concept of 'competence' has generated so much opposition and resistance within some sectors of the British social work training establishment; far more helpful would it have been if the traditional label 'incompetence', so mercilessly applied to so many social workers in the last three decades, had generated a similar opposition and resistance within the social work training establishment as a whole. We must now accept the challenge of competences; we may have to 'tolerate the uncertainty and ambiguity' sometimes associated with them (Cooper 1992); social work students and the profession to which they aspire cannot afford to do otherwise.

References

Aldridge, M. (1994) *Making Social Work News.* London: Routledge.

Amiel, B. (1993) 'Lady Bountiful's lethal little society list.' *The Times* 11th October.

Berger, P.L. and Luckmann, T. (1967) *The Social Construction of Reality.* London: Allen Lane.

Boyatzis, R. (1982) 'The competent manager.' Quoted in T. Conway and S. Willcocks (1993) In 'Search of competence: A management development programme for the NHS.' *Journal of Training and Development 3,* 2, 48–53.

Braye, S. and Preston-Shoot (1995) *Empowering Practice in Social Care.* Buckingham: Open University Publications.

Bridge Childcare Consultancy Service (1991) *Sukina: An Evaluation Report of the Circumstances of her Death.* London: Bridge.

Brown, J. (1991) 'Judgement on Rochdale child sexual abuse investigation, 1990.' *Daily Telegraph,* 8th March.

Burton, V. and Goudge, P. (1992) 'A question of competence.' *Community Care,* 21/9/92.

Cannan, C. (1994) 'Enterprise culture, professional socialisation and social work education in Britain.' *Critical Social Policy 42,* 5–18.

Care Sector Consortium (1992) *National Occupational Standards for Care.* London: Care Sector Consortium.

Central Council for the Education and Training of Social Workers (1989, 1st edition; 1991, 2nd edition) *Rules and Requirements for the Diploma in Social Work.* London: CCETSW.

Central Council for the Education and Training of Social Workers (1995) *Rules and Requirements for the Diploma in Social Work.* CCETSW Paper 30, Revised Edition. London: CCETSW.

Clyde, Lord (1993) *Report of the Enquiry into the Removal of Children from Orkney in February 1991.* House of Commons, Session 1992/93, Paper 195. London: HMSO

Collins, M. (1991) *Adult Education as Vocation.* London: Routledge.

Committee for Social Work Education and Policy (1995) *Rethinking Social Work Education.* Liverpool: University of Liverpool.

Cooper, L. (1992) 'Managing to survive: Competence and skills in social work.' *Issues in Social Work Education 12,* 2, 3–21.

Field, J. (1995) 'Reality testing in the workplace: are NVQs "employment-led"?' In P. Hodkinson and M. Issitt (eds) *The Challenge of Competence.* London: Cassell

Gibson, R. (1986) *Critical Theory and Education.* London: Hodder

Greenwood, J. (1994) 'Letter to Editor.' *Community Care* 8–14 December.

Hoad, T.F. (1988) *The Concise Oxford Dictionary of English Etymology.* London: Guild.

Hodkinson, P. (1995) 'Professionalism and competence.' In P. Hodkinson and M. Issitt (eds) *The Challenge of Competence.* London: Cassell.

Hodkinson, P. and Issitt, M. (1995) 'The Challenge of competence for the caring professions: an overview.' In P. Hodkinson and M. Issitt (eds) *The Challenge of Competence.* London: Cassell.

Hodkinson, P. and Issitt, M. (1995) 'Competence, professionalism, and vocational education and training.' In P. Hodkinson and M. Issitt (eds) *The Challenge of Competence.* London: Cassell.

Hyland, T. (1995) 'Behaviourism and the meaning of competence.' In P. Hodkinson and M. Issitt (eds) *The Challenge of Competence.* London: Cassell.

Issitt, M. (1995) 'Competence, professionalism and equal opportunities.' In P. Hodkinson and M. Issitt (eds) *The Challenge of Competence.* London: Cassell

Jones, J. (1995) 'Professional artistry and child protection: towards a reflective holistic practice.' In P. Hodkinson and M. Issitt (eds) *The Challenge of Competence.* London: Cassell.

Jordon, W. (1991) 'Competencies and values.' *Social Work Education 10,* 1, 5–11.

Kemshall, H. (1993) 'Assessing competence: Process or subjective inference? Do we really see it?' *Social Work Education 12,* 1, 36–45.

Kirkwood, A. (1993) *The Leicestershire Enquiry 1992.* Leicester: Leicestershire County Council.

Levy, A. and Kahan, B. (1991) *The Pindown Experience and the Protection of Children: A Report of the Staffordshire Child Care Enquiry.* Staffordshire: Staffordshire County Council.

Macrae, D.G. (1968) 'Theory.' In G.D. Mitchell (ed) *A Dictionary of Sociology.* London: RKP.

Melton, F.R. (1994) 'Competences in perspective.' *Educational Research 36,* 3, 285–94.

Miller, C.B. (1995) *Sheriff Miller's judgement on Ayrshire child abuse investigations, in the Petition of 6 families. Respondent: F. Kennedy, Reporter of the Children's Panel, Strathclyde Regional Council.* Strathclyde.

Mitchell, G.D. (1975) *A Dictionary of Sociology.* London: Routledge and Kegan Paul.

National Children's Bureau (NCB) (1993) *Investigation into Inter-Agency Practice Following the Cleveland Area Child Protection Committee's Report Concerning the Death of Toni Dales.* London: NCB.

National Council for Vocational Qualifications (1988) *Agency Training Notes 1. (1988).* London: NCVQ.

Nissim, R. and Simm, M. (1994) 'Linking research evidence in fostering work the art of the possible.' *Adoption and Fostering 18,* 4, 10–16.

Northern Ireland Post-Qualifying Education and Training Pilot Partnership (1992) Post Qualifying Level Competences. Antrim, N.Ireland: NIPQETPP.

O'Hagan, K.P. and Dillenburger, K. (1995) *The Abuse of Women within Childcare Work.* Buckingham: Open University Press.

Phillips, M. (1993) 'Oppressive urge to stop oppression.' *The Observer* 1st August.

Pinker, R. (1994) 'Playing Devil's Advocate.' *Community Care* 24–30 November.

Platt, D. (1994) 'Listen and learn.' *Community Care* 16–23 February.

Rosen, A. (1994) 'Knowledge use in practice.' *Social Services Review,* December, 560–577.

Smalley, R.E. (1967) *Theory for Social Work Practice.* New York: Columbia University Press.

Sommerfeld, D.P. and Hughes, J.R. (1987) 'Do health professionals agree on the parenting potential of pregnant women?' *Social Sciences Medicine 24,* 3, 285–288.

Statham, D. and Carroll, G. (1994) 'Diploma document does not ignore race'. (Letters to Editor). *Community Care* 27th October-2nd November.

Timms, N. (1986) *Taking Care: The Value and Values of Social Work.* Inaugural Lecture, University of Leicester.

Timms, N. (1991) 'A new diploma for social work or Dunkirk as total victory.' In P. Carter and T. Jeffs (eds) *Social Work and Social Welfare, Yearbook 3.* Buckingham: OUP.

Woodruffe, C. (1991) 'Competent by any other name.' *Personnel Management.* September.

CHAPTER 2

Competence in Conciliation Work

Margaret Fawcett and Kate Lewis

Introduction

Marital breakdown is an increasingly common fact of family life. In 1993 there were 165,000 divorces in England and Wales making Britain the country with the highest divorce rate in the European Union. It is now estimated that one in three marriages in the UK will end in divorce, the majority of these occurring within ten years of marriage and happening between parents with young children (Registrar General NI 1992). Over the last decade there has been considerable debate about the extent to which the courts and welfare professionals should be involved with children and their families on separation and divorce. The aim of the new Children Act 1989 has been to provide a consistent set of legal remedies for both private family law and public law. The Act sets out a number of principles which represent a new approach to intervention when parents separate.

- The concept of 'parental responsibility' which continues on divorce and which encourages parents who do not live with their children to maintain a relationship with them.

- The concept of court intervention only when necessary to protect the interests of the child. This has re-enforced the trend of also encouraging parents who are separating and divorcing to agree their own arrangements for their children's' future.

- As under the old law, the child's welfare remains the court's paramount consideration in all cases involving the upbringing of the children.

'The difficulty with the concept of parental responsibility and its operation in law is the premise that parents are willing or able to behave reasonably and responsibly on relationship breakdown' (Wyld 1994). The reality, as the facts below suggest, is that the transitions involved are complex and difficult.

- 'The majority of divorces are obtained by one partner accusing the other of unreasonable behaviour of adultery.'

- 'Most divorces are acutely painful for parents and their children.'
- 'Considerable numbers of fathers lose contact with their children within the first two or three years.'
- 'Over two million children are growing up in either a full-time or part-time stepfamily.' (Walker 1994)

Social workers and probation officers are drawn into work with these families in a number of ways. The court may request a welfare report from a court welfare officer or from a social services department. Parents or other professionals may raise child care concerns where children have been adversely affected by parental separation. Social services departments may also be the first port of call in relation to benefits, housing queries and issues of domestic violence.

Given this diversity of need and the variety of responses that are required from welfare professionals – court reporting, welfare rights, counselling and conciliation work, child guidance and child protection work, it must come as no surprise that there is similar diversity in standards of practice. Wyld (1994), for example, quotes research which shows that there is enormous regional variation in court welfare practice, including the manner of working with separating parents, the involvement of the child, and the quality and content of court reports. Peyton (1994) highlighted difficulties that social workers experience in prioritising competing demands for preventative work alongside child protection work. In terms of marital work it has often meant that welfare rights, counselling and conciliation work have been low on the priority list and dealt with by the most inexperienced workers.

The case study we have selected focuses on conciliation work with a recently separated couple called Mr and Mrs Hobson. They have been married for ten years and have three young children. Conciliation is essentially a process of joint decision making and the settlement of disputes by the parties themselves (Roberts 1991), an approach to practice very much in keeping with the philosophy of the Children Act 1989. In the discussion that follows we are going to explore the actions and the responses of the student social worker in referral taking and the core competencies of *communicating and engaging, enabling, assessing* and *planning and intervening*... At each stage in the process we will look at key issues such as planning joint sessions, managing conflict and balancing different needs and perspectives. Our aim is to demonstrate the principles of conciliation practice with couples in dispute – an approach which will provide numerous opportunities for the student to demonstrate evidence of competence practice.

Referral

The referral to social services came in a Monday morning telephone call from a GP to a duty officer. He had a tearful young mother called Mrs Hobson in his surgery saying she didn't know which way to turn for help. There were problems between her and her husband. Although they had recently separated, the tension and the rows between the couple were getting worse and were beginning to affect her and the three young children. She was finding it difficult to sleep and had asked for tablets. He had prescribed a couple of sleeping tablets and with her permission was phoning to see if a social worker would call with a view to providing support and advice. The duty officer had accepted the referral indicating that as this was a service they had provided in the past, it was likely that a social worker would be in contact once the case had been allocated. Later that afternoon the team leader, who was also a practice teacher, had passed the referral to the student for action.

Competence in the Referral Phase

The manner in which a worker begins work with an individual or a family often determines the effectiveness of the intervention that follows. The student social worker needs to be aware that their own anxiety about taking on new work can create a tendency to rush into action. If this is allowed to happen in a referral where a couple are in conflict, the student can fall into one of a number of traps. They can either become prematurely involved in individual work at the expense of exploring options for engaging both parties, or they can be unwittingly drawn into taking sides in what are often complex and bitter marital disputes – see Table 2.1.

The background information on the Hobson family referral is information which the worker would normally gather during the early assessment phase of work. In the context of this discussion it illustrates the interplay between marital and parenting issues and the strength of feeling evoked when parents separate. In order to respond effectively it is essential during this referral stage that the student undertakes some preparatory work (background reading, discussions in supervision, role-play rehearsal of initial interviews) so that she is informed of the knowledge, values and skills underpinning good practice with couples in dispute.

Knowledge

The *knowledge* required in this referral will include (1) basic information about legislation; (2) an understanding of agency policies and procedures in relation to marital work – prioritisation, referral taking, case recording and reporting; (3) policies and procedures relevant to all family and child care work such as child protection procedures and policies on partnerships with parents; (4) research and literature on the impact of separation and divorce on families; (5) resources and services available for families when parents separate. Much of this information (reference point 1, 2, 3 and 5) is easily accessible as it is part of the everyday business of social services departments. What is essential is that the student recognises that the referral could require a variety of responses depending on family circumstances. For the purposes of this case study we are focusing on 'conciliation work' – helping couples in dispute resolve areas of disagreement in relation to their children. In general terms though, the student should always bear in mind the possibility of needing to respond to other scenarios – domestic violence, allegations of child sexual abuse, a request for marital counselling, problems of debt and financial hardship, a need for advice and guidance on legal and support services. As such they will have to be very clear about what can be appropriately offered within their agency and what needs to be referred elsewhere.

Table 2.1 Hobson Family Background

Mr H	34 years	Store Assistant	Living with parents
Mrs H	32 years	Office secretary (p/t)	Living in family home
Gary	8 years	Living with mother	At primary school
Alice	6 years	Living with mother	At primary school
Stacey	18 mths	Living with mother	Day care with grandmother

Mr and Mrs Hobson separated three months ago following constant arguments and rows usually about money or Mr Hobson's drinking. His low paid job as a store assistant involved shift work and week-end work and Mrs Hobson increasingly resented the amount of time this took away from the family as well as Mr Hobson's binge drinking when off work. The growing hostility between the couple had resulted in Mrs Hobson suggesting a temporary separation 'while they sort themselves out'. Mr Hobson had reluctantly agreed and had gone to live with his elderly parents. Mrs Hobson had remained in the family home with the three children. Most week-ends Mr Hobson spent some time with Gary and Alice at his parents' house and saw Stacey when collecting or returning the other children. The children were often upset following visits to Dad. Alice had become increasingly clingy and tearful, while Gary had become more cheeky and hard to manage. His recent school report had said that he 'had become withdrawn and unable to concentrate in class'.

The situation between the couple reached crisis point following a row at the start of a Saturday visit in which Mr Hobson accused his wife of 'being seen out at a disco with her mates talking to some other bloke'. The heated conversation that followed had soon degenerated into a shouting and screaming match ending only when Mr Hobson stormed out. His parents had telephoned the next day wanting to know what was going on as their son seemed 'pretty cut-up' about things and had spent the entire week-end drinking. It was a distraught Mrs Hobson who referred herself to her GP on the Monday morning requesting help as she didn't know how she could cope any longer with things the way they were.

Developing a theoretical understanding (reference point 4) on what happens in families when parents separate remains the other essential part of the student's knowledge base. With the increase in divorce in the United Kingdom a wide range of research and advice literature is now readily available on the subject (Burgoyne, Ormrod and Richards 1987; Burrett 1993; Coleman 1990; De'Ath and Slater 1992, and Robinson 1993; Wyld 1994). This literature highlights consistent findings about both the process of separation and its impact on children and young people.

Key Research Findings

- Parental separation is not a crisis or isolated event but is part of a process. This separation process is almost always stressful. 'It often results in feelings of grief, sadness, anger, rejection, bitterness and an overwhelming sense of loss for everyone concerned. In the early stages, anger and hostility are commonplace' (Walker 1994).

  Adults are typically at different stages in this process. It is commonplace for one party to want to leave the relationship, while the other party would like the marriage to continue.

- Because of these dynamics, communication and joint decision-making will have often broken down in relation to the children. 'Parents may in fact be too pre-occupied with their own feelings to understand their children's needs' (Mitchell 1985).

- Initially, the majority of children will be distressed by the removal of one parent from their daily lives. In the longer term, a whole configuration of factors will influence the process of the children's adjustment including age, sex, practical arrangements for the care of the children, economic factors and adjustment of the parent with whom the child resides.

- The situation most conducive to children's welfare is 'minimum overt conflict and both parents easily accessible and properly involved' (Schaffer 1990).

It is these well researched findings which will enhance the student's under-standing of this family; negotiating participation and involvement of both parents, facilitating the reduction of conflict, enabling improved communica-tion and joint decision making, providing emotional and practical support and sharing information with parents on children's needs and reactions when separation occurs.

Values

CCETSW's revised Paper 30 makes it clear that students' practice must be 'founded on, informed by and capable of being judged against a clear value base' (CCETSW Paper 30 Revised Ed 1995). The following ethical imperatives are especially pertinent to this case.

RESPECT AND VALUE UNIQUENESS AND DIVERSITY
AND RECOGNISE AND BUILD ON STRENGTHS

'When relationships end there is a frequent need to allocate blame and in our current adversarial system, partners are encouraged to think the worst of each other' (Walker 1994). The challenge for the student adopting a conciliation approach is to demonstrate respect for each party's point of view without taking sides in the disputes or colluding with the bickering between the couple. The feelings of guilt, rejection and failure which are so common at the ending of adult relationships often means that the couple will have lost sight of their qualities as parents. It will be important for the student in their assessment to use every opportunity to recognise and affirm the couple's shared commitment to their children and to highlight the good parenting which had been in evidence such as their joint planning of visiting arrangements for the children.

PROMOTE PEOPLE'S RIGHTS TO CHOICE, PRIVACY, CONFIDENTIALITY
AND PROTECTION WHILE RECOGNISING THE COMPLEXITY OF
COMPETING RIGHTS AND DEMANDS

Parental separation often raises very complex ethical issues because the needs of the adults to separate and end their own relationship does not easily coincide with the needs of children for stability and continuity of parenting. The worker will need to ensure that the views of both adults are listened to as well as the voice of the child. They will want to promote parental choices but will need to ensure that decision-making is not unfairly slanted towards a dominant partner or by a need to settle scores. They will aim to recognise the aspirations of each individual but will need to facilitate negotiations in the light of what is manageable, realistic and workable.

Skills

Working with couples in dispute can tax the student's skills at a number of levels. At the beginning there can be a pressure for both parties to tell their story and have the student on their side. From the very start the student will need to adopt an even-handed approach which equalises time between them and demonstrates respect for each as an individual. Attending and listening, (hearing and understanding the messages clients are sending), normalising (providing appropriate reassurance), mutualising (working towards a shared problem definition), summarising (providing an overview of important themes and concerns) and maintaining a future focus (orientating interaction with the future in mind) will be essential skills which the student will use throughout. As joint work develops faulty communication skills may become apparent. One party may talk too much while the other remains silent. Both may talk together or not at all. Resource material such as Fisher and Ury's (1987) *Getting to Yes* and John Haynes' (1989) video, *Michael and Debbie* can provide helpful tips and techniques on structuring and managing negotiations and dealing with conflict. The student should also be aware that they can feel under pressure to provide answers. Considerable patience and persistence will be required to assist people to find their own solutions based on their ability to negotiate what best suits their family.

Competence in Practice: Communicating and Engaging

Establishing initial contact with Mr and Mrs Hobson

The starting point in this case is likely to be a phone call to Mrs Hobson. It shows a consideration for the sense of crises on Mrs Hobson's part and demonstrates a prompt expression of care and concern. At this stage the student may offer an appointment at the office. It is in this setting that the student will acknowledge the information received from the GP and establish basic information about the family and their current circumstances. An essential task in this first contact is to listen attentively to Mrs Hobson's many concerns without taking sides in the dispute and without getting into significant work. She may say, 'He's still drinking and he's never going to change...' 'We never could talk and now it's just getting worse...' 'He won't accept that I need a life of my own...' 'Every time the children see him they're getting really upset... it might just be better if he didn't call for them...' 'He doesn't listen...' 'I'm at the end of my tether.' Hearing this for the first time can feel fairly overwhelming for the student and mutualising the problems at this stage can lay a very helpful basis for beginning work. 'It seems like this is a difficult time for you all...' 'From what you're saying it sounds as though you and your husband are both very upset and finding it difficult to communicate with each other...' It can also be helpful for the student to summarise what may have been a jumbled account of events and issues. 'From what you've described there do seem to be a number of issues around for you and your husband... the future of your own relationship, his drinking, visiting arrangements and the children's behaviour.'

It is at this stage that the student can introduce the idea of approaching Mr Hobson with a view to arranging a joint meeting. Mrs Hobson is likely to have some initial reservations and the student will need to explain what a 'conciliation approach' means and the benefits to everyone of finding a way of minimising conflict and preventing differences escalating into complicated legal wrangles. The student would hope that the outcome of the meeting would be permission to make initial contact with her husband.

New challenges will present themselves in negotiating contact with Mr Hobson. What reaction will he have to a phone call from a student social worker? How will the initial referral be explained? Does he know that his wife has been to see the family doctor? How should the idea of a conciliation approach be presented to someone who is likely to be angry and upset? It is very helpful if his wife's concerns are presented in a non-judgmental way and if the student demonstrates impartiality by offering a similar half hour appointment to hear Mr Hobson's side of the story. The skills underpinning that session will be very similar to the one outlined earlier. The emphasis will be on listening, clarifying, information giving, mutualising and summarising with a view to a follow-up appointment where the student will see the couple both together.

Planning the first joint session

At the end of these first interviews the student can sometimes feel swamped by the anger and distress of the parties. The challenge of now bringing the couple together in the same room can feel as if it is a fairly daunting task fraught with practical difficulties. Should Mr and Mrs Hobson share the same waiting room? How should the seating in the interview be arranged? What happens if a row breaks out or one of them starts to cry? What if they don't listen to each other? It can be reassuring for the student to know first sessions often go more smoothly than expected.

The clients are trying to impress the student with their reasonableness and they are also using the time to assess whether the student is trustworthy, willing to listen and capable of controlling the session. A session plan such as that outlined in Table 2.2 helps the student 'tune in' and plan for some of the difficulties they have anticipated. On the basis of such careful preparation and planning they can be reasonably confident at the end of the first joint session that they will have successfully communicated and engaged with the couple. Table 2.4 provides a summary of these evidence indicators for each stage of the conciliation process as well as noting material such as the written session plan which can be included in any portfolio of evidence.

Competence in Practice: Enabling

The agenda which Mr and Mrs Hobson had identified at the end of the first session for discussion included visiting arrangements, communication, the children's behaviour and future plans for the marriage. They agreed that in the second joint meeting they would start by talking about visiting arrangements, and it is at this stage that open hostility and conflict can emerge. This is often linked to the growing confidence of the clients in the conciliation process. They will have tested out the student and will be more confident of revealing their agenda and showing some 'hot emotions'. The shift in atmosphere between the couple to one of open conflict can be very disconcerting. The careful preparation of the first session will have built up the student's confidence which will rapidly be replaced by a sense of 'I thought I had it but now I have lost it'. This is where patience and persistence come into play, together with the effective use of supervision. The practice teacher has asked the student to make a process recording of the beginning of the second session and, as it happens, this is when

Table 2.2 First Session Outline

1. **Reception**	Can couple share same waiting room or are separate rooms needed? Alert reception staff. Choose comfortable but neutral venue – preferably not clients' home.
2. **Seating**	Mr and Mrs H angled seating beside each other and facing the student. Student seated nearest the door.
3. **Introductions**	Introduce self as student social worker – first name. Ask couple whether they prefer first or full names. Acknowledge them for agreeing to talk at a time when things are difficult for them as a couple.
4. **Session Outline**	Briefly outline initial contacts. Check basic information, eg names of children, current living arrangements. Emphasise benefits to agreeing to meet before difficulties escalate, normalise process of negotiation by sharing what usually happens, ie 3–4 sessions, 1 hour each with aim of *the couple* negotiating a working agreement facilitated by the student. Make clear distinction between this and a counselling or court-reporting role.
5. **Ground Rules**	Confidentiality – discuss boundaries to feedback to GP (at beginning and end of work); supervision of student's practice. Respectful communication (no interrupting or name-calling). Equal time – each party given the opportunity to have their say.
6. **Agenda setting**	Invite Mr and Mrs H in turn to identify the issues and concerns they wish to discuss. Note these on flip-chart. Give each equal time. Be firm about the other party not interrupting. Keep focus on what can be negotiated rather than the past. Reframe issues using neutral language. Prioritise issues for next meeting; set date and time for next week.

Table 2.3 Extract from Process Recording

	Clients	Student's Perceptions
Mr H:	I want more time with the children – (to me) they could stay over until Sunday evening. Gary has joined a wee boy's league around the corner and I said I would help out – do a bit of coaching... like......	Fear of loss of control. Skills – trying to establish eye contact.
Mrs H:	What the hell are you talking about? I'm pissed off hearing what you want. You don't even stick to what you are getting already... if you don't stop messing about I'm going...	
Mr H:	I don't know what you are talking about... Don't talk rubbish wee girl...	Rising panic. Feeling that the situation is rapidly going out of control. Deciding to intervene.
Mrs H:	That's typical... go on... you know exactly what I'm talking about.	
Mr H:	Oh aye, a mind reader next. If I knew what you were talking about, I wouldn't waste my breath asking questions.	
Student:	Wait a minute. I don't understand what is going on.	
Mrs H:	I'll soon tell you. He left the children last Saturday with his mother and never bothered to tell them or me where he was all day – but I know. He was seen coming out of the Supporters Club at quarter past five and then brought the children round at twenty past six – twenty minutes late...	Emotion – relief. Feeling more in control. Quickly followed by losing the initiative again.
Mr H:	For somebody who's not interested you know a lot about me...	
Mrs H:	I had to. You are so sly. I have enough of you telling everyone including the Welfare how much you care. I'm going to my solicitor and that's it. [Mrs H starts gathering up her bag and putting on her coat. Her husband's face reddens and he says nothing].	
Student:	Mrs H, don't go yet.	

Table 2.3 Extract from Process Recording (Cont.)

	Clients	Student's Perceptions
Mrs H:	Are you wise or what? If you're going to listen to a pack of lies, I'm not… I've more to do with my time.	
Student:	[*Getting up and laughing nervously.*] I don't know about being wise but I'm certainly confused. One minute we're talking sensibly about the future, next minute there are more allegations than confetti at a wedding. [*At this both Mr and Mrs H burst out laughing. I join in not certain what they are laughing at.*]	Reactions instinctive rather than planned. Feel pressure to do something.Not quite sure what I said.
Student:	Okay, okay, let's try and start again. Mrs H… Could you take off your coat, sit down and I'll give each of you a chance to talk… Can I remind you… only one person speaks at a time… [*they both chorus this and start laughing again.*]	
Mrs H:	That line has stuck in my head – do you know that I said that the other night to the kids at dinner time… didn't work with Stacey… she kept on shouting.	
Student:	Maybe it will work with you. Now Mr H… Can you talk us through what happened on Saturday…	

open conflict emerges as Mr Hobson is asked to give his views on current visiting arrangements (Table 2.3).

In the detailed discussion that followed the couple were able to talk over these recent incidents that had caused a lot of tension and ill feeling between them. Mr Hobson talked about recent visits, the pressures of irregular shift arrangements and the fact that he had gone out the previous Saturday for a quick drink and a bet on the Grand National. Mrs Hobson was able to express her fears that Mr Hobson would get drunk and be incapable of looking after the children and this led on to a discussion about communication and the effect of getting information second hand – either through the children or through mates at work. Mr Hobson admitted he had been over the top in his reactions to Mrs Hobson being out at a disco. She, for her part, was very clear that she had a right to her own friends but emphasised that she wasn't seeing anyone else.

At this point the meeting had gone over the scheduled hour and so the student had to draw the session to a close with the couple agreeing that they would meet again next week. In closing the session she was very aware of feeling discouraged because part of the session had got out of control and no issues had actually been resolved. It was only in talking the session over in detail with the practice teacher afterwards that the student was able to see just how enabling her intervention had been.

- Difficult feelings of hurt, mistrust and anger had been acknowledged.
- Important misperceptions had been dealt with.
- Unhelpful patterns of communication had been identified.
- Ground rules for conciliation had been kept to with the notable exception of the outburst at the beginning.

(See Table 2.4 at the end of the chapter for summary of evidence indicators)

It was in the area of managing conflict that the student felt most deskilled. Through looking in detail at the process recording of the incident, she was able to recognise the benefits of a patient persistent approach and the impact of her use of humour in defusing tension during the meeting. The advantages and disadvantages of other techniques were discussed: saying something like, 'let's put it on the shelf for the moment and return to it later', everyone sitting in silence for a moment together, physically changing positions in the room or taking a coffee break. By the end of supervision the student had learnt a vital lesson about professional competence – the value of asking for support and guidance after a difficult interview and the importance of reflecting and analysing one's own practice. On this basis she felt better equipped to deal with the challenges of the next stage in the conciliation process.

Competence in Practice: Assessing and Planning

The work of the third and fourth session will again involve another shift in emphasis for the student. Now that the 'air has been cleared' between the couple, negotiations are likely to begin in earnest. From background reading the student will already be aware that few couples who separate actually plan or discuss in advance across two households. As a result they often end up really discouraged and blaming each other for the tensions and teething problems that inevitably occur. This was very apparent in the second session with Mr and Mrs Hobson and at this new stage in the conciliation process the challenge for the student will be to help the couple plan and generate options around communication, access, the children's behaviour and the future of the marriage. Essential skills will include maintaining a focus on the future not the past, examining the strength and weaknesses of options, clarifying what has been agreed and writing it down in unambiguous language.

Planning

One of the first issues that Mr and Mrs Hobson wanted to sort out was the visiting arrangements for the children. Given the recriminations of the previous week the couple will be looking to the student to help them find a way of moving forward. It can actually ease tension if the student acknowledges the difficulties of the previous session. 'I realise contact is something you both feel strongly about. It seemed to me that last time you had got into something of a "wind up", maybe this time we could approach the issue in another way...'

The couple will often be relieved to admit that last time they were getting at each other and challenging this pattern of communication if it reoccurs will be an important step towards more constructive negotiations. In order to move the discussions forward, a detailed weekly timetable drawn up on the flip chart can be a very useful planning tool for reviewing contact. The children's activities and Mr and Mrs Hobson's work arrangements can be pencilled in and discussed to see where the problem areas are and what alternatives are possible. Keeping a focus on the future and examining options one by one in this organised manner will do much to diffuse tension and facilitate the exchange of good quality information. Agreement on more respectful communication often emerges as part of this planning exercise – no rows in front of the children, no discussion of adult issues during visits and a telephone call to be made if there is a change in Mr Hobson's work arrangements.

Balancing differing needs and perspectives

Throughout these negotiations another area of challenge to the competence of the student will be one of balancing differing needs and perspectives. In addition to balancing differing adult perspectives, balancing is often required between adult needs and children's needs. During negotiations parents can be preoccupied with their own feelings and concerns and will often require help to focus on their children's needs. The student has a number of tools to do this. One is the use of handouts and easy reading material on children's reactions and needs when parents separate; another is to use simple exercises and techniques which effectively bring the children into the room. Asking Mr and Mrs Hobson simply to describe their children to the student is often an important uniting moment for the couple in their negotiations; and asking questions like, 'how would that arrangement feel to Gary and Alice?' or 'what do you think the children would think of that decision when they get older?' can help keep their needs central. Had the couple been faced with the task of parenting older children, then a very real option would have been directly gaining their views and wishes in relation to contact and residence.

Generating options

Because the student is faced with a couple who have very different views about the future of their marriage, this will be another area where she will need to help Mr and Mrs Hobson generate options. One way of doing this will be through developing 'what if' scenarios. 'What if you were to permanently separate? What kind of decisions and arrangements might you need to make?' 'What if you were to live together again, what are the issues which need to be resolved?' The aim of the student is to provide a forum for a preliminary discussion of these issues, and getting into the role of therapist. It is not unusual for couples at this stage to seek further help with regard to their relationship difficulties and the student can advise on the availability of couple counselling in the area.

Competence in Practice: Intervention

The purpose of the final session is to review the intervention strategy of mutually agreed parenting arrangements for Gary, Alice and Sophie while Mr and Mrs Hobson continue to live separately. The role of the student will be to support and sustain the couple through the process of change. Many of the core skills and techniques used in earlier sessions are likely to be just as essential at this final stage – attending and listening, normalising, summarising and maintaining a future focus. However, endings are full of pitfalls where the business of competence is concerned. The atmosphere between the parties in this ending session is likely to swing between discouragement and over-optimism. This can be very disconcerting for the student who simply wants to tidy up loose ends and celebrate a piece of work that is actually finished and 'in the bag'! Competence at this ending stage will in fact require careful preparation and may include a preliminary phone call to each party a day or two before the session and follow-up discussions in supervision on issues which are likely to arise.

As it turned out, a number of difficulties had arisen in relation to contact. On one occasion a visit had to be cancelled because Alice had a chest infection, and on another occasion the children's clothes and belongings had been left behind in their grandparent's house. Both parents also identified concerns about the children's behaviour. Alice had twice woken in the night crying and had told her mother 'I dreamt last night that Mummy and Daddy had an argument and Daddy stopped visiting'. Gary continued to be very cheeky and demanding and had recently asked his father 'Daddy, can I come and live with you?' The student had been made aware of these incidents in her telephone call to the parents and the first challenge will be how to get the final session off to a good start when Mr and Mrs Hobson are feeling a bit discouraged and irritated with each other.

Using the simple technique of looking at what *has* worked in the previous weeks can do much to diffuse tension and set a positive tone to the meeting. Most visits have in fact taken place regularly and on time; hand-over arrangements have generally worked well and no further arguments have taken place in front of the children. These are all tangible signs of the couple's commitment to co-operative parenting and Mr and Mrs Hobson need to be praised for their efforts to create a secure atmosphere for the children. They will also need reassurance that teething problems are inevitable in the setting up of parenting arrangements. The student can facilitate good communication by dealing with the problem areas one at a time, clarifying exactly what went wrong and encouraging a future focus on how such misunderstandings can be prevented from occurring in the future. The student also has an absolutely vital role in helping the parents to understand how children react when parents separate and in helping them find co-operative strategies for dealing with sensitive questions. It will be important that the student has done some background reading and perhaps has copies of one or two relevant articles which can be an extremely useful focus for discussion in the session.

A final task in this review meeting is likely to be some discussion of the future beyond these short term arrangements. The couple have now made an appointment with a counselling agency but the student will also want to help the couple look at and anticipate the likely impact of future developments on current arrangements. A decision to separate permanently, one parent moving to live in new accommodation or a change in work patterns can all cause a strain on arrangements and some preliminary discussions about how potential problems might be handled can prove extremely helpful. The student is in essence trying to prevent over-optimism now that the ending of formal work with the couple is in sight. However, they will want to end the session on a positive note by acknowledging Mr and Mrs Hobson's commitment to the conciliation process and their achievement in setting aside marital differences to negotiate joint parenting arrangements for their children.

Summary

These five joint sessions have been something of a rollercoaster of highs and lows, testing the student's tenacity and persistence to the limits. Each stage of the intervention process of communicating, enabling, planning and intervention has presented its own particular challenges and demands and also provided numerous opportunities for the student to demonstrate evidence of competent practice. A summary of the work undertaken is provided in Table 2.4 which also identifies exemplars of evidence such as the first session plan and the process recording on conflict which are suitable for inclusion in a student portfolio. While the Hobson case study has concentrated on competence in the intervention process, the material will also relate to other core competencies, particularly in relation to the student's own professional development. The work has required the student to review literature and research findings, to make appropriate use of supervision and to evaluate their own practice. In conclusion, this case study in conciliation work has demonstrated competence based on knowledge, values and skills and has illustrated some of the principles of good childcare practice.

Table 2.4 Summary of Evidence Indicators

Core Competence	Practice Requirement	Evidence Indicators	Evidence Exemplar
1. **Communicate and exchange**	Form and develop working relationship with Mr and Mrs H	(1) Establish initial contacts (2) Outline student role (3) Agree control of information (4) Communicate effectively (5) Identify shared, differing perspectives, values and aims	Written plan for first session (Table 2.2)
2. **Enable**	Work with Mr and Mrs H to enable them to identify their own strengths to meet responsibilities and achieve change. Provide information on the legal process. Promote the rights of children and adults	(1) Appropriate form of communication established (2) Areas of conflict acknowledged (3) Users identify own strengths/ weaknesses (4) Careful attention paid to what Mr and Mrs H say (5) Outline court procedures and sources of legal advice (6) Advocate on behalf of Gary, Alice and Stacey	Process Recording of student dealing with high conflict issue (Table 2.3)
3. **Assess and Plan**	Work in partnership with Mr and Mrs H to assess their needs, responsibilities, rights and resources	(1) Take account of all significant and relevant information (2) Respect difference and diversity (3) Balance the differing perspective, needs and resources of Mr and Mrs H with the children's needs	Written outline of parenting agreement

Table 2.4 Summary of Evidence Indicators (Cont.)

Core Competence	Practice Requirement	Evidence Indicators	Evidence Exemplar
		(4) Establish objectives and options for action	
		(5) Identify resources	
		(6) Apply research findings	
4. **Intervene**	Support and sustain Mr and Mrs H through the process of change	(1) Facilitate effective communication	Supervision notes on dealing with impasses
		(2) Assist Mr and Mrs H in the management of conflict and stress	
		(3) Negotiate ground rules for on-going contact	
		(4) Respond to changing circumstances	
		(5) Review effectiveness of arrangements	

References

Burgoyne, J., Ormrod, R. and Richards, M. (1987) *Divorce Matters*. Harmondsworth: Penguin.

Burrett, J. (1993) *To and Fro Children*. London: Harper Collins.

CCETSW (1995) Rules and requirements for the Diploma in Social Work (Paper 30: Revised Edition). London: CCETSW.

Coleman, J. (1990) *Teenagers and Divorce: Tape, Booklet and Trainer's Guide*. Brighton: Trust for the Study of Adolescence.

De'Ath, E. and Slater, D. (1992) *Parenting Threads: Caring for Children when Couples Part*. London: Stepfamily Publications.

Fisher, R. and Ury, W. (1987) *Getting to Yes*. London: Arrow Books.

Haynes, J. (1989) *Michael and Debbie: Video, Booklet and Trainer's Guide*. New York: Haynes Mediation Associates.

Mitchell, A. (1985) *Children in the Middle*. London: Tavistock Publications.

Peyton, L. (1994) 'Provision in N Ireland for young people who are experiencing separation and divorce.' In M. Fawcett and K. Lewis (eds) *The Effects of*

Separation and Divorce on Children and Young People. Belfast: Relate NI Conference Proceedings.

Registrar General (NI) (1992) *Annual Report 1992.* Belfast: HMSO.

Roberts, M. (1991) *A Conciliator's Guide to the Children Act 198.* London: National Family Conciliation Council.

Robinson, M. (1993) *Family Transformation through Divorce and Remarriage.* London: Routledge.

Schaffer, R. (1990) *Making Decisions about Children.* Oxford: Basil Blackwell.

Walker, J. (1994) 'Parenting in the 1990s and the role of fathers post-divorce.' In M. Fawcett and K. Lewis (eds) *The Effects of Separation and Divorce on Children and Young People.* Belfast: Relate NI Conference Proceedings.

Wyld, N. (1994) *When Parents Separate.* London: Children's Legal Centre.

CHAPTER 3

Competence in Residential Child Care

Johnnie Gibson and John Turtle

Introduction

Caring for children in groups, away from their own families, has a long and inauspicious history. The current provision of residential child care is not the outcome of a smooth and continuous progression to an ever improving quality experience. Residential child care has a distant past which casts long shadows, and a recent past that has done little to dispel those shadows. In fact, recent episodes of the abuse of power by adults over young people and the 'blind eye' of managers (Levy and Kahan 1991) show marked similarity with other abuses in the history of institutional care (Robins 1980).

Parker (1988) writes about the consequences of this historical legacy, a 'persistent image of residential child care as nothing more than a repugnant type of institutional life' (p.8). This is no mere academic observation. It is tangible enough to be felt, seen and heard. For children and young people the image becomes manifest in the stigma of not telling friends in school that they live in a 'home'. For regular staff members and students on placement in residential care settings, the image becomes manifest in the attitude of colleagues in other parts of the child care system who view admission to residential care as failure or at best as a last resort. Perhaps the most regrettable manifestation occurs when social work leadership expresses similar views: the Warner Report (1992) quotes one director of social services who said that 'residential child care is a "necessary evil"' (p.7). Warner goes on to say that debate and opinion about residential care today 'is still dominated by historical attitudes towards looking after children: as women's work in which skills are inherent or intuitive and the commitment of the work-force is exploitable' (p.25). Three major reports, (Utting 1991; Skinner 1992; Warner 1992) have each stressed strategic leadership at Government and organisational level as a critical factor in a broad strategy to achieve a positive image of residential child care and to guarantee positive outcomes for children and young people. Another strand in this strategy is the continued development of competent social work practice in residential care settings.

In the context of caring for the whole child the idea of 'competence', meaning 'effectiveness' has great appeal. However, we have some discomfort with the idea of competences which have become the driving force behind training in professional social work. Our discomfort is eloquently summarised by Cannan (1995) in her critique of the competency approach as reductionist; she says that '... it is assumed that competence is the sum of achieved competences...' (p.14). We take the view that the competent residential social worker in child care settings is 'much more that the sum of the parts'.

CCETSW's Paper 30 does not miss this point; it repeatedly emphasises the necessity of integrating knowledge, values and skills. In 1971 Clare Winnicott wrote that children and young people in residential care need 'good experiences of care comfort and control' (p.30). Many interactions in residential child care require that workers provide **care, comfort and control simultaneously**. In the case example which follows we illustrate this integration in two complementary situations. First, we illustrate competence in making an entry to the group living context of residential child care; second, we illustrate competence in responding to an individual in crisis in this particular social work setting.

Group Living: The General Context

Brown and Clough (1989) comment that, 'life in day and residential centres is multi-layered and complex' (p.6). This observation is supported by Douglas (1986), who states that although a residential unit can be referred to as a group 'it is most often an organisation containing many groups' (p.1). A student on placement is expected to evidence competence in this multi-layered and complex organisation of small groups where a primary goal is to 'place the individual at the heart of the system' (Ward 1993, p.158). The range and intensity of activities encountered can be a very intimidating environment in the first few days for a student on placement. Unlike fieldwork settings where students can be afforded some time to acclimatise, adjust and respond to the demands of the setting before meeting clients, no such moratorium can be given in residential child care. From the first day of placement the student can expect to meet clients who are eager to find out about this new adult. Young people have an enormous need to make some sense of any new adult entering their living space, because, entering their world – their living space – is precisely what the new adult is doing. Their unspoken questions will be:

- Do I have anything to fear from this person?
- Will I like them?
- Will they like me?
- Will they respect me?

- Will they be fair in their dealings with me?
- Will they be afraid of me?
- Will they be trustworthy?
- Will they trust me?

These tuning-in questions which are an important pre-occupation of young people are essentially about discovering the value base of adults who are charged with their care. We return shortly in more detail to the subject of values.

Most residential units are busy places. Staff often work a twenty-four hour shift; Figure 3.1 provides a typical day in a residential unit. On the left hand side are tasks and activities arising during specific phases; on the right hand side are designated core themes in residential care and competences which are likely to be necessary.

Table 3.1 is adapted from Clough and Brown's (1989) 'mosaic of groups and groupings' (p.21), commonly found in residential care settings. It shows the potential complexity of the situation to be encountered by the student.

Table 3.1 Groups and groupings in residential settings

Groups and groupings	Signs and symbols of identity/belonging
The residential unit as whole community	Totality of residents and staff
Living together groups	Groups determined by the programme of the unit – mealtime groups, bedroom groups.
Informal friendship groups	Common interests/spontaneous friendships – individual choice regarding whether or not to 'join' – process of acceptance and rejection.
Groups to discuss group living issues	Meetings to discuss shared concerns – frequently symbolises interface between staff and residents.
Staff groups and groupings	(1) Staff meetings (2) Groupings of staff with shared responsibilities, e.g. art and craft. (3) Informal affinity groupings – shared personal interests outside the work situation
Groups and groupings whose membership crosses the physical boundary of the unit	Membership composed of 'insiders' and 'outsiders', e.g. case conferences, family groupings, teams of residential and field social workers.

Tasks and activities	Themes and competences

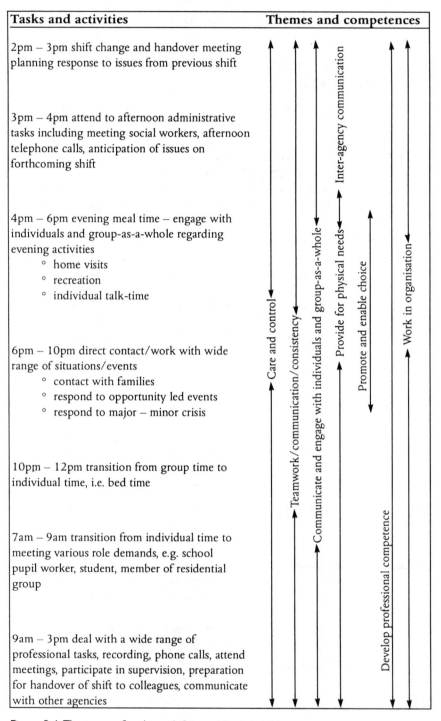

2pm – 3pm shift change and handover meeting planning response to issues from previous shift

3pm – 4pm attend to afternoon administrative tasks including meeting social workers, afternoon telephone calls, anticipation of issues on forthcoming shift

4pm – 6pm evening meal time – engage with individuals and group-as-a-whole regarding evening activities
　　○　home visits
　　○　recreation
　　○　individual talk-time

6pm – 10pm direct contact/work with wide range of situations/events
　　○　contact with families
　　○　respond to opportunity led events
　　○　respond to major – minor crisis

10pm – 12pm transition from group time to individual time, i.e. bed time

7am – 9am transition from individual time to meeting various role demands, e.g. school pupil worker, student, member of residential group

9am – 3pm deal with a wide range of professional tasks, recording, phone calls, attend meetings, participate in supervision, preparation for handover of shift to colleagues, communicate with other agencies

Figure 3.1 The twenty-four hour shift in residential child care

Figure 3.1 and Table 3.1 clearly show that the worker often operates in a public arena. The practice of social work in most other settings can be a private transaction between worker and client/s. In a group living setting, work is carried out in full view of colleagues, other clients, family members and sometimes other visiting professionals. This public arena can be intimidating. However, when development of competent social work practice and team work is a priority, then the public arena becomes a support factor as colleagues share in pieces of work with each other and, as a consequence, learn together.

In the next two sections of this chapter we present a two part case example. In part one, the student records how she enters the living space of the group-as-a-whole and meets the challenge of **communicating her role** and **engaging with members of the group**. She begins the essential transition from being 'the student' to being a student, who, like the residents, has a name, a past, a public life, a private life, a sense of humour, a personality; characteristics that will make her different from other adults charged with the care of the young people, but, unique characteristics through which she will have to give expression to the values embraced by the agency and the staff team. The student also encounters one of the core dilemmas of residential care, that of, 'enabling people to live private lives in public places' (Ward 1993, p.vii). Taken as a whole this two part case study provides opportunity for the student to meet all core competencies.

Case Study – Part One

Entering the group living space
The group living setting described here is a residential adolescent unit. Ten places are provided for the use of social service departments. The young people admitted to the unit are of mixed gender, they are aged between 12 and 18, and there is no selection criteria on grounds of religious belief or ethnic origin. Competence in making effective entry into a group living situation depends on the integration of knowledge, values and skills. The core competences in the first part of the case example are, **communicate and engage**, **work in organisations**, and **develop professional competence**. Before describing the work we need to explore the knowledge, values and skills underpinning social work in residential child care.

Knowledge
The knowledge base which informs social work practice in residential child care is extensive in its range but for convenience can be divided into

(1) utilising theory

(2) essential information

(3) self-knowledge.

UTILISING THEORY

The theory base which informs residential social work practice is extensive, equally daunting for student and practitioner alike. Figure 3.2 is a summary of the theory base that a student might draw on.

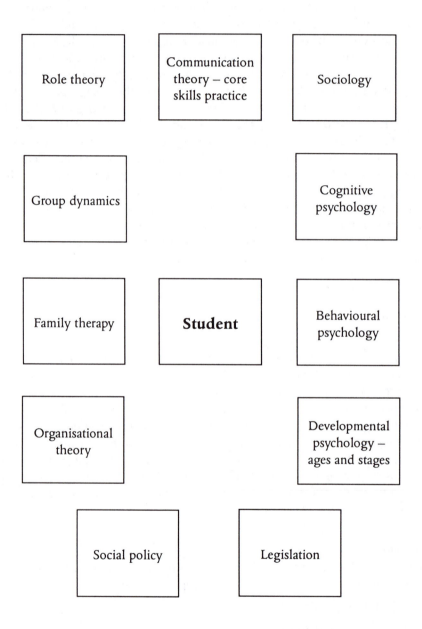

Figure 3.2. The knowledge base

This is most easily understood in diagrammatic form; Table 3.2 presents our view of what constitutes essential information. The list is not exhaustive, neither is it presented in order of priority.

Table 3.2: Essential Information

Nature of the managing agency	Location of policy and procedure documents
Purpose of the unit	Daily routine
Aims and objectives	Key working system
Names of staff	Pattern of meetings
Pen pictures of young people	Physical layout of building
Social climate	Recording systems
Theory base	Values
Care and control policy	Administrative tasks

Peter England (1985) suggests that 'making sense' of human situations is a key task for social workers (p.21). In the first days and weeks of placement the student can expect to spend a considerable amount of time and energy in 'making sense' of how all this essential information fits together to inform the work of the particular unit.

SELF-KNOWLEDGE
'To try and understand oneself is not simply an interesting pastime, it is a necessity of life' (Bannister 1990, p.111). When we accept self-knowledge as a 'necessity' of ordinary everyday life, then it must be regarded as essential in the practice of professional social work. CCETSW's Paper 30 (1995) gives emphasis to 'knowledge of self and use of self' (p.9) as being central in developing professional competence. The importance of self knowledge or insight is explained by Winnicott (1971)

> insight into the feelings of others implies insight into our own similar feelings... when one truly 'understands' human motivation one succeeds in fusing the affects of one's own previous experience with the affects called up by the observation of another's observed behaviour... we are unable to see in others that which for years we have defended ourselves against... because the feelings aroused are too painful and threatening to us. (p.72)

Self-knowledge is comprised of more that affective components. Anti-discriminatory practice also requires that workers take a rigorous approach to self knowledge. Ward (1993) argues convincingly that workers in group care need to be aware of three powerful dynamic relationship forces which, if not managed by the individual worker and by effective **organisational policies** can lead to discriminatory attitudes and practice. His threefold analysis of these 'core issues' in group care includes power, prejudice and dependency. He writes

> power: 'people in group care frequently feel that they are have been placed at the receiving end of a complex set of power-relationships' (p.9)

> prejudice: 'the combination of the structural power held by the dominant groups in society with prejudices held by those groups and which they have the power to enact or enforce' (p.10)

> dependency: 'for many of the people in group care, dependency may be a very fraught area for children, their previous experience of dependency may have been traumatic'. (p.13)

Thompson (1993) makes the point that 'social work practice cannot avoid the question of discrimination and oppression' (p.151). He goes on to issue a challenge that underlines self-knowledge as an essential component in competent social work practice, 'perhaps the most fundamental step towards anti-discriminatory practice that we can take is to become, and remain open and critical in relation to our own practice' (p.153). The articulation and personal identification with a set of values is another ingredient in the worker's inventory of self-knowledge as well as a means of ensuring anti-discriminatory practice.

Values

Levy (1973) has written of 'the tendency in social work literature to list routinely and indiscriminately a series of so-called social work values as if nothing more need to be said for all to understand' (p.2). The clear insistence in CCETSW's Paper 30 that 'values are integral to rather than separate from competent practice' and that 'It is the clear, consistent and thoughtful integration of values in practice, that students must demonstrate' is an injunction that has the potential to bridge the gap between mere itemised lists and values in action. An analysis of personal values is implied in our earlier discussion of self-knowledge. The student needs to be aware of her own values as they will influence the quality and effectiveness of her relationships in the group living context.

Our primary concern in this section is to outline agency and professional values; it is these that the student will have to operationalise in demonstrating competence. Residential child care now has a well developed value base. The impetus for its development comes from at least two sources. First, as a reaction to the abuse and exploitation by adults of young people and second, from the more positive dynamic of the United Nations Convention on the Rights of the Child. The Convention is a 'public avowal by all signatory countries that children are especially vulnerable'. Its ethos is 'to listen to and respect the voice of and needs of the child. For the first time all currently defined rights of children – from protection to self-expression – have been brought together in a single and internationally agreed document' (Kahan 1994, p.28). Drawing from the Convention as well as from other legislation such as the Children Act 1989, Kahan delineates the rights of children in residential child care. These are listed in Table 3.3.

Table 3.3: The Rights of Children and Young People in Residential Care

The right to be heard

The right to complain

The right to see health, education and social work files

The right to contact with others

The right to health

The right to education

Kahan (1994, p.54) defines rights in terms of two categories; 'rights of recipience' and 'rights of action'. A right of recipience is a right that one is entitled to have; for example, all social work clients who enter residential care are entitled to competent social work practice. Active involvement in helping to make decisions about their future care is an example of a right of action. Agencies providing residential services are now required to make sure that residential social workers explicitly inform children and young people and their parents of their rights. Discourse on children's rights cannot exclude the theme of responsibilities. Whilst it is true that, 'some rights do not impose responsibilities on children and young people... the right to protection from abuse is an absolute right' (Kahan, p.56). Other rights do exact responsibilities: the right to privacy requires respect of others' right to privacy in return; so too does the right to have one's property respected; other similar rights with accompanying responsibilities could be listed. This value base of children's rights has proved a powerful mechanism for influencing policy and practice; workers need to make sure that there is no clash between their personal values and the framework of children's rights.

Skills

The use of verbal and non-verbal communication, listening, questioning, pausing, pacing, timing, observing, summarising, planning skills, giving and receiving feedback apply equally in one-to-one social work encounters as in the group living setting. However, in the group living setting there are two important differences. The first of these, the public arena of practice, we have already discussed and will not repeat here.

The second difference refers to intensity and pacing. It is not unusual for residential social workers to operate on the basis of a twenty-four hour (including a sleep-over) period in the facility. Ward (1993) refers to the total shift as the 'unit of work' (p.88); a contrast is drawn with field social work where the unit of work is an individual case. Ward suggests that it is helpful to regard the shift from a process perspective, as having a beginning, middle and end. At the beginning of the shift the worker uses skills to engage with what will become a 'unit of work'. Information gathering skills are to the fore at this stage; information about what happened during the previous shift and information about work to be done during the forthcoming shift. Anticipation and rehearsal skills will also predominate at this beginning stage; based on information from colleagues who worked the previous shift, the student will need to ask herself what is the anticipated mood of individuals and of the group-as-a-whole? Depending on what work needs to be done with individuals the student can begin a private cognitive rehearsal of how best to engage with individuals and the group. In the middle part of the shift the student will need to engage directly with young clients in carrying out identified work as well as responding to events that require a response. As the shift progresses the worker will need to use planning skills to think ahead to the end of the shift so that she can hand over to another set of colleagues. What we have described here can be defined as the macro process of the shift. There is also the micro process. By this we mean the myriad encounters that take place between workers and young people during the period of the shift. Each of these has its own beginning, middle and end; the quality of each such encounter will contribute to a residential unit that communicates a climate of warmth, acceptance and safety or of suspicion and detachment, a place in which there is no emotional investment.

The following section of the chapter is the student's account of entering the group living space of the adolescent residential unit. At the end of the student's note we analyse her practice in terms of the core competences that are relevant to the work, and the knowledge, skills and values which underpin the competences. Successful entry into the adolescent group living situation necessitates competence in the ability to *communicate and engage*.

Student Notes   Daily Diary: 3 Sept. 1995

> *This was my first time entering the young people's group. Actually moving into face-to-face contact in the environment of their living space left me feeling quite anxious. I was aware that I needed to appear relaxed, yet I also knew that the young people might test out this new adult to see how I would react. Part of my anxiety was based on how would I make good social contact with the young people and part was based on would I be able to respond to stressful situations that I knew were bound to arise. I did not want to make mistakes that would*

either create difficulties for the young people or that would incur the disapproval of colleagues.

When I entered the living room there were five young people present watching TV and chatting. I had already been introduced to each of them very briefly during my induction period. I said hello, smiled and sat down on the nearest available seat. I was pleased that my voice sounded confident but no-one said anything to me, in fact some of then didn't even glance at me. The sense of isolation, of not having a relationship base with any of them was quite unnerving – for a moment or two I felt very like an intruder. Like the young people I too have a 'right' to be here but I am aware that I have to earn that right by showing respect. I decided that it was up to me to initiate the contact. I asked one of the young people whom I met before, 'Did you enjoy your home visit?' To my relief he said, 'Yea, it was good. I stayed overnight and my dad is going to decorate my room'. I was then able to continue the conversation along the lines of what his preferences were regarding decor, sport and leisure activities. One of the other young people then asked me, ' Are you the student?' I said, 'Yes I am', and went on to say that I would be here for four months. I also said that my purpose in being here was to learn about what it was like to live in residential care.

They did not seem terribly interested. One of the boys asked did I play sport. I replied, 'I'm not good at sport but I really enjoy swimming, do any of you ever go to the leisure centre?' One replied that he went weight training. I said I wouldn't mind trying that. There was some amusement and I laughed as well, my comment led to a couple of the lads turning around a little in their seats to face in my direction and to look at me directly for the first time. I soon began to feel that I was beginning to be included. There were lots of questions but I was not asked anything that I felt awkward about answering. A member of staff then came in to inform us that some others were going out to town. As I left the room one of the of the girls, whose name is Mary, asked another worker, in what I felt was a hostile tone, if 'the student was going on the outing'. The worker asked me, I said 'Yes I am'. Mary looked away and did not seem too happy. I felt uneasy about this and knew I would need to consult with colleagues and practice teacher about what happened. The group broke up to organise for going out and I took a few moments in the office to think over my reactions.

Commentary

The student has confidently begun to *communicate her role and to engage directly with the group and with individuals*. The practice requirements: **form and develop working relationships with children... and groups,** can be met at this stage, and the following evidence indicators can be identified:

- **establish initial contact and the reason for contact with children... carers and groups**

- **communicate effectively with children... carers and groups**
- **develop working relationships with children... carers and groups**

This is the very beginning stage of relationship building, a crucial phase in entering group care. All other work with individuals, sub-groups and the group-as-a-whole stand on the success of this stage. This process of relationship building has been described by means of the following process model which is quite easily remembered (Dickson *et al.* 1993, pp.161–172):

> *acquaintance: literally the act of meeting other people either in voluntary or non-voluntary association.* Dickson comments that 'one of the most powerful factors in developing meaningful fellowship with another person is the ability to demonstrate that you evaluate them highly... this can be accomplished simply by being physically present' (p.164).

> *build-up: the core process at this stage* can be described as mutual discovery of the 'attitudes and beliefs' (p.166) of the various partners in the relationship set. Judicious self-disclosure is an important skill at this stage. Too much self-disclosure and other partners may be overwhelmed, too little self-disclosure and other partners are deprived of information that will enable the next stage.

> *consolidation:* during this phase participants typically look for ways of maintaining 'variety and interest in being together' (p.167).

> *ending: either through break-up* or planned ending of association.

In the recording of her entry to the group living space the student's actions can be analysed against the first two stages of this framework as she begins to 'get acquainted' and we witness 'build-up' as she becomes involved in a process of mutual and appropriate self-disclosure. The student shows a mature sense of self knowledge. She is aware of potential sources of stress, feeling isolated and vulnerable and feeling a sense of discomfort at Mary's hostility. She is aware of territory: it is their living room, she is the outsider 'joining' the group, she is aware of her own feelings and the source of these. She has an understanding of the children's rights *value base* and *is aware of the need to show respect.* She displays *good use of knowledge* and uses this to engage directly with one of the boys by talking to him about his home visit. She also *uses knowledge to inform her thinking* about being part of the team, i.e. not wanting to earn the disapproval of colleagues. The student has made good use of relationship-building skills through her physical presence, through giving information, through initiating conversation, through humour, through tone of voice and physical control of her anxiety – 'I was glad that my voice sounded confident' – the student shows skill in active listening as she correctly 'hears' the hostility in Mary's communication.

Arising out of this piece of work the student recognises that three other competences begin to have relevance. First, assess and plan. Assessment and planning are constant and sometimes very immediate elements in the thinking processes of residential social workers. The student has begun to gather information that will contribute to assessment of immediate, short and long term goals. Second, her developing understanding of team work will help her to gain competence in work in organisations. Third, her sense of self-knowledge and her recognition of the importance of bringing her feelings about Mary's hostility to her practice teacher during supervision will enable her to develop professional competence and provide evidence for doing so. The section which follows now is part two of the case example in which the student responds to a crisis in Mary's life.

Case Example – Part Two

Competence in responding to crisis in the group living context
Many situations will require an immediate response from a student in residential placement. A student may not have time to consult with other workers. These situations can be seen as crises that intrude into and disrupt the routine, or as opportunities that can offer a deeper understanding of the young person being cared for, and opportunities for the young person to learn mature and healthy ways of coping with problems.

CRISIS
We will assume that the student is now at the end of week four of her placement. The hostility which the student initially encountered has lessened but the student has not really engaged yet with Mary. The pace has been slow and the student has encountered Mary's mistrust of adults. Another young person, Jill, comes to the student and informs her that Mary is cutting herself in her bedroom. An immediate response is required.

Knowledge
For the sake of uniformity we use the same three categories as for competence in entering the group-living space (1) essential information, (2) self-knowledge and (3) utilisation of theory.

ESSENTIAL INFORMATION
What we provide here is a check list that a student will need to be aware of in responding to a situation of reported self-injury. This essential information can be sub-divided into the three categories of (1) information about the specific context, (2) worker self-check list, and (3) post incident procedural requirements.

(1) Information about the specific context

- What is the name of the young person reported as injured?
- What is the exact location of the young person?
- Where is the first aid equipment kept and where is that in relation to the location of the young person?
- Has another member of staff been informed?
- Where is the nearest phone in case an ambulance is required?
- What is the young person's legal status in care?
- Is this a characteristic response for this particular young person?
- What are the significant events or concerns in this young person life?
- Are other young people involved?
- Has the young person taken any substances?
- Where are the other young people at the moment?
- If the situation requires the immediate intervention of more than one adult, are other staff free to attend?
- Will the remainder of the group require supervision or can they be left alone; if they require supervision who will do this?

(2) Worker self-check list

- What am I feeling right now – am I in control of myself?
- Can I cope with the sight of blood and physical injury?
- Am I competent in first aid?
- What will I say on first point of contact with the young person?
- What is my relationship with the young person concerned?
- Have I made sure that another adult has been informed?

(3) Post incident procedural requirements

- Has the incident been written up?
- Has the young person's social worker been informed?
- Have arrangements been made to relay the information about the episode to parents, and other residential workers including the young person's key worker?
- Has a risk assessment been undertaken?
- Has someone talked through the episode with the young person?
- Is there need for psychiatric or psychological consultation?

SELF-KNOWLEDGE

A student finding a teenager who is involved in self-injury will need to be aware that this can provoke personal reactions including shock, denial, anger, disgust and pity, or a reluctance to see the episode as nothing more that attention-seeking behaviour. An understandable initial reaction can be that of fear, because of the amount of blood or the number of cuts or because the cuts are facial. Young people do not contrive self-injurious behaviour simply as a means of getting attention. Fundamentally, the student must be prepared to ask 'what do I feel about what has happened'? There is a good reason for doing so. If the student's answer is that they are annoyed, or disgusted, or repulsed and that they believe that the behaviour is designed as an attention-seeking strategy, then that response will inevitably act as a block on the student's ability to see self-injury for what it is: a communication of distress. A young person who self-injures is in crisis; we turn now to crisis theory as the final element in the knowledge base particular to such an episode.

UTILISATION OF THEORY

Crisis theory is acutely relevant to residential work with troubled adolescents and workers need to be knowledgeable about its application. Crisis can be defined as an 'upset in a steady state'. In response to some hazardous or traumatic event the individual experiences a sense of helplessness, of not being able to cope or solve problems in their usual adaptive way. As Coulshed (1991) observes, 'If a human being is overpowered by external, interpersonal or intra-psychic forces... then harmony is lost for a time', (p.68). With children and young people it may be that they have never learned healthy and adaptive ways of coping. Adult response to young people in crisis is vitally important, 'the outcome of a crisis is greatly influenced by the actions of the adult who handles it and it is the adult's attitudes and techniques that influence how a youngster responds' (Budlong, Holden and Mooney 1993, p.15), or, as Davies (1982) puts it, 'every unhappy incident with a resident, every unfortunate occurrence within a group can be used by staff and worked with as a vehicle for learning', (p.55). Drawing on the work of Coulshed we have assembled the following summary of crisis theory and how workers can respond:

> Crisis is generally self-limiting with a beginning, middle and end. A rise in tension in relation to some stressor is the main characteristic of the beginning phase, habitual ways of problem solving are called on and found to be deficient; tension increases.

> The final phase is reached when the problem is solved or discharged in some way, perhaps by mobilising additional resources or, perhaps, as we will see in the case of Mary, by turning the problem inward and acting aggressively against the self.

At first contact or first interview the worker needs to focus on the present circumstances. It is important to establish what happened and what were the circumstances that led up to the crisis.

The next phase of intervention by the worker is to try and enable the client to state what is the most pressing issue and then to decide steps that can be taken to resolve this.

During this early phase the worker seeks to communicate hope and optimism.

Once the client's thinking has been concentrated on the immediate issues it may then be helpful to broaden out the exploration of circumstances, 'Has this ever happened before?' What solutions have worked in the past?

Reviewing progress and working toward ending the crisis intervention constitute the final phase.

Responding to crisis – student notes

I was upstairs in the house. Jill came to me and said that Mary had a piece of blade from a safety razor and was in her room cutting her arm. I asked Jill to go and tell another member of staff that I would be at Mary's room and could they check in with me as soon as possible. I was quite definite in my tone of voice and instruction to Jill, and was confident that Jill would do as I asked. For a brief moment I wondered if I was being 'set-up' by Jill as she knew that Mary had been quite hostile to me. I went to Mary's room and knocked on the door. There was no answer. I was aware of Mary's right to privacy and that that is really part of the culture of the unit. I felt quite anxious – not knowing whether to go on in or wait. I knocked again. This time there was an answer. I was anxious for Mary's safety and anxious for myself as I did not know what I would find inside the room. Another factor in my anxiety was that Mary had remained very distant from me; I had no sense of a relationship with Mary at all. Not only had she remained distant but had been openly hostile toward me. I could not make out what Mary said after my second knock on the door. It did not sound like 'come in'. I opened the door anyway.

Here is some of the dialogue with my thoughts and observations.

MARY: 'What do you want?'

Mary just gave a quick glance and looked away. I was relieved to see her sitting up on the bed. Her tone of voice was angry and hostile. There was quite a lot of blood and I could see she still had the blade in her hand.

ME: 'Can I come in?'

I had decided I needed to stay but also felt I needed some permission from Mary. If she had told me to get out I would have told her that I would send one of the staff to her.

MARY: 'If you want – but there's no point.'

Mary seemed less hostile. I asked if I could sit down on the bed beside her. I still kept a bit of distance from her. I was very relieved that she stopped cutting herself and had actually set the blade down.

ME: 'Mary, I'm here because Jill told me that you were hurting yourself. I know she told you that she was going to get someone. What you're doing looks sore. Do you want to talk to me about what's wrong? I've got plenty of time to listen – and I won't lecture at you.'

One of the other staff arrived and asked if we needed help. I said that I would call if I needed to. Mary gave me another quick glance. She looked at the staff member as if to say 'okay' and we were left alone again. There was a long silence. I broke it by the following comment.

ME: 'Mary, I don't know you all that well but I want to tell you that talking about things really can help and this makes me feel that you are being really hard on your self.'

I was beginning to feel that the distance put up by Mary had suddenly gone. I was worried that this might frighten her.

MARY: 'I do this more than you think. The staff just don't know about it.'

Mary rolled up her sweatshirt and showed me previous scars. They looked quite old.

MARY: 'I used to do it at home but my Ma never knew. She was always out with her friends.'

ME: 'Perhaps you would have liked her to notice?'

Mary looked at me intently but said nothing. I was aware that Mary had had a home visit yesterday. I also knew from discussion at handover that the last time Mary cut herself was following a home visit. Other questions were coming quickly to my mind but I did not want to push, yet on the other hand I felt that Mary was ready to talk.

ME: 'Mary there are other things I would like to ask you but I'm not sure that I should just at the moment.'

She shuffled a bit on the bed and started to pick at the blood on her arm. There was quite a long pause which was broken by Mary.

MARY: 'Go ahead – I don't mind.'

ME: 'I know that the last time you cut your arm was after a home visit'. (*I paused here before going any further – I was looking for some sign that I should go on. I got a glance from Mary and a slight nod.*) 'I also know that your dad was at home at the same time.' (*Mary was watching me intently*).

MARY: 'Did you know that I told Karen (key-worker) that I hate my dad?'

ME: 'No I didn't know that. Is that why you are cutting yourself?'

MARY: 'It's because of what he done to my sister. He called at the house yesterday when my ma was out. There was just me and him in the house. I want to say things but I can't.'

At this point two other girls arrive at the bedroom door. They were not too sympathetic toward Mary. I had to quite firmly ask them to leave. I was glad of the momentary distraction to give me a little thinking time. I was struck by the determined note in Mary's voice when she said 'I can't'.

ME: 'Mary you say there are things you want to say but can't. Do you think you might be able to write them down?'

MARY: 'I really hate my dad. If I wrote things down who would have to see it?'

ME: 'Who do you think you could allow to see it first?'

MARY: 'My key-worker, Karen.'

ME: 'Do you understand that Karen would probably have to tell your social worker.'

MARY: 'Yes I know that – would my Ma have to be told?'

ME: 'I don't know but I can find out for you.'

MARY: 'Karen is on duty tomorrow; I can ask her then. Will you get me something to write on – and an envelope?'

I agreed to this and then asked Mary if she would now let me clean up her arm. I also told her that I would like her to give me the piece of blade. I really was very unsure about doing this. I knew she could easily get another piece but I felt it was an important sign of caring for her that I removed the dangerous object. She handed it to me and we went downstairs.

Commentary

In her response to Mary in crisis, the student illustrates many aspects of residential child care which we have described and discussed above,

- the necessity of having a personalised value base that convincingly communicates respect for individuals.
- the ability to respond to the opportunity-led orientation of this work setting.
- the tension between the public and private aspects of the setting.
- the need for workers to have well developed self-knowledge.
- the ability to draw from a wide range of theories.
- the ability to put individual clients at the 'heart of the system'.
- the ability to quickly identify with the philosophy and working practices of the unit.
- the ability to use core social work skills in a wide variety of formal and informal settings.

The student demonstrated integration of values, knowledge and skills. She convincingly communicates values of respect and acceptance in all her actions with Mary, from knocking the bedroom door to the whole tone of her intervention. The student utilises knowledge in various ways: she knows and acts on the importance of informing a colleague about what is happening; she draws on information obtained at the handover meeting about Mary's home visits; she is acutely aware of and listens to her own internal dialogue of anxiety about her self as well as anxiety about Mary; she draws on her knowledge of crisis intervention theory and responds to the immediacy of what is happening with Mary; she works toward helping Mary identify adaptive coping mechanisms. The student's recording conveys the impression of a good use of core skills.

Written evidence of competence in group care

With regard to written evidence of competence in all social work settings we think it important to contextualise this requirement by repeating some of the points of emphasis contained in CCETSW's Paper 30. We do so because our experience suggests that producing evidence of competence creates strong temptation for students and practice teachers to compartmentalise placement experience, i.e. seeing competences as nothing more than discrete and separate tick lists, whereas significant emphasis in Paper 30 is that of integration of knowledge, values and skills. For example, Paper 30 states that 'competence in social work is the product of knowledge, skills, and values... students must be assessed for their understanding of knowledge and theory, and their integration of values in the context of their application to practice...', and a final comment with which we strongly agree reminds practice teachers that they '... must seek evidence of the integration of knowledge and values in students' practice'.

Of course they must, and to that injunction we add that practice teachers must also enable students to achieve this important integration. We turn now to examine the student's written comments in regard to each of the core competences.

Communicate and engage

This competence requires that students **communicate and engage with organisations and people within communities** to promote opportunities for children, adults, families and groups, at risk or in need to function, participate and develop in society. Two practice requirements are directly relevant; **form and develop working relationships with children, adults, families, carers and groups and communicate and engage... and seek to minimise factors which cause risk and need**. Here is how the student provides evidence of this competence:

> I was aware from pre-placement preparation, which included a visit to the unit and directed reading that I would not only have to *communicate and engage with the ten individuals in the unit but also with the group as a whole*. Similar episodes to that which I recorded on my first entry into the group living space happened time and again. Through these points of

contact I increased my range of responses so that by the end of placement I was not just 'the student' but an individual who could carry out a range of functions, e.g. someone who would socialise with the residents, a carer, an authority figure and someone who was there to carry out agreed pieces of work with individuals.

I became aware of the various types of groups that make up the totality of a residential unit. I believe that I have been successful in *communicating*, engaging with individual young people as well. Mary was, for example, initially quite hostile toward me. I came to understand that this is a characteristic way that Mary responds to new adults. When I responded to Mary in crisis I was very aware of this and out of respect was ready to leave her room if she had so indicated. With Mary I communicated concern and respect, I engaged her in the beginning of a problem solving sequence and I promoted an opportunity for her to function in a more adaptive way. I used knowledge about Mary as an individual as well as knowledge of crisis theory to shape my intervention, I dealt with the immediate issue and through use of open questions, silence and active listening I helped Mary to communicate her thoughts and feelings about a recent experience which had caused her distress.

Promote and enable

This competency is defined in Paper 30 as **promote opportunities for people to use their own strengths and expertise** to enable them to meet responsibilities, secure rights and achieve change. Specific practice requirements are **to promote the rights of children and adults at risk or in need... provide information and advice to individuals, families, carers and groups... provide opportunities for learning and development to enable children to function and participate and to enable people to use their own strengths and expertise to meet responsibilities, secure rights and achieve change**.

The student provides evidence of this competence as follows.

There is a very strong awareness in this unit among young people and workers of rights and responsibilities. When I first made entry to the group living space I was acutely aware of this – I recorded that I felt a bit like an outsider. From personal conviction I believe I do show respect anyway, but I took my lead from other workers in this unit and made sure that I communicated respect and interest in my dealings with the young people. On occasions when young people infringed the rights of others and had to be enabled to think about meeting their responsibilities, I was able to confront such issues in a way that *promoted their ability to think and plan how they might do things differently next time and so achieve change.* As time went on and I took on a wider repertoire of roles and tasks I found that in the daily context of group care there was ample opportunity for me to meet several evidence indicators for this competence and its practice requirements e.g. *assisting children to represent their own rights.* This was done in many informal discussions with the young people when they seemed to use me to check out ideas that they wanted to discuss with key-workers or social workers – I helped them rehearse their approach; advocate directly with and on behalf of children – this happened through young people asking me to raise issues on their behalf at staff meetings; assist children to participate in decision making about arrangements for daily living and personal care – work in relation to this evidence indicator happened every day as young people talked about their plans or, as sometimes happened, I had to tell them about sanctions that had been imposed and talked through how they were going to manage temporary restrictions on liberty and learn from the experience. In my beginning contact with Mary and in subsequent work with her I believe I fully met the practice requirement of *enable people to use their own strengths and expertise to meet responsibilities, secure rights and achieve change.*

Assess and plan

This competence is defined as **work in partnership to assess and revise people's circumstances and plan responses to need and risk**; among the practice requirements the most relevant are that students **work in partnership to assess and review people's needs, rights, risks, strengths, responsibilities and resources... work in partnership to identify and analyse risk of harm, abuse or failure to protect**. The student details her evidence of competence in the following way.

> From this placement I have learned that assessment in a group care setting is a continuous activity. The evidence indicator of: *identify and evaluate the purpose of assessment* has had real meaning for me in this placement as has that of *gathering recording and evaluating information to make assessment.* For example, there is the immediate assessment process of watching one's own interventions with individuals and groups and assessing the impact of these; then there is the process of formal assessment as requested, for example, by a court. There is also the assessment of situations like Mary in crisis. In the latter I was very aware of assessing what Mary needed from me: care, protection and someone who could help her draw on her strengths and find adaptive ways to cope with her distress. I was able then to communicate this episode to the rest of the staff team and to Mary's social worker, in doing so I believe I contributed to analysis of risk and harm, thus ensuring that

the agencies concerned did not fail in their statutory and legal requirements to protect Mary. In preparation for a meeting to discuss Mary's future home visits I undertook a joint assessment with Mary which included a range of options. I was thus able to work in partnership with Mary and from this exercise I was able to formulate and present an assessment and options for action.

Intervene and provide services

This competence requires students to **intervene and provide services to achieve change, through provisions or purchase of appropriate levels of support, care, protection and control**. Five practice requirements give further definition to this competence; four are particularly pertinent: **contribute to the direct provision of care, support and protection; support and sustain children, young people through the process of change; sustain and maintain working relationships with individuals and groups; contribute to the care protections and control of people who are a risk to themselves or others**. The student details her evidence in the following way.

My role in this unit involved me in the direct provision of services. Because of the increase of children and young people in residential care who are listed on the child protection register and who as a consequence are subject to child protection plans I was very aware of *care protection and support*. I contributed directly to this in my work with Mary. I initially provided her with an atmosphere in which she was assured that I would not lecture her, an atmosphere which conveyed respect and acceptance, an atmosphere which showed that I was not shocked or panicked by her actions (even though I was feeling anxious myself) and an atmosphere that did not retaliate for the hostility that I had experienced from Mary. Removing the blade from Mary is an example of protection and care. I believe I communicated that I valued Mary as a person and did so without being possessive of her. As we entered into a partnership I provided her with a working relationship which continued to show acceptance but which challenged Mary to draw on her strengths and abilities. Through this work with Mary I met other evidence indicators, for example, *assist children and adults to express their emotional needs through the process of change... provide emotional support to sustain children and young people through the process of change*. I attended and contributed to Child in Care Reviews and was thus involved in *planning programmes of personal care for children and young people in group care settings*.

Throughout the placement several other evidence indicators occurred with regularity and proved to be strongly characteristic of residential child care, for example, *negotiate and agree aims, expectations, roles and ground rules for on-going work with children, young people, adults, carers, and groups*. The unit had a basic number of rules and expectations. For the most part these were accepted by the young people but, as most adolescents will, they did try to find ways round rules and to dilute or change expectations. I had good experience of working with this adolescent phenomenon (which is probably accentuated by the numbers of workers and young people involved, i.e. compared to a family, the demands on communication in a residential unit about decisions concerning rules, care plans etc., are multiplied many times). Other evidence indicators which were regularly met were: *challenge behaviour that creates risk and establish boundaries and expectations; maintain and review agreed boundaries and expectations of behaviour; assist people to develop greater control over their own behaviour; assist people to change behaviour harmful to themselves and others; respond to expressions of emotional needs from children, young people... throughout the development and maintenance of a professional social work relationship.*

Work in organisations

Paper 30 states this competence very briefly as **contribute to the work of the Organisation**. There are three practice requirements. In the following paragraph we discuss the one that has most direct bearing in this placement: **demonstrate capacity to work as an accountable and effective member of the organisation in which placed**. The student comments as follows.

On this placement I became very aware of interdependence between team members and between the team as a whole, the host organisation and with other professionals outside the agency. At daily handover meetings and in teams meetings I believe I went through a process of becoming an effective team member by describing my contact with the young people and by openly communicating things that were difficult for me, for example Mary's hostility and distance and by actively seeking advice from colleagues. When Mary was in crisis I was very aware of not taking over from the Key-worker who was not on duty. I made sure that the information was passed to the Key-worker. This is one example of effective team work. In joining with the resident's group I was aware of being a representative of the staff team and quickly understood that I needed to be seen as part of that team whilst retaining my own individuality. I contributed to the work of the organisation by completing written records such as Untoward Incident forms of episodes such as Mary's self-injury, by taking minutes of meetings and by contributing items for team meeting agendas.

Develop professional competence

The final core competence in CCETSW's Paper 30 requires that students show evidence of ability to **manage and evaluate own capacity to develop professional competence**. The practice requirements are; **use supervision effectively... exchange, process and report information... contribute to the resolution of professional dilemmas and conflicts, balancing rights, needs and perspectives... respond to unexpected opportunities and problems; make decisions** and finally **contribute to the maintenance, critical evaluation and development of own professional practice, knowledge and values**. Here is how the student evidences her achievement of this competence.

> I had not previously worked in a residential child care setting, therefore much of what was expected of me was quite new. I believe I have achieved this competence in three ways; from using supervision, from directed reading and from watching and working with experienced workers. I found that I had to make good use of supervision as one opportunity to think through the numerous events of each day. I was surprised at the emotional intensity of a residential child care setting, and found that I actually needed to talk about the emotional components of the wide range of relationships in which I became involved. I found it helpful to prepare for supervision by thinking about thoughts and feelings that I had about the various roles that I had to take on.

As far as direct work with the young people was concerned these roles grouped under the headings of care, control and focused pieces of work. By using supervision as an opportunity for personal reflection I learned that in this setting I needed to develop competence in using skills in informal as well as formal settings. Using supervision in this way enabled me to identify and develop strategies, for coping with stressful situations; for example, I felt quite confused by Mary's hostility toward me. This made me doubt myself and made me think that I had done something to her. Realising that this was Mary's typical response to new adults and that she had understandable reasons for not immediately trusting adults helped me to maintain an attitude of respect toward her. The situation with Mary enabled me to make connections between practice dilemmas and research findings about children in residential care. Research shows (Millham, Bullock, Hoşie and Haak 1986) that children in residential care can lose contact with family members, yet Mary comes from a family where there has been sexual abuse and neglect. On the one hand Mary needs and has a right to protection but on the other hand has a right and need to see her mother – even though it is thought that her mother may have know about the abuse to Mary's sister. This was resolved by having supervised access visits between Mary and her mother.

This placement gave me many opportunities to meet three particular practice requirements associated with this competency, first, *responding to unexpected opportunities*. I found that the young people were very willing to talk about matters of concern to them at all sorts of odd moments during the day. It was possible to talk these situations through and at the end of the conversation to reinforce that they had, for example, used good thinking skills to solve problems. The second practice requirement that was very evident on this placement was make decisions. I found that I was constantly involved in making decisions; these included individual decisions which only I could make; for example, about whether or not to intervene in conflicts between the young people in the group living context. Other decision making events took place in groups such as the staff team or in inter-agency settings such as Child Protection Case Conferences which had multi-disciplinary membership. The third practice requirement which occurred frequently was exchange, process and report information. I was surprised at the amount of information that is generated in this social work setting. Every day involved *information exchange*, within the unit between staff and the manager, within each shift team and between the shift teams; also between young people and the workers. Outside the unit other professionals also need to be kept informed and involved, so too do parents and other family members.

I believe that the placement enabled me to meet the following evidence indicators:

- prepare for and use supervision effectively
- identify personal stress and develop coping strategies
- contribute to meetings and decisions making
- record, evaluate and store information
- make creative use of opportunities to achieve positive change
- make and record decisions within agency decision making processes.

Conclusion

As in like all other social work settings, good practice in residential child care is informed by an ever expanding corpus of knowledge. The translation of that knowledge into social work tasks and activities is dependent on the use of skills soundly based on professional values. Debate about the value of residential child care is likely to continue for some time to come (Skinner 1992). In the meantime we acknowledge that the service has major developmental hurdles to overcome (Gibson 1995). Notwithstanding these observations our experience confirms that good residential child care placements can provide students with a rich opportunity to develop competence in social work practice and are a setting in which all the practice requirements of CCETSW's new Paper 30 can be fulfilled.

References

Bannister, D. (1990) 'Knowledge of self.' In M. Herbert *Psychology for Social Workers*. The British Psychology Society and Macmillian Publishers Limited.

Brown, A. and Clough, R. (1989) *Groups and Groupings. Life and Work in Day and Residential Centres*. London and New York: Tavistock/Routledge.

Budlong, J., Holden, M. and Mooney, A.J. (1993) *Therapeutic Crisis in Residential Youth and Child Care*. A training pack produced by Family Life Development Centre, College of Human Ecology Cornell University Ithaca NY, NY.

Cannan, C. (1995) 'Enterprise culture, professional socialisation, and social work education.' *Journal of Socialist Theory and Practice in Social Welfare 42*, Winter 94/95, 5–18.

CCETSW (Central Council for Education and Training in Social Work) (1995) *Rules and Requirements for the Diploma in Social Work, Paper 30*. London: CCETSW.

Coulshed, V. (1991) *Social Work Practice. An Introduction*. London: Macmillan.

Davies, L. (1982) *Residential Care: A Community Resource*. London: Heineman.

Dickson, D., Saunders, C. and Stringer, M. (1993) *Rewarding People. The Skills of Responding Positively*. London and New York: Routledge.

Douglas, T. (1986) *Group Living. The Application of Group Dynamics in Residential Settings*. London: Tavistock.

England, H. (1986) *Social Work as Art: Making sense for Good Practice*. London: Allen and Unwin.

Gibson, A.J. (1995) 'Residential child care in Northern Ireland: confronting old images and planning for partnership with parents and families.' *Northern Ireland Journal of Multi-Disciplinary Child Care Practice 2*, 4, 26–39.

Horne, M. (1987) 'Values in Social Work.' In *Community Care Practice Handbook*. Aldershot: Ashgate.

Kahan, B. (1994) *Growing up in Groups*. London: HMSO.

Levy, A. and Kahan, B. (1991) *The Pindown Experience and the Protection of Children: The Report of the Staffordshire Child Care Inquiry 1990*. Staffordshire County Council.

Levy, C.S. (1973) 'The value base of social work.' *Journal of Education for Social Work 9, 34–42*.

Millham, S., Bullock, R., Hosie, K. and Haak, M. (1986) *Lost in Care. The Problems of Maintaining Links Between Children and their Families*. Aldershot: Gower.

Parker, R. (1988) *Residential Care: The Research Reviewed*. London: National Institute for Social Work.

Robins, J. (1980) *The Lost Children: A Study of Charity Children in Ireland 1700–1900*. Dublin: Institute of Public Administration.

Skinner, A. (1992) *Another Kind of Home – a Review of Residential Child Care. The Social Work Services Inspectorate for Scotland*. Edinburgh: HMSO.

Thompson, N. (1993) *Anti-Discriminatory Practice*. London: Macmillan.

Utting, W. (1991) *Children in the Public Care. A review of Residential Child Care*. London: HMSO.

Ward, A. (1993) *Working in Group Care*. Birmingham: Venture Press.

Warner, N. (1992) *Choosing with Care. Report of the Committee of Inquiry into the Selection Development and management of Staff in Children's Homes*. London: HMSO.

Winnicott, C. (1971) *Child Care and Social Work*. Hitchin: Codicote Press.

CHAPTER 4

Competence in Mental Health Social Work

Jim Campbell

'It is only practice which is founded on values, carried out in a skilled manner and informed by knowledge, critical analysis and reflection which is competent practice' (CCETSW Paper 30, 1995)

Introduction

Paper 30 provides students working in the mental health field with a framework for demonstrating competent social work practice. In this chapter the theme of competence will be explored in the context of case material referred to a student social worker located in a community-based mental health placement. Although there is a great variety in the types of referrals to be found in mental health social work, the material chosen for analysis in this chapter is fairly typical, and allows for a discussion about the nature of chronic mental illness, the needs of the person with the illness as well as their carer and family members. The discussion starts with the early period of engagement through to intervention with the family.

An analysis of key aspects of the student's practice with the family will take place for *each* of the four competences – **communicate and engage, promote and enable, assess and plan, intervene and provide services**. The remaining two core competences – **working in organisations** and **developing professional competence** – will be discussed and integrated throughout this analysis. In addition, practice requirements and performance criteria for the core competences will be identified where appropriate. Competent social work practice is only possible when the practitioner can achieve a synthesis between the 'doing' of social work, and the theories and ideas which inform professional activity. For this reason, the discussion of core competences takes place alongside a body of knowledge which the student should acquire.

Case Material

Brief history

Susan Jones (33) and her cohabitee John Smith (35) live in a public authority terrace in a run down inner city area. Susan's two children from a previous marriage, Jill (13) and Tom (10) live with the couple. Susan has a long history of mental disorder which began with an acute psychotic episode following the birth of Jill. Since then she has had twelve admissions to psychiatric hospital, over half of which have been on a compulsory basis. The original diagnosis of schizophrenia has been occasionally questioned by psychiatrists, but remains. For the last five years Susan has received visits from her community psychiatric nurse who administers a long-acting depot injection, designed to counteract delusional thoughts of persecution, and to monitor the use of oral tranquilisers. She is reviewed by psychiatrists at an outpatients clinic on a monthly basis.

John, who is long-term unemployed, met Susan ten years ago when they were in psychiatric hospital. He was receiving treatment for depression. He has had no recent admissions to hospital. He has struggled to hold the family together, particularly at times of crisis when Susan's mental state deteriorates. He has a caring relationship with his stepchildren but finds it hard to address their demands for consistent attention and resources. Despite this impoverished environment, Jill and Tom have managed to do reasonably well at school. There is little support from any extended family.

Current circumstances

Susan has just been discharged from psychiatric hospital after another compulsory admission. Prior to admission she had expressed thoughts of suicide and paranoid ideas about being pursued by persons unknown. The hospital-based social worker has referred the family to the community team and the 'case' has been allocated to the student.

Reason for referral

The multidisciplinary team in the hospital are concerned at Susan's unbroken cycle of relapse and admission over the years. They are requesting social work involvement as a preventative measure.

The recognition of a number of key features in this case should stand out for the student social worker on reading the details of this referral. These include the chronic nature of Susan's mental illness, potential difficulties for her children, at home and at school, and the impoverished living environment faced by the whole family. More positively, John appears to have been an essential support for the family. The problem of non-attendance at school could well be the consequence of disruption to the family created by Susan's ill-health.

Communicate and engage

A major challenge in working with people with mental health problems is in understanding the depth of the client's human distress and its impact on the worker's awareness of 'self'. In dealing with the painful stories expressed by this family, there may be an understandable temptation by the student to ignore these emotions and, at times, their strange and bizarre thought processes. This response may have a number of causes. The psychoanalytical concepts of transference and countertransference (Yelloly 1980), for example, help explain how our past lives create psychological blocks which prevent us from listening to the needs of others. Sociological perspectives can also reveal popularized discourses on 'madness which may mistakenly inform social work practice (Dallos and Boswell 1993). It is essential that the student recognises the complex influences affecting her/his professional judgement; this will help in refraining from making generalized assumptions about this family's experience of mental illness.

Such personal insights will complement the Paper 30 value requirement which asserts that students must demonstrate **'respect and value uniqueness and diversity'** and **'Promote people's rights to choice, privacy, confidentiality and protection…'**. As part of a commitment to a sound value base for practice it is crucial that the student should not reinforce or replicate Susan's experiences of being deprived of individual freedom and opportunities for decision-making. In the early stages of **engagement** the student should enter the relationship with Susan with an openness and willingness to listen. This sense of honesty, combined with a genuine commitment to helping, will lay the foundation for **promoting** Susan's rights and wishes and **enabling** the family to reestablish their lives following her discharge from hospital. Susan's recent experiences in being detained in hospital will have damaged her self-esteem and trust of professionals. There is a very real possibility that she will perceive anyone associated with mental health services as a sinister, controlling threat to her personal freedom and the well-being of her family. In order to restore her self-belief and confidence in the student as a caring figure, Susan should be contacted first so that *her* feelings and hopes can be explored. The student should offer to visit Susan's home for the first interview because it will probably feel more secure for her than the potentially threatening surroundings of yet another institution – an office in a social services department.

In the initial communication with Susan the student should be competent in using generic, interpersonal skills which are just as appropriate for interventions with people who have mental health problems as other groups (Tilbury 1993). It is inconceivable that a student working in the mental health field could be assessed as competent without an able demonstration of interpersonal skills – questioning, clarifying, listening, empathising, reflecting, sustaining, restating, controlling, summarizing and non-verbal communication. For Susan, who may be experiencing abject feelings of loss and abandonment, the student must be able to demonstrate an ability to listen, empathise and reflect back, if the client's emotional pain is to be recognised and addressed. The student should be careful to describe the purpose of their involvement in language which is non-threatening, jargon-free and which makes sense to the client. Susan may not have had good experiences of meaningful communication with professionals in the past. It may be that her capacity to understand the student's role may be limited by her disturbed mental state and/or the side effects of psychotropic medication. A consistent, empathic and non-threatening approach can prevent Susan from relapsing (Falloon *et al.* 1982; Leff and Vaughn 1985). Skills in active listening, clarifying and restating the purpose of the social work intervention will provide a necessary sense of consistency to the interaction between the student and Susan.

The student should endeavour to 'communicate effectively' with various parts of the family system (Dallos 1991) and allow Susan, John, Jill and Tom to have space to speak for themselves. As a way of 'tuning in' to the needs of the family members, the student should ask these questions:

SUSAN:

- Can she talk of her experiences of breakdown and incarceration?
- Can she be allowed to express her feelings about loss of role as a wife and mother?
- What are the effects of stigma on her identity and personal confidence?

JOHN:

- Can he express anger about the role and expectations of caring for the family?
- Has he had an opportunity to talk about losses in his life?

JILL AND TOM:

- What are their feelings and experiences of the stigma associated with the mental illness in the family?
- Are their life-cycle needs being met?
- How good is the relationship with their mother and step-father?

As the social work process moves towards **assessment** and **intervention**, the student should consider 'contacting community resources' as a way of broadening the system to help alleviate the stigma experienced by the family (Mayo 1994).

Effective communication with other agencies and professionals is required in this referral. The student should 'establish contact... and communicate effectively' with the multidisciplinary hospital team and other agencies (family and child care social workers, education and welfare officers). They should make early contact with key professionals to explain the purpose of intervention and, if need be, prepare to renegotiate role where conflict with community psychiatric nurse (CPN) and psychiatrist occurs. Even in these initial stages, this willingness to be flexible should not preclude an assertive defence of the social work role as part of competence in **working in organisations** and towards **developing professional competence**. Intraprofessional rivalry and conflict is commonplace in the mental health field so students should be able to listen to the views of other professionals but also be competent in clarifying reasons for particular assessments and strategies for intervention. There are a variety of situations which offer the student opportunities to 'communicate effectively with other... professionals':

(1) By telephone, negotiate with the community psychiatric nurse (CPN) a mutually agreed visiting timetable and occasional points of contact for the purposes of review.

(2) Prepare a report, which can be copied to other professionals, which details the initial assessment and proposed interventions.

(3) In supervision, discuss the significant issues gained from an initial assessment (Susan's mental state, stability of relationships in the family, proposed interventions), in preparation for a formal multidisciplinary meeting about Susan and her family's progress since discharge.

Promote and enable

Paper 30's value statement also provides encouragement for the student to empower members of the family. To be competent the student should be able to '**identify, analyse and take action to counter discrimination, racism, disadvantage, inequality and injustice**'. A knowledge of systems of discrimination often faced by people with mental health problems is an essential prerequisite if the student is to be equipped to challenge oppression.

It has been argued that the social construction of images of disability shape professional discourses about the behaviour of clients and reinforce wider systems of discrimination (Foucault 1965; Oliver 1993). The student should therefore be able to move beyond oversimplified explanations for Susan's behaviour and begin to understand the way in which social inequalities shape the services she and her family receives. There is, for example, evidence that social class influences the diagnosis and treatment of mental disorders (Goldberg and Huxley 1980; Newton 1988; Pilgrim and Rodgers 1993). The fact that many people with mental health problems are unemployed and in receipt of welfare benefits, indicates a *de facto* experience of unequal opportunity. Racism and sexism are pernicious influences on the provision of many services for people with mental health problems (Brown and Harris 1978; CCETSW

1991; Corob 1987; Dominelli and McLeod 1988; Fernando 1988; Newton 1988; Pilgrim and Rodgers 1993). What emerges from such literature is evidence of multi-layered, overlapping systems of inequalities, the effects of which may have to be contended with by this family in their everyday lives. The student should be not only able to demonstrate an awareness and understanding of the dimensions of such discrimination, they should demonstrate competence in how they have challenged their own prejudices and oppressive social structures. Social work agencies in the mental health field are gradually moving towards an acceptance of the need to redress such imbalances of power. Theories of user empowerment (Braye and Preston-Shoot 1995; Croft and Beresford 1993; Monach and Sprigs 1994) for example, offers the student a framework which can address discrimination within organisations in purposeful ways which can empower service users.

In this case the student should consider a number of opportunities for 'promoting the rights' of this family, bearing in mind that careful attention must always be paid to establishing prior agreement and moving at the clients' pace. For Susan, as with other women, her experience of the psychiatric system may have left her stigmatised and degraded; subjected to stereotypical ideas about her loss of role as a mother and carer for her children. There needs to be careful attention to how the student recognises the internalised prejudices they may be bringing to practice. For example in the way she/he views the roles and relationships, they may be using assumptions which reinforce the 'patriarchal ideology'. Attention to Susan's needs can be achieved through a sensitive, non-judgmental interviewing style which acknowledges this history of discrimination. Susan should be allowed to revisit any past 'bad' experiences of psychiatry and any shame she might have of failure as a mother and wife. Self-confidence can emerge if clients' grief and anger can be contained by the student, but this entails patience and an ability to sustain a fundamentally caring relationship. Moving beyond the interpersonal relationship between the student and Susan, her rights may be further **promoted** by the use of community-based resources. It would be appropriate, for example for the student to 'facilitate access' to a woman's' group in the local area for Susan, either through a direct referral or by providing Susan with the information to 'enable her to use her own strengths and expertise to achieve change'.

Much of the literature on empowerment describes how the failure of adequate information, and a lack of technical knowledge about how to access services, results in structured inequality for social work clients. Discrimination caused by generalized prejudices about disability, gender, race, class, sexual orientation, age and religion further compounds these failings of systems of welfare. The social and economic circumstances of this family suggest that the student has further opportunities to demonstrate competent anti-oppressive practice. John's role as carer for the family should be readily acknowledged as legitimate and meaningful. Resources from both statutory and voluntary sectors should be assessed and used to support him. The student should gain a thorough working knowledge of the welfare rights system in order to alleviate the family's poverty and 'directly provide information and advice to the family'. She/he should:

- maximise the family's income level by encouraging legitimate benefit claims
- advocate on behalf of the family with fuel boards and the DSS
- improve access to services
- provide information about services (Blackburn 1992, p.74)

When acting on behalf of the family the student should ask whether she/he has

- the family's consent to be their advocate?
- an agreed plan which prioritises which problems are to be addressed and solved?
- clarified and clearly presented the issues to the service provider?
- confirmed that the receiver be in a position to meet these requests?

Assess and plan
ASSESSING MENTAL ILLNESS
An important task for the student will be their assessment of the impact of social circumstances on Susan's mental state. There is little doubt that what has become known as the 'medical model of mental illness' will influence the practice of the student in working with this family. Despite doubts about its scientific status (Clare 1980; Newton 1988; Pilgrim and Rodgers 1993; Sedgewick 1982; Sheldon 1984), the student will find themselves using the medical model because it seems to provide a convenient epistemology which apparently strengthens practice judgments and helps them 'demonstrate capacity to work as an accountable and effective member of the organisations in which placed'. Hudson (1982) describes the intricate relationship which exists between mental health social workers and other psychiatric team members in the assessment and diagnosis of mental illness. A sound grasp of the psychiatric system of classification will enhance multidisciplinary working and help towards a full assessment of the client's problems. The student should be aware of the symptomology of paranoid schizophrenia – thought disorder, auditory hallucinations, delusions, flatness or incongruity of mood – in order to make a judgement about Susan's current mental state, and communicate this to other professionals.

The need for a system of psychiatric classification is important for the care and treatment of sufferers, but the discourses which accompany the label often deny the existence of the diversity of human experience and contingent choices made by clients. The student should be aware of the possibility that too close an attachment to this perspective may lead to a simplistic assessment of Susan's mental disorder; an illness to be treated rather than a problem to be solved. For this reason the student should 'identify and evaluate the context and purpose of assessment' and consider, for example, whether aspects of of Susan's illness may be socially constructed. The variation in the social work profession's acceptance of the 'illness model' (Tilbury 1993) will allow the student to make choices about alternative perspectives when assessing the complex social circumstances of this family. The medical model is a significant but not comprehensive guide to understanding disturbed mental states and alternatives to this approach should become part of the student's practice repertoire.

The broad collection of writers on 'anti-psychiatry' (Sedgewick 1982) have delivered critical insights into the social construction of mental illness and penetrating analyses of the way in which professionals protect their power at the expense of clients' rights. These social critiques, although often insightful, provide limited guidance for practice. Other models of mental illness, however, offer useful concepts which may be applicable to the circumstances of this family. For example, an awareness of how aspects of mental illnesses develop through learned behaviour (Sutton 1994; Sutton and Herbert 1992; Trower, Casey and Dryden 1988) might help the student consider whether at least some aspects of Susan's thoughts, feelings and behaviour are conditioned by the social circumstances of 'being ill'– she may have lost the will to be proactive in making decisions because this is not expected of her by family members and professionals. The student might consider theories of loss and grief rather than using the illness paradigm, to explain a understandable changes in Susan's mood created by personal conflict within the family.

Assessment of risk

The student's understanding of Susan's mental illness will also inform crucial decisions about risk (Hudson 1982; Sutton and Herbert 1992; Tilbury 1993). Competence in assessing risk in the mental health field involves a detailed calculation of a number of variables. The concern that Susan may take her life, or the lives of others, should be an important aspect of the student's assessment. It is therefore important that she/he is aware of a knowledge base which can support skills in assessing such risk – past history of parasuicide, history of mental disorder, a history of chronic social disorganisation. The immediate circumstances of risk in the client's life, including evidence of recent disruptions to close relationships, debilitating life events, verbal or written expressions of intention to commit suicide, access to alcohol, drugs and firearms, indicate high risk. Although Susan's history of mental illness indicates a risk factor in this case, there are protective factors – a caring partner and children, regular visits from professionals, and limited times when Susan will be alone at home.

Nevertheless, the student should be vigilant in observing and reporting changes in Susan' mood, thought process and expressions of intent to self-harm or injure others.

As part of the **assessment** it is important to gauge what levels of risk exist in the family and how much therapeutic work can be managed by the student. Particularly in the early stages of **assessment**, the student social worker should prepare well for supervision as an essential prerequisite for **developing professional competence**. A judgement about the involvement of other key professionals or support mechanisms should be made by the student as part of competence in **working in organisations**.

An awareness of the roles of various mental health professionals should be combined with skills of negotiation and advocacy if intervention is to be purposeful. A major concern for the student should be if Susan's mental state begins to deteriorate; tell-tale symptoms may include retarded emotional responses and depressive mood, or conversely, overactive or bizarre thought-processes. If this is the case there should be immediate discussion with the CPN and her psychiatrist, perhaps leading to the arrangement of a quick outpatient's review. In the case of relapse causing risk or harm, the student should ensure that increased monitoring visits take place, and that John is aware of the student's concern and support. Ultimately a statutory response may be the only alternative left to be considered available to the student.

The statutory role

A knowledge of existing mental health law will inform the student's judgement about statutory intervention if and when Susan's mental state deteriorates. The various national mental health laws (DHSS 1983; DHSS 1984; DHSS 1986) have established more substantive rights for patients, and their nearest relatives, and created an independent professional role for the Approved Social Worker (ASW) (Campbell 1995; Gostin 1975; Olsen 1984; Prior 1992; Sheppard 1990). Although at times subject to criticism about role and function (Bean 1986; Kerfoot and Huxley 1994; Prior 1992), the creation of such professional responsibility for the ASW has enabled mental health social workers to use knowledge, skills and values to assess, intervene and protect the rights of clients, particularly around the contentious period prior to compulsory admission to hospital. It is essential that the student is conversant with the ethos and relevant principles of the legislation, and the duties and responsibilities of the ASW. Although the student will not be qualified to carry out statutory duties (only practitioners who have completed a specialised post-qualifying programme to become ASWs can carry out applications for assessment, for example), they will need to know when it is appropriate to consult their supervisor and ASW. The basic conditions are that

- Susan is suffering from a mental disorder at that moment.

- There is a substantial likelihood of serious physical harm to herself or others.
- The situation is so serious that it requires her detention in hospital.

The student should also assess other relevant factors which can help the ASW make a judgement about whether a statutory response is appropriate or not:

- Is Susan informed about the possibility of a detention in hospital?
- Is the nearest relative (John) informed and agreeable?
- Are there alternatives to a detention in hospital, including community support/referral to a hostel?

Although the final decision about the detention in hospital will not be the student's, there is a great deal they can do to humanise the experience for Susan and her family by providing an explanation about how the risk is viewed and what action is being proposed. 'Working in partnership with families to identify and analyse risk of harm' may avert the need for a statutory response – attention to well-thought-out planning can prevent the repetition of breakdown and hospitalisation. With the client's permission it may be reasonable to accompany Susan to her outpatient's appointment to update and agree original plans with her psychiatrist. Consistent and complementary visiting arrangements agreed by the student and CPN means that the family's social care and physical needs are monitored and resources organised accordingly. It might emerge that John feels that Susan may be more 'manageable' if extra support is provided for him: a home help service, or a referral for attendance for Susan at a psychiatric day hospital.

Planning

The theme of 'working in partnership' is crucial to competence in **planning**. Because of the debilitating nature of schizophrenia – disorder of thought often accompanied by the negative symptoms of reduced motivation and loss of affect – there is a need to move at Susan's pace and engage the family in managing levels of harmful stress. It is important to help individual members protect their own needs and interests to prevent the family becoming totally enmeshed in the management of the mental disorder. One way of achieving this stability is through the use of contracts with family members (Sutton and Herbert 1992). Contracts can facilitate the student 'Identifying with service users, carers and other professional, required and available resources to meet agreed objectives and options'. With the permission of individual members of the family the student should develop a contractual agreement which meets their needs and the student's statutory obligations:

(1) The student should agree to a visiting timetable to monitor Susan's mental state and rehabilitation. Susan should be encouraged to use the session to discuss issues arising from her compulsory admission to hospital, and what future services might be appropriate as the contact with the student develops.

(2) The student should interview Jill and Tom to **assess** their developmental needs and progress at school.

(3) John should be given the opportunity to express his needs as a carer – does he need more material and emotional support?

(4) The student should explore the use of the contract to engage the family in a programme of education about 'stress and schizophrenia'. This would include the provision of short information sessions by the student or the CPN about avoiding excessive criticism and conflict in dealing with Susan.

The use of contracts can help **assess and plan** interventions which can be approved in a formal way by the student and the family. It is important, however, that the student does not simply become a 'technician' who manages family conflict or gatekeeps resources. The painful slowness of Susan's thought process and intermittent fears of persecution, John's struggle to provide as best he can for his partner and step children, the possible shame and frustration which Tom and Jill harbour about their mother's mental illness – these are all changing personal and social circumstances, to be carefully and sensitively considered in each contact with the family members.

Intervene and provide services

Competence in providing services for this family will hinge on the student's awareness of the way in which decisions by policy makers impinge on organisations and ultimately individual practice. For example, the related themes of 'deinstitutionalisation' and 'community care' which emerged during the last twenty-five years have significantly influenced the shape and delivery of social services for people with mental health problems (Bean and Mounser 1993; Busfield 1986; Rodgers, Pilgrim and Lacey 1993). The accelerated closure of psychiatric hospitals in the 1980s and 1990s has coincided with broader changes in the organisation and delivery of health and social services (Langan and Clarke 1994; Payne 1995). The key objectives for community care post-Griffiths have been summarised as:

- the promotion of domicilary, day and respite services to enable people to live in their own homes.
- support for carers by service providers.
- the proper assessment of need and case management.

- the development of a flourishing independent sector.
- greater accountability by service providers
- the introduction of a funding structure which would lead to better use of taxpayers' money. (Malin 1994, p.6)

These substantial changes have affected the structure of social welfare organisations and social work practice. The management of packages of care introduces the student to the pressures and conflicts of **working in organisations** at a time of financial stringency. The student should be able to use skills in decision-making and processing information to further the **development of professional competence**. His or her assessment of the family's needs will be a crucial factor in the negotiation of resources, 'managing packages of care', as well as 'directly contributing to the provision of care support and protection' for the family. In engaging with such a wide range of problems, the student should have a flexible approach to problem-solving, using a diverse skills-base.

There are a number of ways in which the student can make this policy environment work to the benefit of the family and 'Contribute to the provision of an effective and safe physical, environment for individuals, families and carers'. Using skills in advocacy and negotiation (Braye and Preston-Shoot 1995; Challis 1994; Payne 1995), the student should liaise with a care manager if John requires domicilary support. The student should present a clear assessment of prioritised need, based on the physical and psychological stress of caring, and the possibility of breakdown and institutional care for Susan.

In working with other agencies the student will need to be strategic in finding out which key personnel should be contacted and what their organisational responsibilities are. If the family requires assistance with poor housing conditions, it is important that the student is aware of the local housing department's policy and procedures, and which housing officer deals with such matters. If necessary the student should use her/his professional authority to seek additional supporting evidence in the form of a sympathetic letter from Susan's GP or consultant psychiatrist. Once contact is made between the student and the officer who is managing the resource, then the student's competent use of interpersonal skills – in clarifying, explaining, confronting – will be important in the decision which could benefit the family. The student should review the family's income from state benefits and determine full 'uptake'. It would be appropriate, for example, to discuss with the social fund manager the case for a grant if it can be shown that such assistance would prevent a further hospital admission for Susan. There is little doubt that consistent attention to such 'practical needs' will help generate confidence in the helping relationship with the family.

The student should also consider the possibility of directly providing therapeutic services for the family as a way of supporting their emotional needs. Therapeutic skills are often used by mental health professionals to help solve social and psychological problems; and despite a sense of mystique and technical expertise which is sometimes associated with these interventions, the student should not be reticent in acquiring and applying such skills with this family. As part of the requirement to **developing professional competence**, supervision should always be sought before planning detailed therapeutic interventions. The choice of therapy will depend on the student's personal and professional ideology, as well as the problems presented by the family.

There are a number of therapeutic approaches available to the student, which would be relevant in this case. Trower, Bryant and Argyle (1978) use theories of behaviour modification to develop social skills training for people with mental illness. Competence in this approach would include the student assessing Susan's social deficits and problem behaviours, and contracting to time-limited, uncomplicated tasks. For example Susan's reduced drive and loss of confidence will have left her unable to perform basic functions. A short programme in time management might reduce these social deficits. A cognitive therapy approach may be used to help John overcome depressive ideas or negative self-images which he holds about himself (Trower *et al.* 1988). In both of these forms of intervention the student needs to be convinced that there is an agreement with the client about the nature of the problem, that the identified problem can be measured and that there is a commitment to the fulfilment of agreed tasks. Skills in questioning, clarifying, sustaining and controlling are therefore important. The psychoanalytic tradition offers quite different approaches to problems of mental health (Yellolly 1980). As with many other theories applied to social work practice, the student should not feel obliged to understand and practice all of aspects therapy; this would be ill-advised without full and rigorous supervision. There are, nonetheless, many significant analytical concepts which have relevance, particularly in counselling practice (Coulshed 1991). A non-directive counselling approach could well be applied by the student as a way of helping individual members of the family express emotions of loss, grief and guilt about the problems of the past and their hopes for the future.

In conclusion, competence in **intervening and providing services** entails an imaginative and flexible approach by the student in devising pragmatic strategies to solve problems presented by this family. Because the needs of the family are complex, the student should be prepared to become both a manager of and negotiator for resources, as well as being a counsellor – someone who can be consistently available to the individuals as needs arise.

Conclusion

In the introduction to this chapter it was argued that Paper 30 is organised around the principle that practice cannot be understood if it is abstracted from the values, knowledge and skills which help define competence. In this chapter the details of a family experiencing a severe and chronic mental illness in one of its members is used to illustrate the intricate balance between knowledge and practice which the student needs to grasp in order to make sense of competence. The chapter seeks to provide the student with a broad sweep of existing theories to enable them to grasp the types of dilemmas they would experience in practising with this family, from engagement through to intervention.

What emerges in this account is a notion of competence which is client-centred, and yet not oblivious to structured forms of discrimination. Although necessarily brief and selective, the discussion of the Paper 30 competences, practice requirements and evidence indicators in this chapter reveal opportunities for the student to empower clients and access wider social systems in addressing the family's need. The ideas of adaptability to change and flexibility in choice of interventions which pervade this discussion are essential if the needs of mentally ill clients are to be addressed through social work practice. An imaginative use of the Paper 30 competences can help students move away from a passive, pessimistic view of the limitations of mental health social work, and towards practice which is progressive and challenging.

References

Bean, P. (1986) *Mental Disorder and Legal Control*. Cambridge: Cambridge University Press.

Bean, P. and Mounser, P. (1993) *Discharged From Psychiatric Hospitals*. London: Macmillan/MIND.

Blackburn, C. (1992) *Improving Health and Welfare Work with Families in Poverty: A Handbook*. Buckingham: Open University Press.

Busfield, J. (1986) *Managing Madness*. London: Hutchinson.

Braye, S. and Preston-Shoot, M. (1995) *Empowering Practice in Social Care*. Buckingham: Open University Press.

Brown, G.W. and Harris, T. (1978) *The Social Origins of Depression*. London: Routledge and Kegan Paul.

Campbell, J. (1995) 'The role of the approved social worker in a changing policy environment.' *Personal Social Social Services in Northern Ireland*, SSI Paper No. 54.

CCETSW (1991) *One Small Step Towards Racial Justice: The Teaching of Anti-Racism in Diploma in Social work Programmes*. London: CCETSW.

CCETSW (1995) *Paper 30*. London: CCETSW

Challis, D. (1994) 'Care Managment.' In N. Mallin (ed) *Implementing Community Care*. Buckingham: Open University Press.

Clare, A. (1980) *Psychiatry in Dissent*. London: Tavistock.

Coulshed, V. (1991) *Social Work Practice: An Introduction*. London: Macmillan.

Corob, A. (1987) *Working with Depressed Women*. Aldershot: Gower.

Croft, S. and Beresford, P. (1993) *Getting Involved: A Practical Manual*. London: Open Services Project.

Dallos, R. (1991) *Family Belief Systems, Therapy and Change*. Milton Keynes: Open University.

Dallos, R. and Boswell, D. (1993) 'Mental health.' In R. Dallos and E. McLaughlin (eds) *Social Problems and the Family*. London: Sage.

DHSS (1983) *The Mental Health Act*. London: HMSO.

DHSS (1984) *The Mental Health (Scotland) Act*. London: HMSO.

DHSS (1986) *The Mental Health (Northern Ireland) Order*. Belfast: HMSO.

Dominelli, L. and McLeod, E. (1988) *Feminist Social Work*. London: Macmillan.

Falloon, I.R.H., Boyd, J.L., McGill, C.W., Razani, J., Moss, H.B. and Gilderman, A.M. (1982) 'Family management in the prevention of exacerbations of schizophrenia.' *New England Journal of Medicine 306*, 1437–40.

Fernando, S. (1988) *Race and Culture in Psychiatry*. London: Tavistock/Routledge.

Foucault, M. (1965) *Madness and Civilisation*. New York: Random House.

Goldberg, D. and Huxley, P. (1980) *Mental Illness in the Community: The Pathways to Psychiatric Care*. London: Tavistock.

Gostin, L. (1975) *A Human Condition*. London: MIND.

Hudson, B.L. (1982) *Social Work with Psychiatric Patients*. London: Macmillan.

Kerfoot, M. and Huxley, P. (1994) 'A survey of approved social work in England and Wales.' *British Journal of Social Work 24*, 311–124.

Langan, M. and Clarke, J. (1994) 'Managing in the mixed economy of welfare.' In J. Clarke, A. Cochrane and E. McLaughlin (eds) *Managing Social Policy*. London: Sage.

Leff, J.P. and Vaughn, C.E. (1985) *Expressed Emotions in Families: Its Significance for Mental Ilness*. New York: Guilford.

Malin, N. (ed) (1994) *Implementing Community Care*. Buckingham: Open University Press.

Mayo, M. (1994) 'Community work.' In C. Hanvey and T. Philpot (eds) *Practising Social Work*. London: Routledge.

Monach, J. and Spriggs, L. (1994) 'The consumer role.' In N. Malin (ed) *Implementing Community Care*. Buckingham: Open University Press.

Newton, J. (1988) *Preventing Mental Illness*. London: Kegan Paul.

Oliver, M. (1993) *Disabling Barriers – Disabling Environments*. Milton Keynes: Open University/Sage.

Olsen, R.M. (ed) (1984) *Social Work and Mental Health: A Guide for the Approved Social Worker*. London: Tavistock.

Payne, M. (1995) *Social Work and Community Care*. London: Macmillan.

Pilgrim, D. and Rodgers, A. (1993) *A Sociology of Mental Illness*. Buckingham: Open University Press.

Prior, P. (1992) 'The approved social worker – reflections on origins.' *British Journal of Social Work 22*, 105–119.

Rodgers, A., Pilgrim, D. and Lacey, R. (1993) *Experiencing Psychiatry: Users' Views of Services.* London: Macmillan/MIND.

Sedgewick, P. (1982) *Psychopolitics.* London: Pluto.

Sheldon, B. (1984) 'A critical appraisal of the medical model in psychiatry.' In R.M. Olsen (ed) *Social Work and Mental Health: A Guide for the Approved Social Worker.* London: Tavistock.

Sheppard, M. (1990) *Mental Health: The Role of the Approved Social Worker.* Sheffield: JUSSR.

Sutton, C. (1994) *Social Work, Community Work and Psychology.* London: BPS.

Sutton, C. and Herbert, M. (1992) *Mental Health: A Client Resource Pack.* London NFER.

Tilbury, D. (1993) *Working with Mental Illness: A Community-Based Approach.* London: Macmillan.

Trower, P., Bryant, B. and Argyle, M. (1978) *Social Skills and Mental Health.* London: Methuen.

Trower, P., Casey, A. and Dryden, W. (1988) *Cognitive Behavioural Counselling in Action.* London: Sage.

Yelloly, M.A. (1980) *Social Work Theory and Psychoanalysis.* Wokingham: Van Nostrand Rheinhold.

CHAPTER 5

Competence in Child Protection

Kieran O'Hagan

Introduction

The pursuit of *competence* in child protection has been accelerated by a catalogue of disasters and official enquiry reports criticising professionals for *incompetence*. Many of the reports highlight areas in which competence was not attained; in, for example, response to child abuse crises, multidisciplinary cooperation, knowledge of relevant law, comprehensive assessment, communicating with children, engaging men, assessing risk, etc. A substantial body of recent literature and research, new laws and government publications have all contributed towards understanding of competence in child protection work. But this has not necessarily led to greater opportunity for students to attain such competence; on the contrary, it may have limited their opportunity for doing so.

This is the first of two chapters on child protection. It will begin by exploring this apparent irony, in the light of stipulations in CCETSW's new paper. It will then use an actual case to concentrate upon the core competences required in the initial *referral phase* of child protection work. Referral taking is a crucial phase, often posing similar ethical and practice dilemmas to those which will inevitably arise in later phases. Competent referral taking makes a major contribution to competence in *investigation* and *intervention*. The **knowledge values and skills** underpinning competence in referral taking will be provided, and the competence will be demonstrated in practice.

Child protection: giving student opportunities

There is enormous diversity of opinion amongst practice teachers in social work agencies on the question of how much responsibility should be given to students on placement. In respect of child protection and family and childcare placements in particular, however, opinions and practice are more consistent: responsibility is minimal, and many students are deprived of real opportunity. The nature and extent of criticism levelled against child protection agencies over many years has been such as to induce extreme caution in those responsible for student placements in child protection settings. Some practice teachers and/or their managers believe that unqualified staff should not have any responsibility for any child protection task; some may take a less extreme view, and stipulate that second year students be permitted to take child protection *referrals*, but should never be permitted to carry out an *investigation*. Others believe that students may observe an investigation taking place, and may participate in a very limited capacity. No practice teacher or manager is likely to permit a student to carry out a child protection *intervention*. The principal reasons for these prohibitions (which vary enormously throughout UK child protection agencies) is a conviction that child protection work is too complex and dangerous for students, and a fear that if a student were permitted to undertake such work and erred in some way, the consequences could be disastrous, for child, student, practice teacher, and agency alike.

Such fears by those held personally accountable for student practice in child protection are understandable. But it is imperative for practice teachers and their line managers to realise the consequences of these prohibitions, particularly on the professional development of the student, on their level of confidence and, of course, on the opportunity for them to fulfil child protection competence requirements. Obviously, students should never be given sole responsibility for child abuse cases; conversely, they should not be given placements in family and childcare teams without exposure to, and supervised practice in, at least some aspects of child protection work. CCETSW's new paper frequently stipulates practice requirements and evidence indicators, many of which can ideally be met in the earliest phases of child protection. Here are some examples of those requirements:

> **establish initial contact and the reason for contact...communicate effectively with children, adults, family...identify and evaluate the roles, responsibilities, policies and potential contributions of agencies...assist people to clarify goals...promote the rights of children...establish rights, statutory requirements and organisational responsibilities and priorities...**

CCETSW recognises the complexities of *decision making* which it identifies as a practice requirement, and, in one of its many evidence indicators of this requirement (extremely pertinent to child protection) it states: **Determine which decisions can be made within own remit and which require prior consultation with colleagues and other professionals.**

One particular decision making task allocated to most students in child protection placements (first and second year) is that of referral-taking. Students taking referrals often have to make many decisions, and quickly too, in order to gain the information upon which an investigation may be based. Despite the extreme caution mentioned in the opening paragraphs of this chapter, many practice teachers will be happy to allocate this task, providing they or colleagues will be available if unforeseen difficulties arises. Both practice teacher and student may perceive referral taking to be the least problematic phase of child protection work (as do, regrettably, many experienced practitioners). It is, in fact, potentially a major problematic area as this chapter will demonstrate, and it is the foundation stone upon which investigations are planned and carried out. The more competent and comprehensive the referral-taking, the greater the opportunity for competent investigation. Child abuse referral taking presents multiple challenges to the unwary student, yet correspondingly, numerous opportunities to demonstrate evidence of competences. *Anonymous* child abuse referrals are the most complex and difficult referrals of all, but their unique characteristics and challenges actually maximize opportunity to demonstrate competence.

Competence during the referral phase of child protection

Child protection work begins long before contact with parent or child. Responding effectively to a child abuse referral for example, necessitates competence, based upon certain **knowledge, values, and skills**. Anonymous referrals are particularly demanding in respect of attaining competence; such referrals are quite common in child protection work. Of the six core competences which now constitute the principal goal of social work training, four of them are most likely to be required in nearly all child abuse referral-taking; these competences are:

- **communicate and engage**
- **enable and promote**
- **develop professional competence**
- **work in organisations**

A worker accepting a referral is expected to be able to **communicate with and engage** the person making the referral; a worker will often have to **enable** the referrer to answer pertinent questions; knowledge and experiences gained during the referral taking should make a contribution towards the worker's **developing professional competence**; referrals are made in an organisational context, with regard to the policies and guidelines of the agency; the worker taking the referral therefore, must be able to **work in organisations**. Each of these core competences will be required to some extent in referral taking generally; all of them will be necessary in coping with anonymous referrals in particular, which are more prevalent, challenging, and complex. This chapter will concentrate on one actual anonymous referral.

CASE EXAMPLE

The duty officer (hereinafter referred to as the 'student') takes a call from a woman, speaking from a public telephone. The woman refuses to give her name; her voice betrays fear and anxiety:

> A don't want to give my name... A want to tell you 'bout these two kids... Mark and Marie Wharton... 25 Bedford Street... they're bin badly done by... they're only weeins... the mother takes erself off... she leaves em with a stranger... a tell ya... that guy minding those kids... you can hear 'im yellin and the kids screamin... somebudy gotta do somethin!

On paper, this may not seem much of a challenge; in a social services office, however, it may render an inexperienced worker as anxious and as fearful as the referrer herself seems to be. A major prerequisite of competence in referral-taking is an adequate knowledge base. This needs to be explored in detail.

Knowledge

The **knowledge** base underpinning effective referral taking consists of (1) basic information, (2) understanding, (3) self-knowledge.

BASIC INFORMATION

The most important information required is:

(1) the law pertaining to child protection (i.e., Children Act, Ss.42–52) and in particular, the statutory obligation to investigate all child abuse referrals (Children Act, 1989, S.47, 1(b)).

(2) the particular department's policy and procedures on child abuse referrals and responses to them (usually contained in child protection handbooks, made available on placement).

(3) the department's policy on *Partnership with parents* in child protection work (since implementation of the Children Act, most social services departments have formulated such a policy).

(4) knowledge of the areas to be explored in referral taking generally.

(5) Child abuse enquiry reports which have identified poor referral-taking as a contributory factor in the chain of events leading to the deaths of children, or to the unjustified removal of children (e.g., Blom-Cooper 1985; Brown 1991; Butler-Sloss 1988; Clyde 1993; DHSS 1974; Ferguson 1993; Greenwich 1987; Lambeth 1987; NCB 1993).

(6) Child protection research findings, in particular, DSS (1995).

(1), (2) and (3) are quite straight-forward: in addition to being available in the agency's literature, such knowledge will be demonstrated daily by other more experienced workers. Also, many such demonstrations in the past will have been recorded in available files. In respect of no. 4 (knowledge of the areas to be explored), policy, departmental procedure, and referral forms will guide workers to some extent. Although such guides may vary in different parts of the UK, basically they should require the worker to establish in so far as is possible:

- person making the referral
- age, sex, and ethnicity of child being referred
- position of child in family
- whether or not child is disabled in any way
- identity of alleged abuser
- type of alleged abuse
- location of child at time of abuse
- location of child at time of referral

In addition to these basic factors, five specific lines of enquiry should be made:

(a) about the nature and extent of the alleged abuse

(b) about the circumstances surrounding the abuse

(c) about the family, extended family and significant others

(d) about the welfare of the child: their emotional, social, psychological, educational and physical wellbeing

(e) about the involvement (and reasons for it) of other childcare agency.

(*All these necessary enquiries are encapsulated in Table 5.1.*)

UNDERSTANDING

The importance of each of these information factors (Table 5.1) in enhancing understanding of the referral is self-evident; they also help determine the appropriateness and urgency of an investigation. For example, if the above enquiries reveal it is a referral about a 14-year-old hit by a neighbour for playing football outside their front door, that should not concern social services at all; if, however, it turns out to be a referral about a six-month-old baby frequently beaten by her mother's new boyfriend, it should be treated with the utmost urgency. Generally, the younger the child, the greater the danger; and, the closer the relationship between child and alleged abuser, the greater the vulnerability of the child (O'Hagan 1989, 1993; Sgroi 1982). We may look at any of the

Table 5.1 Components of Referral-taking Task

Person making referral	Age of child	Place of child in family	Ethnicity of child	Disability of child	Perpetrator	Type of abuse	Location of child at time of referral	Location of child at time of alledged abuse
relative	0–2 years	youngest	Caucasian	physical	mother	physical	home	home
neighbour	2–5 years	oldest	Afro-Carribean	sensory	father	emotional	school	neighbour's home
friend	5–10 years	middle	Asian	psychological	stepmother	social	surgery	relative's home
GP	10–12 years	other	other	emotional	stepfather	psychological	clinic	street/neighbourhood
teacher	12–16 years				grandparent	sexual	neighbourhood	school
HV					sibling	failure to thrive	nursery	nursery
comm. nurse					aunt/uncle	ritual	hospital	foster home
police					neighbour	satanic	unknown	residential home
psychiatrist					professional		other	other
child					putative father			
anonymous					cohabitee			
other					babysitter			

above information factors and pinpoint additional significant variations; for example:

(1) A referral made by a professional (e.g., teacher, health visitor, etc.) is likely to be less complicated and less challenging than a referral made by a relative or neighbour.

(2) Many children are of an age and understanding enabling them to tell workers precisely what happened to them (e.g., adolescents); infants and some categories of disabled children are unable to do so, and are particularly vulnerable to abuse.

(3) Alleged physical abuse is relatively simple to explore in referral taking (i.e., wounds, bruises, burns, etc.); other types of abuse may be much more difficult to explore.

(4) Generally speaking, abuse in the child's home is more serious and difficult than abuse in other locations.

SELF-KNOWLEDGE

It is important for workers to be aware of precisely how certain features of the referral taking task impacts upon them, and how that impact may affect the quality of their response. Workers should carefully explore this question in practice and in reflection, with the help of Table 51. Which referrer, for example, is likely to pose the greatest challenge to them? Does the answer depend upon the style or status of the referrer? A confident, assertive, demanding GP... a timid, inarticulate friend or neighbour? In attempting to respond to the information provided by the referrer, which category of child poses the greatest difficulty? A referral about a new born, or a referral about an adolescent boy (or any other age category? Which alleged perpetrator will be the most problematic? Mother, father, cohabittee, grandfather... etc? What type of abuse is instinctively regarded as difficult: sexual abuse? neglect? emotional abuse, etc. Asking these questions is important, but even more so is the reason behind the answers; these may be any of the following: 'I am apprehensive about taking a referral from a GP because GPs always seem to be confident and demanding and I find it difficult to cope...' or: 'I would find it emotionally difficult, and therefore even more difficult to concentrate in listening to a referrer telling about some infant being sexually abused...' It is this kind of exploration and the sharing of findings with the practice teacher which will make a significant contribution to *developing professional competence.*

Let us now return to the actual case. It should be readily apparent that for anonymous referrals, additional basic knowledge, understanding, and self-knowledge is required.

KNOWLEDGE NEEDED IN RESPONDING TO ANONYMOUS REFERRALS

Competence will more easily be attained if the student is aware of the challenge and prevalency of anonymous referrals, and of available literature demonstrating competence. Besharov (1990) and Thorpe (1994) have provided convincing evidence of their prevalency, and O'Hagan (1989, 1993) has analysed anonymous referrals in practice, and provided guidelines for coping with them. O'Hagan and Dillenburger (1995) are particularly concerned about anonymous referrals alleging abuse or neglect by single parent mothers. They contend that such referrals and the way in which agencies often respond are an intrinsic feature of abusive childcare and child protection systems.

UNDERSTANDING ANONYMOUS REFERRALS

A student encountering an anonymous referral for the first time will very quickly achieve a significant *understanding* of the nature of such referrals. Much of this understanding will come on hearing the referrer's words, tone, mood, warnings, threats, apprehension and/or fear. At the outset, the student should keep an open mind on whether or not this is a genuine referral. It may be a malicious referral, which is not uncommon, but on the other hand it may be genuine. Either of these possibilities will become more apparent if the student succeeds in **communicating and engaging** with the referrer. Assuming for the moment that it is genuine, the student should understand that:

(1) The referrer's tension, apprehension, and fear, are reasonable; she may be taking considerable risks in expressing her concern about the children.

(2) The referrer may find it difficult to use a phone at any time, to speak to any person; therefore it's likely to be extremely difficult for her to ring a social services department (particularly from a call box) to make a child abuse referral; the point is that most referrers need help and support, not just help in saying what they want to say.

(3) Following on from that point, the referrer may give the very strong impression that they want to get the referral over with as quickly as possible and put the phone down; but in fact, they will most often welcome a well timed, suitably toned interjection, alleviating them momentarily of the considerable burden of speaking.

SELF-KNOWLEDGE IN RESPONDING TO ANONYMOUS REFERRALS

We have seen the importance of self-knowledge in how we respond to child abuse referrals generally. Self-knowledge acquires greater significance in coping with anonymous referrals. First, the mere fact that this is only a voice without a face, without a name, alleging or hinting at something terrible happening to small children – how does that impact upon the worker, particularly a student? Or, the referrer's anxiety and haste, or forcible demand to remain anonymous, or barely concealed warning that if nothing's done, 'you (*or your agency*) are in trouble!' Whatever the impact, the student should learn precisely how that impact affects the quality of their response to the referrer; for example, does the referrer's anxiety and fear make the student anxious and fearful (thereby seriously limiting the student's capacity for logical and objective responses)? Or, does the referrer's hint of something terrible happening to the children pre-occupy the student to the exclusion of all other necessary enquiries? Anonymous referrals are significantly different and more challenging than ordinary referrals, and this fact alone makes comprehensive self-exploration vital.

Values

The value base for child protection work in general and for response to this anonymous referral in particular consists of more than the paramountcy principle, i.e., 'the welfare of the child is paramount'. The welfare and rights of the mother, and the welfare and rights of the person making the referral, have both got to be considered. The mother has the right not to be prejudged on the basis of an anonymous referral. An agency which responds immediately to the referral as it stands, by rushing out to investigate, will generate an enormous crisis for the mother, thus risking incapaciting her caring adequately for the children she is allegedly neglecting. The referrer too has rights; the right to be listened to and taken seriously; the right to be helped and comforted (if needed) during her probable ordeal in making the referral; the right not to be forgotten if the referral leads to an investigation and intervention, and she holds herself responsible for some drastic resolution (e.g., court proceedings, children permanently removed, etc.). CCETSW's revised Paper 30 spells out the ethical imperatives in social work practice; here are some most pertinent to this case:

(1) **Identify and question one's own values and prejudices.** For the case in question, the student needs to be particularly rigorous in exploring his/her attitude to single parent mothers, fragmented families, mother–cohabittee relationships, particularly in the light of the current widespread prejudice towards one parent families and the discriminatory legislation and policies which have evolved from such prejudice (O'Hagan and Dillenburger 1995)

(2) **Promote people's rights to choice, privacy, confidentiality and protection, while recognising and addressing the complexities of competing rights and demands.** This reaffirms the necessity of careful assessment; its recognition of competing rights and demands is especially realistic.

(3) **Identify, challenge and deal with discrimination...**

(4) **Practise in a manner that does not stigmatise or disadvantage either individuals or groups.**

Skills

Using the broad definition of the term 'skill' provided in the first chapter, the skills required for referral taking (including anoymous referrals) are implicit in much of what has been written above: (1) listening skills; (2) accurate interpretation (of words, voice, tone, emotion, attitude); (3) empathy (crucially important to convey to the referrer that you understand and 'feel' the likely predicament they are in); (4) patience (avoid putting referrer under any pressure whatsoever); (5) pacing and sensitivity (uttering words or sounds of encouragement at the appropriate time; (6) discipline and control (enabling the exercise of the above skills, and, continuous awareness of, and being able to respond within, the bounds of legal obligation and departmental procedure); (7) written recording (contemporaneous); (8) report writing (necessary for future consultations, case conferences, submission to court etc.); computer literacy (eliciting, adding to, correcting, updating existing files on computer; creating new files).

Achievement of Competence

Communicate and engage

Let us now explore precisely how the student progressed in her attempt to achieve competence. The following account of events is based upon detailed recordings made by the student during and immediately after the referral was completed. We will assume that the student, through college training, placement supervision, the studying of texts (including some of those mentioned above), and previous attempts at supervised referral-taking during the placement, has had the opportunity to acquire essential **knowledge values and skills.**

'I don't want to give my name...' is the first utterance of the anxiety-laden referral. The student realises that, despite the difficulty created by anonymity, she must respect the demand for anonymity. The student says 'Okay... that's all right', and listens carefully to the remainder of the referral. She notes the increasing anxiety and fear in the referrer's voice, and the lack of detail and context of the message; she knows she firstly has to deal with the anxiety and fear. She occasionally and gently interjects with 'okay... right... I see...' She then says slowly, genuinely, reassuringly:

> Look that was really helpful... I don't know who you are, but that's not important... You've done the right thing... I'm sure it wasn't easy... we *will* look into it... could I ask you... could you give me a little more information... I mean about the kids... that would be appreciated... could you do that...

The student has significantly reduced the tension and burden carried by the referrer: she has acknowledged and praised her effort; she is not going to press the referrer about her identity; she is not going to adopt a morally censorious tone about the 'nastiness' of anonymous referrals; in effect, she has begun creating a relationship and atmosphere facilitating **communication and engagement, enabling** the referrer to provide much more information.

> She checks that the referrer has sufficient money for the coin box; she invites the referrer, if she so wishes, to recall her and reverse charges (fumbling for more money in a telephone booth can easily regenerate anxiety). The referrer declines, saying she has enough money for a while. The student encourages the referrer at numerous points as she begins attempting to explore the five specific areas and necessary factual data (Table 5.1). It is not yet time to embark upon a straight question and answer session; she encourages the referrer to give additional information in her own way, at her own pace. The referrer relates the following:
>
>> The children are Marie, aged approximately eight months, and Mark, aged three. Their mother is Jean Wharton, 24, a single parent mother. They live in a council tenement block; they were placed there six months ago.
>>
>> The referrer says that Jean works in a fish and chip shop three to four times a week, and that some male is looking after the kids. He has been heard by neighbours (including the referrer) yelling at the kids, and the kids have been heard screaming.

Most of the factual data of Table 5.1 is provided here, including the key point of alleged perpetrator. Precise data (dates of birth etc.) can be traced later.

The student again thanks the referrer. She again invites the referrer to phone in and ask for reverse charge. The referrer says 'no... it's all right...', but the student is a little concerned that she might lose her if she is still having to put money in. She suggests phoning the referrer (as it's a public telephone, that will not betray the referrer's identity). The referrer agrees. The student phones her immediately. The referrer replies immediately, and there is a noticeably more relaxed tone in her voice. The student also feels a little more relaxed.

The student proceeds, tactfully, sensitively, patiently, to explore the five core areas (Table 5.1). This cannot be done systematically or sequentially, or even directly; rather, the student must explore intuitively, with a language and tone far removed from scientific enquiry:

> 'Now those screams you mentioned... that must be worrying... does it sound as though the kids are being hit... or is it just when he yells at them?'

'Oh he hits Mark... I know that for fact.'

'Right... has any bruising or injury been seen on him?'

    'I haven't seen any... but that doesn't mean he isn't hitting him... I know he hits that kid.'

'How often do you know he hits them?'

    'Anytime he's there and she's not.'

'Have you've never known a night when he was there and he didn't hit Mark?'

    'Not recently.'

'Do you know is he the father of either of the children?'

    'I don't think so.'

'Is he living there?'

    'He stays overnight.'

'How long has he been staying overnight?'

    'I'm not sure... at least a month.'

'Do you think he hits Marie?'

    'No... but she cries a lot.'

'What kind of cry?'

    'Whingy cry...'

'When?'

    'When her mother isn't there?'

'Have you heard her cry whingy-like often?'

    'Yes, nearly every night he's there.'

The student pauses for a few seconds. The referrer sounds genuine. It sounds as though she is a next door neighbour, and that she would like to vindicate her allegation by saying so, but she may be afraid of the consequences. The student does not press her further on this point. The student asks are the children seen often? When? Where? By whom? Yes, they are often seen, on the way to nursery, or to the shop at the corner; seen by neighbours including the referrer; and *sometimes* they do look unhappy. Yes, sometimes they look happy too, with their mother. No, they haven't been seen with unexplained bruises;

Mark has been seen with cuts and scratches just like any other kid; no, that's not what she (the referrer) is concerned about...she's just very worried about the mother leaving then in 'the hands of this guy and hearing the kids screaming and whinging all the time he's there'. Yes, Mark does play with other kids, 'normal enough'. Does the referrer know anything about Jean's family of origin? No, except that she keeps in contact with her mother, and her mother occasionally visits. Does the referrer know of any other health or social services people involved with the family? Yes, she's seen a health visitor at the home. Does the referrer or her neighbours know anything about this male who looks after the children? No, except that he looks younger than Jean, and he doesn't want to talk to anybody. The student asks the referrer if there is any additional information she has, but hasn't been asked about. She concludes the referral taking by once again thanking the referrer, acknowledging the time and trouble she has taken for *the sake of the children*, and promising that the case will be referred to her senior. She reminds the referrer of her name again, asking her to take a note of it, and also asking her to contact her again if she thinks she has forgotten to tell her something, or if any additional information arises.

The student completes a referral form and report, and records in writing the whole process of interaction between herself and the referrer, in as much detail as she can recall (crucial for the provision of evidence: see below). **She consults with her Practice teacher.** There are three possible leads towards gaining further information: (1) computer records; (2) she knows the health clinic serving the area; (3) she thinks she knows the Nursery that the child Mark probably attends. There is a voluminous file on Jean Wharton, but the last entry was six months ago. The practice teacher tells the student they should not spend precious time reading through the whole history at this point but to concentrate upon **gaining information about the present situation of the children.** It is agreed that the student traces both the health visitor currently involved with the family, and the Nursery apparently attended by Mark, and consults with both of them. If the identity of the male emerges, the practice teacher will enquire of the police about any significant record.

The student contacts the health clinic and traces the health visitor currently involved. The health visitor has been making regular contacts. The children's last developmental screening took place two months ago; results were normal. The health visitor is aware of the presence of 'a male friend' and believes his name is Michael Greer but doesn't know anything about him. His unannounced arrival has caused her a little concern. He is, she thinks, 'so young and immature'. She has not seen him abuse the children in any way, but she has never seen him make any positive contribution towards the children's welfare on the few occasions he's been there during her visit. The student asks the health visitor has she noticed any overall deterioration in the children's condition, no matter how slight, since the arrival of Michael Greer; do they appear less happy, less vocal, mobile, curious, spontaneous? Have either of them been more whingy?

The health visitor cannot remember any significant specific changes; the children's development remains within acceptable limits, though she is conscious of the lack of warmth and caring in the relationship between them and the newcomer, and believes this may have implications if he remains.

The nursery teacher is much more forthcoming about Mark. Yes, she has noticed a definite deterioration in him during the past few weeks. He and his mother are not getting there on time. Mark is less confident than he was, more withdrawn or, at least more preoccupied, than he was; not a happy preoccupation, apparently. He doesn't play as much and as well as he used to; he doesn't laugh as much as he did; he has become clingy to the nursery teacher. Michael Greer has collected him at the nursery on a number of occasions. He has not shown any enthusiasm in going home with Michael Greer.

The practice teacher checks on records and discovers a Michael Greer age 22 who had committed petty offences as a juvenile (when he was 13). He contacts the police to make further enquiries; Michael Greer actually had a caution from the police for sexual offences against another consenting juvenile when he was 17 (masturbation and oral sex). He has not had contact with the police since.

Concluding the referral phase

Both practice teacher and worker are approaching the end of the **referral** phase of this particular case. The practice teacher decides that an **investigation** is warranted, and convenes a meeting for professionals already involved or likely to be involved at some point in the future. The **investigation** is the subject of the following chapter. This chapter will now address the written evidence required for each of the core competences demonstrated in practice.

Written Evidence of Competence in Referral Taking

Written evidence of competence is usually preceded by (1) providing a context, i.e., an outline and summary of the case (in addition, in this particular case, the student will provide a descriptive account of the process of interaction between herself and the referrer; she will also give a brief account of the consultation with her supervisor, and subsequent contact with other agencies); (2) relevant **knowledge values and skills** through which competence is achieved.

The **knowledge values and skills** underpinning competence in child abuse referral taking (anonymous referrals in particular) are provided on pages 89–95. In providing written evidence of competence, the student should refer to whichever part of that section has been most helpful in (1) enlightening her about the task of referral taking generally and anonymous referrals in particular; (2) increasing her confidence to take on the task; (3) making her aware of necessary skills in referral-taking. *The legal and ethical context of competence achievement should always be provided.*

Let us now consider the explanations of each core competence and the *Practice Requirements and Evidence Indicators* stipulated by CCETSW, and, the student's written evidence of the same, based upon the work previous pages have described.

COMMUNICATE, AND ENGAGE

The core competence **communicate and engage** is explained in the revised Paper 30 by the following:

> Communicate and engage with organisations and people within communities to promote opportunities for children, adults, families, and groups, *at risk or in need*, to function, participate, and develop in society. [my italics]

Here are some of CCETSW's *Practice requirements* for this competence: (1) form and develop working relationship with children, adults, families, carers and groups; (2) communicate and engage with communities and seek to minimize factors which cause risk and need; (3) contribute to networking with and between individuals, agencies, community resources and other professionals.

The student refers to the evidence of this competence as follows:

> I established a relationship with the referrer, and **engaged her and communicated with her** to elicit necessary information for the completion of the referral. In so doing, I promoted the interests of the welfare of the children. The means by which these achievements were made are as follows:

> I exercised discipline and control and avoided being overwhelmed by the nature of the referral. I did not allow the referrer to project her anxiety and fear onto me. I realised on initial contact that I had to allay her anxiety and fear (or at least minimize it) in order to establish a meaningful relationship, which would allow me to explore with her the contents of the referral. I minimized her fear and anxiety by:

> - accepting and respecting her wish for anonymity
> - listening without interruption to what she initially wanted to say
> - encouraging, reassuring and thanking the referrer for that initial information
> - emphasising that what she was doing was right and in the children's best interests
> - relieving her of the expense and inconvenience of paying into a public telephone box

- empathising with and being sensitive to referrer
- being patient, encouraging her to respond to my queries in her own way, at her own pace.

In accordance with the evidence indicators for this competence, I believe I succeeded in:

(1) establishing initial contact and the reason for contact (although referrer took the initiative of contacting, I fullfilled the responsibility of **establishing** contact and enlightening referrer about the extent of information required, i.e., appropriate reason for contact)

(2) communicating effectively

(3) forming and developing working relationship

(4) establishing contact with other professionals.

(**Note:** students must guide the assessors to the precise location, i.e., page number and/or paragraph, in their practice portfolios, where each of the practice requirements has been fulfilled, each evidence indicator provided, and each core competence has been achieved.)

PROMOTE AND ENABLE

This core competence is explained in the revised Paper 30 by the following:

Promote opportunities for people to **enable** them to use their own strengths and expertise to meet responsibilities, secure rights and achieve change.

Here are some of the *Practice requirements*:

(1) Promote the rights of children and adults at risk or in need in the community.

(2) Provide information and advice...

(3) Enable people to use their own strengths and expertise to meet responsibilities, secure rights and achieve change.

The student refers to evidence of this competence as follows:

I was conscious at the outset of an enormous imbalance of power between us: she was anxious and frightened and anonymous; she probably perceived me as confident, official, and formidable. I had to alter that imbalance. By attempting to minimise the referrer's anxiety and fear and establish a relationship with her (see above) I enabled the referrer to function more effectively in her contact with my department.

I attempted to transform an atmosphere of tension and haste into one of calm and trust, thereby enabling her to exercise her responsibility as a citizen to inform the authorities about children she believed were at risk. As the contact increased, I enabled the referrer to provide precise detail and context with the information she was providing, and I enabled her to communicate more objectively, accurately, impartially, and responsibly than she did in the opening minutes of first contact (see original utterance by referrer, and conversation between referrer and myself). The means by which this competence of *promoting and enabling* was achieved include all those means listed above in respect of *communicate and engage.*

In accordance with a number of evidence indicators for this particular competence, I believe I succeeded in:

(1) assisting referrer to express her own... needs and perspectives (the referrer needing to express her concern about children from her particular perspective)

(2) assisting referrer to clarify goals... in meeting responsibilities and achieving change (to the children's situation)

(3) assisting referrer to choose to spend much longer on the phone than she intended, in order to provide the necessary information that would be more likely to bring about necessary change

(4) promoting the rights of children (to be referred to statutory agencies if one believes they are at risk).

DEVELOP PROFESSIONAL COMPETENCE

This core competence is explained in CCETSW's revised Paper 30, as follows:

Manage, evaluate and develop own capacity to develop professional competence

Here are some of the *Practice requirements*:

(1) exchange, process and report information

(2) contribute to the resolution of professional dilemmas and conflicts, balancing rights, needs and perspectives

(3) respond to unexpected opportunities and problems

(4) make decisions

(5) contribute to the maintenance, critical evaluation and development of own professional practice, knowledge and values.

The student refers to evidence of the competence as follows:

> As soon as I spoke to the referrer, I realised this was going to be an anonymous referral during which the referrer was likely to be highly emotional and defensive. I knew that, initially, I would be under great pressure merely to jot down what the referrer was saying, ask no questions, and let her put the phone down. I was conscious that her agitation, anxiety and fear about what she was doing was challenging me enormously, and that from the outset, I needed to exercise a good deal of discipline and control. I felt a certain agitation myself, possibly indicative of the fact that the referrer was, despite my effort, projecting some of her anxieties onto me. I am aware that all these experiences were key factors in my **decision making**, namely, to attempt to sustain contact with the referrer, and to attempt to alter the crisis atmosphere surrounding the referral, into an atmosphere and relationship which would facilitate a **professional exchange of information on behalf of children** for whom the referrer was genuinely concerned.

> As the information increased and the children's circumstances became clearer (in hearing from both referrer and professionals), I felt unease because the children's mother knew nothing about it. A substantial proportion of this information was indicating that the children were being subjected to some form of abuse. She had the right to know about these allegations, and the right to respond to them. I had read the department's policy on partnership with parents, and the obligation on workers to be honest and frank with parents. I often felt during this referral-taking task that I was doing the opposite. I was conscious of the amount of unsubstantiated child abuse referrals made against single parent mothers, and that although the alleged perpetrator is (as was the case in this case) the male cohabittee, that single parent mothers often bear the brunt of child protection investigations. I was also conscious, however, of the very high rate of incidence of physical abuse of children perpetrated by boyfriends of single parent mothers (Margolin 1992). I helped to resolve these dilemmas by reiterating in my own mind that (1) the more thorough the referral taking was, the less risk of inflicting an unnecessary and unwarranted investigation upon the mother; (2) if allegations were being made about the care of her children, she had the right to expect the agency concerned to rigorously examine any information supporting those allegations; (3) that I had a duty to record and explore any referral about children at risk, or children in need, or children being harmed.

> In accordance with a number of evidence indicators relating to this competence, I believe I succeeded in:

(1) fulfilling the referral-taking role and responsibility delegated to me

(2) writing out a detailed recording of the whole process of referral taking, including the interactions between myself and referrer

(3) identifying conflict and ethical dilemma in coping with this actual referral (i.e., the welfare of children – the rights of parent(s)

(4) recognising the problematic nature of anonymous child abuse referrals

(5) creating opportunities to surmount the difficulties of anonymous referrals

(6) collecting, clarifying, verifying, and organising information pertinent to decision making when referral taking was completed

(7) determining when I needed to consult and be guided by my practice teacher (i.e., when conversation with referrer was finished)

(8) reviewing and utilising research and literature on anonymous child abuse referrals, about the children of one parent families.

WORK IN ORGANISATIONS

This core competence is explained in CCETSW's revised Paper as follows:

Contribute to the work of organisations

The main *Practice requirement* is: **Demonstrate capacity to work as an accountable and effective member of the organisations in which placed.**

The student refers to evidence of this competence as follows:

Before attempting to take on the responsibility of accepting an anonymous child abuse referral, I prepared myself through supervision, and learnt much from my practice teacher about the problems and pitfalls of coping with anonymous referrals. I read and remembered the agency's procedures and guidelines on child abuse referral taking, and attempted to adhere to these as I carried out the task. I supplemented this reading and learning by familiarising myself with literature and research on the subject generally. Throughout this work, I was conscious of the fact that I was a member of a team, directly responsible to my Practice teacher, and that I was carrying out statutory duties in relation to child protection, for which my agency was responsible. I was also conscious of the fact that child protection work is a multidisciplinary responsibility, and that I would inevitably be contacting, consulting and working with professionals in other agencies. I was in effect a representative of my agency, to both the person making the referral, and to agencies which would later be involved. In this capacity as representative, I endeavoured to work as efficiently and professionally as I may; I attempted to elicit as much pertinent information as I could, conscious of the fact that the more pertinent it was, the greater its contribution to the multidisciplinary effort which would follow.

In accordance with a number of evidence indicators, I believe I succeeded in:

(1) being accountable for my own behaviour and practice within the organisation (i.e., consulting with and answerable to my Practice teacher)

(2) understanding, and implementing policy and procedures on referral-taking (Table 5.1)

(3) contributing to the development of organisational policy and procedures on child abuse referral-taking by implementing that policy and procedure, and making available completed referral form, and detailed recording of my work, which could be considered with others by those with the responsibility for monitoring and developing policies and procedures

(4) contributing to the planning and allocation of the work of the team and organisation, by comprehensive, accurate referral taking, including consultation with other agencies, thereby enabling Practice teacher and/or team manager to assess more quickly the seriousness and degree of urgency of the case, and the amount of time and human resources likely to be needed for investigation).

Supporting evidence

The demonstration and written evidence of competences in this chapter can be supported by numerous appendices. These may include sections from relevant child protection law and from departmental child abuse policy and procedures; a copy of the actual referral form completed (wholly anonymised of course); a copy of Table 5.1; various sections from the detailed recording and report made immediately after the referral was taken.

There is far more evidence of specific competences provided here than would normally be required. But it is important at this early stage of implementaton of the revised Paper 30, to highlight the virtually unlimited potential for demonstrating competence even in such an initial phase of child protection work. All these four competences and many of the evidence indicators are transferable and applicable to the later phases of child protection work, and indeed, to every other area of social work practice.

Conclusion

The goal of competence in child protection work begins with referral taking. This is a task normally given to all social work students in their childcare and child protection placements. It is an excellent opportunity for students to learn of the nature of the task, and of the challenges and complexities which particular categories of child abuse referrals pose. Anonymous child abuse referrals pose a major challenge, and this chapter demonstrates the ample opportunity students have, in coping with such referrals, to accumulate evidence of specific competences. Like all other social work tasks, competence in dealing with child abuse referrals depends upon a considerable body of knowledge, values and skills. Self-knowledge is particularly important in dealing with anonymous referrals. The core competences in child abuse referral-taking may apply to referral-taking in all areas of social work practice; and they remain important goals in investigation and intervention. But it is highly unlikely that they will be achieved in those later phases if they have not been achieved during the referral phase. This fact is abundantly clear in all the child abuse enquiry reports: comment and analysis of those reports have always concentrated upon incompetence in the investigative and intervention phase, but careful reading of them will expose various incompetences during the referral phase. Investigation is often only as competent as the quality of information obtained beforehand will allow. It is hoped that this chapter will help students to demonstrate the core competences which accurate, comprehensive child abuse referrals necessitate.

References

Besharov, D. (1990) *Recognising Child Abuse: A Guide for the Concerned.* Washington: Free Press.

Blom-Cooper, L. (1995) *A Child in Trust: Jasmine Beckford.* London: Brent.

Brown, Justice (1991) Judgement on Rochdale Child Sexual Abuse Investigation, 1990. *Daily Telegraph* 8 March.

Butler-Sloss, E. (1988) *Report of the Enquiry into Child Abuse in Cleveland, 1987.* London: HMSO.

Clyde, Lord (1993) *Report of the Enquiry into the Removal of Children from Orkney in February 1991.* House of Commons Session 1992/93, Paper 195. London: HMSO.

Department of Health and Social Security (DHSS) (1974) *Report of the Committee of Enquiry into the Care and Supervision Provided in Relation to Maria Colwell.* London: HMSO.

Department of Social Services (1995) *Child Protection: Messages from Research.* London: HMSO.

Ferguson, H. (1993) 'The manifest and latent implications of the report of the Kilkenny incest investigation.' *Irish Social Worker 11,* 4, 4–7.

Greenwich (1987) Protection of Children in a Responsible Society: The Report of the Commission on Enquiry into the Circumstances Surrounding the Death of Kimberly Carlile. London: London Borough of Greenwich, Greenwich Health Authority.

Lambeth (1987) Whose Child? The Report of the Public Enquiry into the Death of Tyra Henry. London: London Borough of Lambeth.

Margolin, L. (1992) 'Child abuse by mother's boyfriends: why the over-representation?' *Child Abuse and Neglect 16,* 541–551.

National Children's Bureau (NCB) (1993) *Investigation into Inter-Agency Practice Following the Cleveland Area Child Protection Committee's Report Concerning the Death of Toni Dales.* London: NCB.

O'Hagan, K.P. (1989) *Working with Child Sexual Abuse.* Milton Keynes: Open University Press.

O'Hagan, K.P. (1993) *Emotional and Psychological Abuse of Children.* Buckingham: Open University Press.

O'Hagan, K.P. and Dillenburger, K. (1995) *The Abuse of Women within Childcare Work.* Buckingham: Open University Press.

Sgroi, S. (1982) *Handbook of Clinical Intervention in Child Sexual Abuse.* Lexington: Lexington Books.

Thorpe, D. (1994) *Evaluating Child Protection.* Buckingham: Open University Press

CHAPTER 6

Competence in Risk Analysis

Greg Kelly

Introduction

In the last twenty years social work in the United Kingdom has become increasingly concerned with the assessment and the management of child abuse. The issue at the heart of this process is the estimation of the risk associated with placing or leaving children in a particular situation. Risk in this sense means the danger of something going wrong – usually the children being abused or further abused. The public, political and professional pressures generated by the succession of tragic situations where children have died have led child care social work to be dominated by the fear of wrongly assessing risk. This preoccupation with the prevention of the negative – abuse – rather than the promotion of the positive – the support of vulnerable families – has been increasingly recognised and criticised in recent years (Dartington Social Research Unit 1995; Thorpe 1994). The Children Act 1989 can be seen as a means of trying to redress the balance by emphasising the role of social services in supporting 'children in need' and by making the grounds for court action – that the child has suffered or is likely to suffer 'significant harm' – more exacting. However, the government has emphasised that it continues to see protection of children from abuse as a prime duty of the child care services. In the context of this chapter it is especially worth noting that the legislation now specifically requires and permits agencies to consider the likelihood of a child suffering harm in the future (Children Act 1989 Section 31 (2)). This formally places risk assessment at the centre of the responsibilities of social workers in child care and, as we shall see below, this is reflected in the competences required by CCETSW'S revised Paper 30.

Risk assessment is most often discussed in the context of social work in child care. This is, arguably, because of the high profile that has been the lot of social work in child care and because of the clear statutory authority social workers have, in their own right, to take action on behalf of children. This should not, however, detract from the importance and applicability of risk assessment to other areas of practice. Under the provisions of the mental health and community care legislation, it is the social worker's responsibility to participate in the assessment of the risks to clients and others associated with community placements. These provisions clearly indicate the worker's responsibility to take action or to contribute to decision making based on an estimate of the future harm that is likely to befall a client or that a client is likely to inflict. Much of the core knowledge, skills and values associated with risk assessment, therefore, are transferable across client groups.

Before proceeding to consider the core competences which risk assessment enable us to meet, it is worth making a general point – a note of caution. Assessing risk is essentially trying to make an informed guess about what is likely to happen in the future – to predict the likelihood of a particular outcome – usually undesirable; for example, will this child suffer further abuse if left in the care of her parents? Risk assessment with its technical language and its striving for objectivity can mask the fact that the essential nature of what is being attempted is to base a decision on what we think is likely to happen in the future.

Some reflection on how difficult this is in other areas of human endeavour can be helpful in getting a fresh perspective on the nature of the task. For example, in both economic and weather forecasting the deployment of enormous scientific resources lead to very modest and frequently inaccurate forecasts. In social work we are often dealing with volatile individuals under severe environmental pressure, with fluctuating personal resources and social support, and whom we often do not know very well. This should make us cautious about our capacity to assess accurately the risk associated with a particular situation. We have to make decisions and assess the risk associated with them, but our practice should be informed with a caution born of the inherent difficulty of the task. This can be difficult when we are placed in the role of professional 'experts'. Decisions are often the result of the deliberations of what can be seen as panels of 'experts' – case conferences. Recent developments in practice, which have emphasised client participation and negotiated agreements, are recognition of the inadequacy of reliance solely on professional opinion as the basis for action.

Core competencies to be evidenced

Risk assessment should form a part of all stages of intervention but it is particularly central to the assessment process where initial decisions have to be agreed. This is recognised in CCETSW's Revised Paper 30 (CCETSW 1995) where risk features prominently in the core competence: 'Assess and Plan – **Work in partnership to assess and review people's circumstances and plan response to need and risk**' (CCETSW 1995). This will be the central core competence to be evidenced in this chapter but we will also give particular consideration to **Working in Organisations and Developing Professional**

Competence. These and the other core competences which are relevant to risk assessment are reviewed below.

Assess and plan

Three of the five 'Practice Requirements' within this core competence mention risk directly: **'Assess and review people's... risks'**; **'work in partnership to identify and analyse risk of harm, abuse or failure to protect'**; **'work in partnership to negotiate and plan responses to assessed... risks...'** The two remaining practice requirements are integral to risk analysis and management – **'work in accordance with statutory and legal requirements'** and **'work in partnership to develop packages of care, protection and control'**.

Communicate and engage

Effective communication and engagement with clients and with other professionals are the basic building bricks of any assessment process. This core competence is particularly important in the assessment of risk where the social worker will often need to discuss particularly sensitive areas. The practice requirements specifically mention the need to **'communicate and engage with people in communities and seek to minimise factors which cause risk and need'**.

Working in organisations

Assessment and management of risk is central to the responsibilities of all statutory social services agencies. Work in the area of risk can provide at least part of the evidence needed for all the practice requirements in this section of Revised Paper 30. Voluntary and community work agencies have very varying degrees of responsibility for the assessment and management of risk. This needs to be taken account of in assessing competent practice. Competent practice in a social services department might not equate with that in a local community work initiative.

Developing professional competence

Risk assessment and management should provide the student with clear opportunities to meet all the practice requirements within this core competence. Situations that require risk assessment are often the most professionally demanding. Students therefore need to **'use supervision effectively'** and to **'exchange, process and report information'** in these situations.

Intervene and provide services

This chapter will concentrate on the assessment phase and will not cover intervention in detail. However, some of the practice requirements within this core competence are applicable to the management of risk, especially, **'Contribute to the care, protection and control of people who are a risk to themselves or others.'**

Evidencing Competence

In reviewing these core competences it is striking how many of them and their practice requirements can be evidenced by a coherent piece of work in one specific case; in this case, assessment and management of risk. Students should feel encouraged to see the wide applicability of practice in this area and its centrality to current social work practice. Often the difficult task for practice teachers and students is to identify work which students can take responsibility for or contribute to. Account must be taken of the agency's responsibilities to its clients, to the public and other agencies and professionals.

In this chapter risk analysis will be used to concentrate on the core competences central to it: **Assess and plan; Working in organisations; Develop professional competence.** This will be done by taking the material gathered in the course of the investigation into the anonymous referral detailed in Chapter 5, considering the application of a risk analysis framework to it and then looking at how this assessment might be used in the context of the decisions that need to be taken in relation to the case. The space available precludes detailing the practice and the associated competence in gathering the material through visits and interviews with parents, children and other professionals. In a practice placement the student's skills in communicating/engaging, promoting/enabling could be evidenced through agency records, process recordings and live observations. Her whole approach should provide evidence of a commitment to a value framework.

Values

In this as in many suspected child abuse situations the student is faced with value dilemmas that need to be recognised, discussed in supervision, worked with and then evidenced using examples from practice. Clearly, in child abuse situations the family's right to 'choice, privacy and confidentiality' has to be set beside the children's right to protection. At one level, this may be resolved by the need to consider the welfare of the children as paramount. However there are other important values governing child care practice. 'There are unique advantages for children in experiencing normal family life in their own birth family and every effort should be made to preserve a child's home and family links' (Department of Health 1989). The resolution of value conflicts in child protection has become a continuous struggle. These conflicts need to be negotiated on a case-by-case and, at times, on a day-by-day basis within cases. Children, parents, the hierarchy within one's own organisation and other professionals will all have a contribution to make to these discussions. Value issues specific to risk assessment will be discussed below.

Case History

Referral

As detailed in Chapter 5, the local social services office received an anonymous referral alleging that Jean Wharton's children had been left in the care of a male stranger, and that the children had been heard screaming, and this male stranger had been heard yelling at them. It transpired that this stranger, Michael Greer, was Jean's new boyfriend, and that he had been caring for the children three or four times a week while Jean was working in a local fish and chip shop.

The investigation

The initial visit was carried out by an experienced social worker, a practice teacher, accompanied by the student. They agreed that the practice teacher would take lead responsibility with the adults and the student would attend to and observe the children. They arrived when Michael Greer was alone with the children: the children appeared to be very distressed, scantily dressed, and Mark had a bruise on his forehead. Marie cried ceaselessly; her nappy was unchanged; her legs were very inflamed; she appeared hungry. Mark seemed relieved at the attempts by the student to engage him. He appeared wary of Michael. The practice teacher and student confirmed that the children had been left with Michael on a regular basis and that he was, indeed, Jean's new boyfriend.

Michael said the bruise was caused by Mark slipping and hitting his head against a small coffee table. Given Mark's stature and the height of the coffee table the practice teacher and student did not believe him. He was extremely anxious, claiming that he was only doing Jean a good turn, enabling her to earn a few pounds.

On checking records it emerges that Michael is known to both the social services and the police; he was a persistent juvenile offender, who had committed offences of violence.

On a subsequent visit later in the day, the social worker and student met Jean Wharton; the house had been tidied; Michael was not there; the baby was asleep and Mark was in his mother's arms throughout the visit. The social worker stated their concerns. Jean was aggressive and initially uncooperative. She denied that the children had been abused in any way but eventually agreed to a medical examination.

The two children were medically examined, accompanied by their mother. The paediatrician believed the bruise was non-accidental. He suggested that they were neglected to some extent, although their physical health was reasonable. The findings were shared with Jean who was shocked by them and denied any knowledge of Mark's injury. She insisted that Michael was not now living with her, and that she would try to make other arrangements for the children to be cared for when she is working. She remained very wary of social services and refused the offer of a family aide.

Action

A case conference was held. The student, supported by the practice teacher presented the information collected, and, the opinions formed during the investigation. This provided evidence of competence in assessment and planning, working in organisations, developing professional competence. At the conference it was agreed that while care proceedings should not be instituted the children's names should be entered in the child abuse register and a full assessment completed.

Summary of background information emerging during assessment

The following information was gathered by the student in the course of a number of visits and other contacts with Jean.

> Jean has been largely disowned by her family, though maintains intermittent contact with her mother who lives at the other end of town. Her father is dead. She has known Michael only a few weeks. Their relationship is stormy.

> Jean's upbringing was characterized by poverty, violence, heavy drinking, and criminal activity. Her father died when she was very young; her mother remarried, and her stepfather sexually abused her. He seldom worked, periodically battered Jean's mother and the children, including Jean, and engaged in petty crime.

> Jean was the second youngest of six children. She attended a school for maladjusted children. She was placed in care in a children's home when she was 15 after repeatedly running away from home. She remained there for two years.

> When she left care she tried living again at home, but this was unsuccessful. She was seen by most of the family as the source of conflict, and it had the effect of uniting her mother and stepfather against her.

> The children have different fathers, neither of them living with Jean. She receives no maintenance from either of them. She has refused to tell the Child Support Agency of the identity of the fathers; she is frightened to do so, having periodically been beaten by one of them. She has been compelled in the past to seek refuge in Battered Women's Units.

After the initial case conference Jean paid a neighbour to care for the children when she was working. She attended most, but not all of the appointments made for her by her health visitor at the child development clinic. Mark's development continued to give some cause for concern but Marie achieved her developmental milestones.

Jean is hard working, and, in many respects, committed to the children. She is of average intelligence, although semi-literate due to the social and educational deprivations brought about by her upbringing and abuse. Jean has a good singing voice and was once a member of a church choir; she has not attended choir or church since Mark was born. She showed herself to be emotional and volatile during the assessment period, prone to yell at the children when she perceived them to be defiant and troublesome. She became somewhat more accepting of social services involvement and would share her feelings with the student, who was close to her in age. However, the social worker never felt confident that she was being open about her relationship with Michael who, she maintained, was not living with her, although he was frequently in the house and a neighbour reported rows late at night.

Task

In readiness for the review case conference – two months after the original referral – the practice teacher asks the student to prepare an analysis of the risk associated with Jean continuing to care for her children, using the material collected during the assessment process, and contained in the report prepared for the case conference.

Risk Analysis

The knowledge base

One of the basic problems that social work has as a discipline is the lack of a generally accepted theoretical framework for the facts and knowledge its assessment processes generate. Without such a framework it is difficult to interpret facts and use knowledge in a consistent way and workers can be thrown back on their own accumulated knowledge from practice or 'common sense'. This will inevitably vary greatly between workers and lead to great variations in practice. There is much research evidence that this is the case (Packman, Randall and Jaques 1986; Rowe, Hundleby and Garnett 1989; Farmer and Owen 1995). In a recent study of case conferences the authors conclude, 'One very striking point about the assessment process was its apparent lack of theoretical reasoning' (Farmer and Owen 1995). Others make similar points about the failure to consider the degree of risk in any coherent way (Corby and Mills 1986). In part these failings are attributed to the multi-disciplinary nature of case conferences and perhaps the need to maintain consensus among the professionals. However, social services and social workers, as the lead agency in child abuse, have a particular responsibility to develop and use frameworks that have the potential for providing a base for rational decision making. There is now an abundance of material attempting to point the way (Brearley 1982; Corby and MIlls 1986; Dalgleish 1991; Farmer and Owen 1995; Murphy-Berman 1994; Stone 1993).

We have discussed above the inherent difficulty in assessing risk. One aspect of this is knowing what factors to consider in attempting to assess the chances of a particular, usually unfavourable, outcome. Given the child abuse tragedies of the 1970s and 1980s it was understandable that workers and agencies should welcome lists of characteristics that would help them distinguish abusing from non-abusing parents.

Checklists

Most basic texts in child abuse (Stainton-Rogers, Hevey and Ash 1989) and many agency procedures contain lists of attributes of carers variously called 'risk factors' or 'predisposing factors' that are said to be associated with abusive parenting.

These lists are fraught with difficulty. They are usually drawn from two sources:

(1) research studies that have looked at characteristics of abusing or neglecting parents (Lynch and Roberts 1977; Steele and Pollock 1968).

(2) studies that have examined the factors that experienced professionals actually use in their decision making (Dalgleish 1991; Meddin 1985).

Both sources suffer from the same fundamental weakness – they are based on experience and study of populations that have actually abused their children and are not studies of the population as a whole. We know from Lynch and Roberts (1977) that early parenthood was a significant factor among the abusing parents they studied but we do not know the incidence of child abuse among the general population of early parents. If we assume it is a small minority then, in any given situation, we must say that, although early parents are over represented among abusing parents, the likelihood of any particular parent abusing their child on the basis of being an early parent is small. Therefore its use as a 'risk' or 'predisposing' factor is severely limited.

The risk factors generated from practitioners tend to emphasise:

(1) the severity of the current abusive incident or harm

(2) the assessment of the parents

(3) parental cooperation with the agency (Meddin 1985; Dalgleish 1991).

These are essentially operational and practical considerations, and they too must be employed with caution, in a dynamic rather than a static way. Parents frequently complain of being labelled by the agency on the basis of how they were at the time of the abuse – their lowest point. Parental cooperation is a particularly difficult criteria to apply and can lead to discriminatory practice against families who want to remain independent of social services. Discriminatory practice is a possibility that always has to be carefully guarded against in risk assessment, where facts from a person's history may be used to inform current decisions.

A third and more tentative group of USA studies (Burrell, Thompson and Sexton 1994) have sought to identify factors associated with a parent's 'child abuse potential' as measured on a rating scale. They identify:

- stress

- family resources

- social support.

This chapter and the case study has concentrated on the physical abuse and neglect of children and not included sexual abuse; but it is interesting to note, in commenting on risk factors, that one of the most widely used checklists of risk factors – Finklehor's for sexual abuse – has not been validated on re-examination (Bergner, Delgado and Graybill 1994). Only one factor from eight, low family income, proved predictive of abuse in a follow-up study.

Thus checklists must be used with extreme caution but decisions have to be made and risks assessed. Their relevance and the weight they are given must be determined by our knowledge of the family we are assessing, and where possible their importance should be discussed with the family. For example, how significant is it for Jean herself that she is cut off from her own family and in the words of the checklist appears to be 'socially isolated'? However, even at the end of this process, social services still have the responsibility to protect children – both from abuse and from unwarranted separations from their families – so they will have to take decisions in uncertainty, based on opinion and with imperfect knowledge. If this is done within a clear framework, decision making is less likely to be arbitrary and it will be more robust in the face of scrutiny by the courts.

A risk assessment framework

Despite more modern attempts that are specifically tailored to child abuse (Dalgleish 1991) an early general model of risk developed by Brearley (1982) has the advantage of working from clear definitions and first principles and this does much to illuminate the difficulties in risk assessment. It also has the advantage of being applicable across different client groups. Brearley applies the model to various case examples. In this presentation the Brearley model has been amended and adapted based on experience of teaching and its use by students and staff.

Risk is defined as: 'the chance of loss or the occurrence of an unfavourable or undesirable contingency' as a result of a decision or course of action. Risk can also involve the chance of gain or a 'desirable contingency' and in some decisions such as moving a child from residential care to substitute family care the possible gains need to be brought into the equation. In social work, however, our preoccupation is usually with minimising loss.

In everyday life our common sense approach to risky decisions is to look at the 'pros and cons'. What are the factors that are likely to make this used car a good buy and those that might make it an expensive mistake and on the balance of these we decide. Brearley's model gives some sophistication and precision to this common sense approach. He invites us to look at the 'hazards' (cons) and 'strengths' (pros):

A **'hazard'** is defined as, 'any existing factor which introduces or increases the possibility of an undesirable outcome'. Rusty bodywork is a hazard to the undesirable outcome of buying a poor second hand car – it makes that more likely. The presence of a violent male partner is a hazard to the undesirable outcome of children being physically abused.

A **'strength'** is defined as, any factor 'which reduces the possibility of an undesirable outcome'. Low mileage is a strength against the undesirable outcome of buying a poor second hand car – it makes the undesirable outcome less likely. Moving close to mum and supportive extended family should be a strength against the undesirable outcome of children being neglected. This encouragement to consider and list strengths clearly is of great importance given social workers' natural problem focus.

Brearley increases the sophistication of the model by distinguishing between: 'predisposing hazards' and 'situational hazards'. In the analysis that follows, the term **'background hazards'** is used instead of 'predisposing hazards'. This is to take account of the problem of attributing too much predictive force to factors where the likelihood that they will 'predispose' a parent to abuse is not known with any certainty.

'Background hazards' – are factors of a general nature in a person's background that make an undesirable outcome more likely. It is useful to pinpoint factors from a person's background which, in the context of the particular case, may accelerate the stress they feel or adversely affect their confidence, and so have an adverse effect on outcome. For example, Jean's own poor experience of parenting as a child. Work with her should focus on whether that experience has left her with a poor model of parenting which she adopts.

'Situational hazards' – These are factors specific to the current circumstances which make an undesirable outcome more likely. Jean's lack of available child care provision could be classified as a situational hazard. A reasonably resourced agency should be able to help in this area.

The distinction between predisposing and situational hazards is useful in that it encourages decision makers to focus on where the problems are and to focus on those that they can alleviate. There may, however, be a degree of arbitrariness as to which category a particular hazard is assigned. For example, an alcohol problem may be viewed as predisposing if it is long standing and there is little possibility or intention of tackling it during the timespan of the decision, but, if it is of recent duration and an appointment has been made for treatment, it may be categorised as situational. The important point is that it is listed as a hazard.

Brearley then recommends listing background, situational hazards and strengths in columns along with the feared, undesirable outcome(s) – i.e., **'dangers'**. Setting it out in this way helps give a visual representation of the material but it should not lead to a simple totting up procedure where the strengths and hazards are totalled and the decision goes with the longest list. One strength – a supportive family network can be a strength against a long list of hazards, and one hazard – a violent alcoholic partner can undo what otherwise seems a safe situation. The framework is to aid the balanced presentation of knowledge, to promote informed discussion. It does not make the decision; that still needs negotiation and professional judgement.

Evidence

The Brearley framework for the analysis of risk as modified by the considerations set out above is used to interpret the case material set out in the case study. It is presented below with a commentary. This would constitute evidence of competence in assessing risk.

Commentary

In presenting the analysis the student should note and, where appropriate, elaborate on the following points.

(1) The risk being assessed is that associated with the children remaining in the care of their mother. A fresh analysis would have to be completed for a different decision, for example, removal to care, as hazards, strengths and dangers would all be different.

(2) The dangers to the children include the danger of suffering emotional abuse which is often neglected because of the problems in defining it precisely and recognising it (O'Hagan 1993).

Table 6.1 Risk Analysis: Case Study

Analysis on Proposed Decision: That the Children Remain in the Care of Their Mother

Name	Background Hazards	Situational Hazards	Strengths	Danger
JEAN	Poor parenting experiences in childhood	Poor child care facilities	Mostly evidence of a close relationship with the children	The child care she provides will be neglectful or abusive of the children
	History of conflict with her own family	Continued 'stormy' relationship with Michael	Responded positively to the crisis caused by the allegations	That she will form unstable/ violent partner relationships
	History of unstable and violent partner relationships	No family support	There have been no further signs of abuse or neglect to the children	That she will lose her children to care
	Single parent	Tolerated poor/abusive child care from partner	Has a job and keen to work	
	Poverty		Cooperated with social and health services to form good relationship with the student social worker	
			Intelligent. Good singer, former contact with the church	

Table 6.1 Risk Analysis: Case Study (Cont.)

Name	Background Hazards	Situational Hazards	Strengths	Danger
MICHAEL	Criminal record Record of violence Has been responsible for the children when child suffered alleged abuse	Little known of him and his background Poor child care skills 'Stormy' relationship with Jean Has poor/abusive relationship with Mark No relationship with social services	Offered and attempted to care for the children when Jean was working	Will physically abuse the children Will contribute to a violent partner relationship with Jean that will contribute to the emotional abuse of the children
MARK and MARIE	Already suffered abuse and neglect Absence of their father Living in poverty	Poor relationship with Michael Mother having difficulty finding adequate child care Cut off from their extended family	Have a good relationship with their mother who has shown she can be protective of them Satisfactory contact with the social services and child health services Their care has improved since the referral. There have been no further suspicions of abuse There will be continued social services support for the family	Will be further abused or neglected Will suffer emotional abuse as a result of the violent atmosphere in the home

(3) In completing the analysis it should be discussed with the client(s). This is the most important safeguard against using background material in a discriminatory manner. Jean's period in care is not listed as a background hazard because she enjoyed it and takes strength from it. To have included it as a hazard would have been discriminatory.

(4) The framework allows the inclusion of the differing types of background and current factors highlighted in the literature. It is however, essentially a listing, and, discussion is needed about the dimensions of many of the factors. For example, the seriousness of the abusive incident and the neglect of the children.

(5) The most worrying feature that emerges from the risk analysis is Jean's shadowy relationship with Michael. In most other respects Jean has responded well to the crisis and shows affection and concern for her children.

(6) There are considerable strengths and safeguards in the situation and the analysis would suggest that the risk associated with the children being cared for at home is acceptable albeit with continued support and supervision from the social and health services.

The risk analysis has a number of **advantages** over the way information is often presented in case conferences (Farmer and Owen 1995). First, it ensures that the strengths in the situation are given appropriate weight. In the crisis and abuse-fixated atmosphere of child abuse case conferences, the strengths in the family can be overlooked. Second, it can look at and enable consideration of each of the individuals and encourage a degree of specificity as to where the difficulties currently lie. Third, by separating background from situational hazards it can help the decision makers focus on those areas they can have an impact on and enable them to consider how the situational hazards could be remedied. For example, in this situation the paucity of child care facilities available to Jean and her continued isolation from her family could become targets for future work. Fourth, in the spirit of openness under the Children Act it should enable a more focused discussion with parents about the agency's precise concerns and allow them to see that their strengths are recognised and appreciated.

The **problems** with the framework are:

First that it is static and accordingly, therefore, fails to take account of changes that will occur over time. Also it does not lend itself particularly well to expressing the dynamic relationships within families; the framework should be seen as only one tool in an assessment.

Second that it can lend itself to a totting up approach with insufficient attention being given to a fundamental weakness or an overriding strength in a situation.

Third that the use of background or predisposing hazards is problematic. Used uncritically these can lead to serious discriminatory practice with parents feeling that they are being judged because of disadvantages they suffered in their past. If they are shared with parents and their views taken into account this can be a safeguard. They must not be used as the sole determinants of decision making and should rather inform a decision made on the grounds of current concerns and performance.

Conclusion

With the growth of statutory responsibilities and the significance which protection from abuse has assumed in social work in the last 20 years the assessment of risk has become central to much social work practice. It is a complex task that requires the application of core social work skills; it requires a familiarity with the relevant specialist knowledge base and it calls for a careful consideration of the values issues because of the potential for discriminatory practice. For these reasons students will normally only contribute to the assessment, but that contribution, accompanied by its presentation within the organisation, in multi-disciplinary settings and possibly in court, can provide high quality evidence of competence in at least four of the six core competences required by Revised Paper 30:

> **Communicate and Engage, Assess and Plan, Working in Organisations and Developing Professional Competence.**

References

Bergner, R.M., Delgado, L.K. and Graybill, D. (1994) 'Finkelhor's risk factor checklist: a cross-validation study.' *Child Abuse and Neglect 18*, 4, 331–340.

Brearley, C.P. (1982) *Risk and Social Work*. London: Routledge and Kegan Paul.

Burrell, B., Thompson, B. and Sexton, D. (1994) 'Predicting child abuse across family types.' *Child Abuse and Neglect 18*, 12, 1039–1049.

CCETSW (1995) *DipSW Rules and Requirements for the Diploma in Social Work, Revised edition*. London: CCETSW.

Corby, B. and Mills, C. (1986) 'Child abuse: risk and resources.' *British Journal of Social Work*. (1986) 16, 531–542.

Dalgleish, L. (1991) Assessment of Perceived Risk in Child Protection. Address to First International Conference on Risk Assessment in Child Protection. Leicester: NSPCC.

Dartington Social Research Unit (1995) *Child Protection and Child Abuse: Messages From Research*. London: HMSO.

Department of Health (1989) *The Care of Children.* London: HMSO.

Farmer, E. and Owen, M. (1995) *Child Protection Practice: Private Risks and Public Remedies.* London: HMSO.

Lynch, M.A. and Roberts, J. (1977) 'Predisposing factors within the family.' In V. Carver (ed), *Child Abuse: A Study Text.* Milton Keynes: Oxford University Press.

Meddin, B. (1985) 'The assessment of risk in child abuse and neglect case investigations.' *Child Abuse and Neglect 9,* 57–62.

Murphy-Berman, V. (1994) 'A conceptual framework for thinking about risk assessment and case management in child protective service.' *Child Abuse and Neglect 18,* 12, 193–201.

O'Hagan, K. (1993) *Emotional and Psychological Abuse of Children.* Buckingham: Open University Press.

Packman, J. Randall, J. and Jaques, N. (1986) *Who Needs Care? Social Work Decisions about Children.* London: Basil Blackwell.

Rowe, J., Hundleby, M. and Garnett, L. (1989) *Child Care Now: A Survey of Placement Patterns.* London: BAAF.

Stainton-Rogers, W., Hevey, D. and Ash, E. (1989) *Child Abuse and Neglect, Facing The Challenge.* London: Batsford.

Steele, B.F. and Pollock, C.F. (1968) 'A psychiatric study of parents who abuse infants and small children.' In R.E. Helfer and C.H. Kempe (eds) *The Battered Child.* Chicago: University of Chicago Press.

Stone, M. (1993) *Child Protection: A Model for Risk Assessment in Physical Abuse/Neglect.* Surrey County Council.

Thorpe, D. (1994) *Evaluating Child Protection.* Buckingham: Open University Press.

CHAPTER 7

Competence in Health Care

John McLaughlin

Introduction

Changing demographic trends in Britain over recent years, particularly the growing numbers of people in the very elderly age group (75–85), have made increased demands on health and social care services. While the number of people aged 75 and over requiring in-patient treatment continues to rise, average lengths of stay in hospital have shortened dramatically (Parker 1990). The current trend in government policies, particularly post-Griffiths, to constrain public expenditure and minimise length of stays in hospital, has major implications for social work role and task. Shorter in-patient stays and greater patient turnover has meant that effective assessment and discharge planning skills by hospital social workers are becoming increasingly essential (Blumenfield 1986).

Recent studies in Scotland and the US have further suggested that effective discharge planning can also contribute to cost-containment through early intervention resulting in earlier patient discharges (Connor and Tibbitt 1988; Spano and Lund 1986). The White Paper, 'Caring for People' (DoH 1989), saw proper assessment of need and good case management as the cornerstone of high quality care and a method of flexibly tailoring services to individual requirements to assist people to remain at home. Hospital placements, because they represent an important interface between institutional care and care in the community, offer social work students excellent learning opportunities to develop effective assessment skills which are sensitive to the needs of both patients and carers, and to demonstrate core competences in the provision of social work services.

Competence in hospital social work with vulnerable older people
When older people are admitted to hospital it is normally in situations of crisis; for example, caused by the traumatic onset of illness, a severe fall in the home, respiratory difficulties or strokes. The consequences of such traumatic events for all concerned requires a competent response from the hospital social worker

(Bergman 1976; Getzel 1982). The core competences normally required in the course of this process are:

- communicate and engage with the patient/family/key multi-disciplinary professionals
- promote the rights of the patient/family
- enable expression of concerns/needs/preferences
- assessment of needs and the planning of an appropriate 'package of care'
- intervention to ensure the agreed services are provided that will support patient/family through change and adaptation
- work in the organisation as an accountable and effective member of the multi-disciplinary team
- develop professional competence.

Case Study

Jim Brown (76) and his wife Peggy (73) live in a two-storey terrace house in an inner city area. They have one daughter, Betty (47) who lives 20 miles away and is separated with no family.

Jim worked as a labourer and enjoyed reasonable health. However, two years after he retired he suffered a heart attack and developed breathing difficulties. Weekends are a special time for Mr Brown when he meets up with his friends at the local pub for a drink and play darts. He doesn't have any hobbies but enjoys gardening.

Peggy Brown worked until retirement as a 'dinner lady' in the local primary school. Although she suffers from quite severe arthritis in her hips, Peggy has managed to get around reasonably well. Lately, however, the condition has worsened and she now uses a walking stick which is particularly necessary when climbing the stairs. Peggy also suffers from angina which becomes rather severe when she is required to walk any distance or when she is worried or upset.

Jim and Peggy are visited regularly by their daughter, Betty, mostly at weekends, and a very close and caring relationship exists between them. Betty separated from her husband three years ago and lives alone in a council house. Since the break-up of the relationship, Betty has become heavily dependent on alcohol and is now attending Alcoholics Anonymous. She is presently unemployed and suffers from periodic bouts of depression. The AA meetings are a great source of support and she attends regularly three times a week.

Last week Mr Brown was admitted to hospital where he was diagnosed as having suffered a stroke. He has lost the power on the right side of his body and the Consultant on the ward is of the opinion that his functional impairment is likely to be permanent, but should improve with intensive rehabilitation.

Knowledge

The requisite knowledge base for working with sick and disabled older people in hospital with complex psycho-social needs and their carers may be classified as follows:

(1) Contextual, legislative, procedural.

(2) Medical conditions and their psycho-social implications.

(3) Self-knowledge in relation to illness and disability.

(4) Methods and theories for practice.

Contextual, legislative, procedural

CONTEXTUAL

The student should have an understanding of the policy framework of community care proposals (e.g. Griffiths' Report (1988)) regarding purchaser–provider split; community care plans; complaints procedures etc.; and the subsequent White Paper 'Caring for People (1989) and its six key objectives including 'care management' proposals.

LEGISLATIVE

The student should have an understanding of the aims of protection and enablement as expressed in the legislation; and the powers and duties of local authorities to provide for care/treatment.

The following pieces of legislation are central to the area of physical disability:

(1) The definition of disability (National Assistance Act (1948) s29).

(2) Gathering and dissemination of information (Chronically Sick and Disabled Persons Act (SDPA) (1970) s1 and Disabled Persons Act (DPA) (1986) s9).

(3) Assessment of needs (CSDPA (1970) s1; DPA (1986) s4 (a) (b), s8; and NHS and Community Care Act (1990) s47.

(4) Provision of services in the community (National Assistance Act (1948) s29); as extended by CSDPA 1970/DPA (1986)/NHS and Community Care Act (1990) Part III).

(5) Provision of residential accommodation (National Assistance Act (1948)s21).

(6) Residential care and nursing homes (Registered Homes Act (1984)).

(Ball *et al.* 1991, p.30)

Knowledge of the contextual and legislative aspects of community care are relatively easy to access, as many social work departments will have copies of the relevant guides and statutes.

PROCEDURAL
The student should be thoroughly familiar with the hospital department's policy and procedures on assessment and care management. This includes both the **process** and **organisational arrangements** of care management which may vary both within and between agencies.

Assessment, however, is only one of seven core tasks in the process, as Figure 7.1 illustrates.

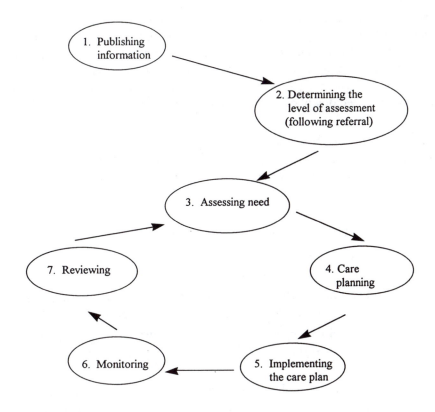

Figure 7.1 The Process of Care Management
Source: Practitioners Guide (SSI/SWSG 1991)

Medical conditions and their psycho-social implications

The student on hospital placements requires knowledge of the effects (physical/social/emotional etc.) of particular conditions and their implications for patients and carers. Basic knowledge of strokes and relevant information therefore will be helpful to the student in the Brown case. The student should also understand and be committed to the promotion of the social model of disability (Oliver 1983; Swain *et al.* 1993). The following reference sources on strokes will be helpful:

- *Epidemiology*: Ebrahim (1990); DoH (1994).
- *Diagnosis, Treatment and Rehabilitation*: Wade (1985).
- *Management and Rehabilitation*: Laidler (1994); Anderson (1992); Youngson (1992); King (1990); Hewer and Wade (1988); Mulley (1985).

Self-knowledge

Working with sick and disabled people in a hospital setting can be an emotionally demanding experience. It can be helpful therefore for the student to discuss their experiences of illness, disability and bereavement with their practice teacher, and explore these areas in a permissive and safe environment. This should considerably reduce anxiety and minimise the risk of the student becoming 'closed down' or 'blocked' in their response.

Methods and theories for practice

Knowledge of, and skills in, counselling, advocacy, crisis intervention and task-centred work will contribute to the achievement of competence.

Skills

The following skills are particularly relevant to hospital social work:

- **Interviewing skills**: Ability to ask appropriate questions; communicate clearly and effectively
- **Counselling skills**: Ability to listen actively and use open questions; ability to use skills such as reflecting, clarifying and summarising
- **Multi-disciplinary work**: Understanding the differing perspectives of other professionals; share knowledge appropriately; work collaboratively
- **Written work**: Ability to write clear, concise and accurate records that can be shared with service users; keep recording up-dated; plan and prepare material well
- **Self organisation**

- **Time management**
- **Work under pressure/understand and manage stress**

Values

Qualified social workers must demonstrate ethical practice. Paper 30 (CCETSW 1995) states that social workers '... must be self aware and critically reflective and their practice must be founded on, informed by and capable of being judged against a clear value base' (p.4). It has identified a number of key value requirements which must be demonstrated in the core competences. The following are central to the Brown case:

- Identify and question one's own values and prejudices

    The student needs to explore her attitude to old, sick, and disabled people and their place and status within a capitalist society.

- Respect and value uniqueness and diversity and recognise and build on strengths

    The student needs to acknowledge and respect the particular needs of old, sick and disabled people and their carers. It will be equally important for the student to promote, encourage and support independence where possible.

- Promote people's right to choice, privacy, confidentiality and protection, while recognising and addressing the complexities of competing rights and demands

    The student needs to recognise each family member's right to express preferences for services which will promote autonomy and personal empowerment. Effective negotiation skills will also be required to address and resolve competing priorities and preferences among family members.

- Practise in a manner that does not stigmatise or disadvantage individuals

    The student needs to be aware of the marginal status accorded to old and/or disabled people and ensure that the expressed needs and preferences of all family members are accurately represented and supported.

Achievement of Competence

Communicate and engage

The social worker (practice teacher) covering the medical ward where Mr Brown is a patient has received the referral through her team leader. It is felt that this particular case would offer the student good learning opportunities and enable her to demonstrate a range of professional competences. The referral form provides brief details of Mr Brown's admission and requests a social work assessment and possible referral to the care manager for comprehensive assessment. At this early stage it will be necessary to establish whether or not the patient is well enough to respond to assessment; this will partly determine whether comprehensive assessment will be required. Early contact can help relatives and carers to 'tell their story' and also reassure them that they will not be left to manage the situation on their own. Good inter-disciplinary liaison and communication with the hospital team will be necessary.

In preparation for the first meeting with Mr Brown the student, with the help of the practice teacher, begins to understand the immense physical impact of a stroke, and the emotional trauma of the condition for Mr Brown. She also 'tunes-in' to her own feelings about the visit and about dealing with possible communication difficulties. Initial visits should be brief and focused, as early days are traumatic and stressful for older sick people. Rehearsal of anxieties can help students considerably in preparing for new situations and should be seen as an integral part of interview preparation (Taylor and Devine 1993). Assessment is not a technical exercise but necessitates good interpersonal and interviewing skills.

On her visit to Mr Brown on the side ward, the student introduces herself and explains the purpose of her visit:

> 'Hello Mr Brown. My name is Helen Johnston. I'm a student social worker based in the hospital. Sister Jones asked me to call with you to see if social services could be of any help to you and your wife when you leave hospital.'

Mr Brown raises his left arm slowly as if to say 'hello' and utters a few slurred words. In a slow and halting fashion, the patient says the words 'wife' and 'afternoon' which the student reframes in the form of a question: 'Your wife will be visiting you this afternoon?' A nod confirms this. 'Would you like me to call with her?' Mr Brown gives the 'thumbs up sign'. Good eye contact with the patient is maintained throughout the brief meeting. The student acknowledges Mr Brown's speech difficulties and reassures him that she will remain in contact with the family during his time in hospital.

The ability to form and develop working relationships with Mr Brown and his family in this early phase should therefore be a key objective for the social work student in promoting good social work practice. Competence in effectively communicating and engaging can also be demonstrated.

Plan of first meeting with Mrs Brown and Mrs Smith.
An interview plan similar to that outlined in Table 7.1 is a useful tool in helping the student mentally prepare for the first meeting. Through this type of focused

preparation, competence in communicating and engaging with Mrs. Brown and her daughter can be rehearsed and eventually demonstrated.

Summaries of the practice requirements relevant to the Brown case and evidence indicators can be found in Table 7.5. An exemplar such as a written plan for the first meeting (see Table 7.1) may be used as evidence of competence. A practice teacher's written assessment of competence during preparatory sessions (e.g. role plays) is also appropriate.

Table 7.1 First meeting with Mrs Brown and Mrs Smith

1. Preparation for interview:	Establish 'preliminary empathy': how Mrs Brown and Mrs Smith might be feeling at this time of crisis. What are the student's own feelings/concerns about interviewing them? Anticipate possible family needs. Rehearse information giving.Study hospital policy and procedures on care management/comprehensive assessment.
2. Multi-disciplinary liaison:	Establish contact and communicate with ward staff. Share appropriate information and social work plans.
3. Introductions:	Introduce self as student social worker. Full name. Mention earlier contact with Mr Brown.
4. Outline of meeting:	Explain referral source and purpose of visit. Encourage relatives to share details about patient's admission. Acknowledge the stress and trauma of Mr Brown's admission for family. Use skills of listening, reflecting, clarifying, paraphrasing etc; open questions; empathy.
5. Information gathering:	Encourage and enable relatives to identify concerns about post-discharge period and anticipated problems. Check family and accommodation details; responsibilities; perceived limitations/constraints/strengths.
.6. Information giving:	Explain: hospital assessment principles of needs-led assessment; care management process/comprehensive assessment. Reassure that Mr Brown will not be discharged until a satisfactory package of care services is in place.
7. Next meeting:	Agree date and venue of next meeting. Two days' time at hospital's social services department.

Promote and Enable

The first meeting with Mrs Brown and Mrs Smith has enabled the student to form an early working relationship and has identified their concerns regarding the discharge period. The family have been reassured that discharge will only take place when a satisfactory package of care services is arranged. Two of the main issues discussed were:

(1) Mrs Smith's concern about how her mother would cope with Mr Brown's multiple needs.

(2) Mrs Smith's own need to attend AA meetings three times a week.

The student has explained the hospital's assessment process in a non-jargonised way and has outlined the care management process and the procedures involved in comprehensive assessment, should this be indicated for Mr Brown. On the basis of the student's initial social report on the family's circumstances and complex needs, the senior social worker decided that a comprehensive assessment will be required. This is **Stage 2** of the care management process **(Determining level of assessment)**.

The student has already sent a completed referral form to the care manager who has agreed to commission a comprehensive assessment. The practice teacher and the care manager confirm that the student will be the key worker in the case. At the end of the first meeting with the family, it was agreed that another meeting would be held in two days' time at the social work department in the hospital. It is important for students to appreciate that relatives need time and space away from the stressful environment of a hospital ward to reflect on the issues which have been discussed. The second meeting can be used to 'revisit' original areas of concern and formally agree and record these as part of the assessment process. A partnership approach can afford the family sufficient time to discuss their needs and enable them to contribute to the decision-making process (Stevenson and Parsloe 1993).

Over the past couple of days, the student has maintained contact with the multi-disciplinary team and has been apprised of Mr Brown's progress. She has also spent time with Mr Brown encouraging him to verbalise and share his feelings of the traumatic experience. Mr Brown has been kept informed by his wife and daughter regarding developments in the assessment process and is reassured that formal help is being negotiated.

DAY 4: MEETING WITH MRS BROWN AND MRS SMITH

In preparation for the meeting, the student has undertaken the necessary tuning-in and has set three objectives:

(1) To explore further family concerns about discharge plans and to establish needs.

(2) To explore and identify areas in which the family could be involved when Mr Brown returns home.

(3) To provide the family with printed information on care management, a volunteer 'Stroke Support Scheme' and on other voluntary organisations for carers.

The session is **observed** by the practice teacher with Mrs Brown's and her daughter's permission. The student provides the following **summary analysis** of the meeting:

Table 7.2 Summary analysis

'I started the meeting by welcoming Mrs Brown and her daughter and thanked them for coming. I then explained the purpose of the meeting and suggested that it might be helpful to explore further and agree specific concerns about Mr Brown's eventual discharge. As they up-dated me on Mr Brown's progress, I maintained good eye contact and periodically used affirmative and supportive statements when progress in Mr Brown's condition was mentioned. As the interview progressed, I got the impression that both women were feeling quite relaxed, as they talked enthusiastically about Mr Brown's condition. I feel I conveyed empathy in this early phase by actively listening and reflecting back on the satisfaction I was picking up from both of them about Mr Brown's progress.

In the next phase of the interview, I sensitively encouraged Mrs Brown and her daughter to **identify the precise concerns** they had about Mr Brown returning home. I used a combination of **open** and **closed** questions to elicit the necessary information.

The concerns are as follows:

Mrs Brown

(1) Getting Mr Brown in and out of bed in the mornings and at bedtime.

(2) Tending to his personal hygiene/toileting (toilet and bathroom are upstairs).

(3) Lighting the fire, shopping, laundry, supper (Mrs Brown has arthritis in hip; husband used to attend to above).

Mrs Smith

(1) Worried about her mother not managing the care demands of Mr Brown.

(2) Fear of the stress of the situation triggering her depression.

(3) Concerned about not being able to attend the AA meetings. May revert to drinking.

(4) Worried about becoming a full time carer for her father.

We then went on to discuss possible **areas where each of them felt they could contribute:**

Mrs Brown

(1) Preparing light breakfast.

(2) Afternoon snack.

Table 7.2 Summary analysis (Cont.)

Mrs Smith

(1)   Live with parents in meantime.

(2)   Prepare meals at weekends.

(3)   Shopping at weekends.

I agreed to provide the care manager with the above information as part of my ongoing assessment. Mrs. Smith had no objection to the care manager and primary care team knowing that she attended AA meetings.

In the final phase of the session, I provided Mrs Brown and her daughter with a departmental leaflet on 'care management' and the role of the care manager. I also explained in simple terms the **needs-led** and flexible approach of the scheme and indicated the probable involvement of the voluntary sector in the **care plan**. I agreed to give Mr Brown a copy of the leaflet on care management and reassured the relatives that I would remain in regular contact with him.

Before drawing the meeting to a close, I gave Mrs Brown leaflets on a local volunteer 'Stroke Support Scheme' and printed documentation from 'Carers National Association' and the 'Stroke Association'. I felt it was important at this early stage that both she and her daughter realised that organisations existed to address the needs of stroke sufferers and their carers. I gave Mrs Brown CNA leaflets on **Attendance Allowance** and suggested to Mrs Smith that **Citizens Advice Bureau** could perhaps provide useful advice on general welfare rights issues. I felt this might be a useful way of encouraging the family to undertake achievable tasks and to help maximize their right to appropriate information and benefits.

The atmosphere of the meeting was very relaxed and informal and the interchange of views, opinions and feelings about particular issues,was open and honest. I believe I communicated effectively with and engaged Mrs Brown and Mrs Smith and enabled them to participate in identifying their specific concerns and personal resources.'

In a subsequent supervision session, the interview with Mrs Brown and Mrs Smith was analysed and evaluated in relation to the stated objectives of the meeting. Throughout the session, the student demonstrated effective interpersonal and enabling skills in assisting the relatives to express their needs and concerns and to identify areas of strength in their own personal resources. An ethos of partnership was evident throughout the meeting and the student had demonstrated competence in enabling Mrs Brown and her daughter to participate in the assessment process. Effective preparation for the meeting had resulted in the student procuring appropriate information on care management and community support agencies for stroke sufferers and their carers. A summary of the evidence indicators relevant to this core competence is contained in Table 7.5. An exemplar such as the summary analysis of the above interview (Table 7.2) can be submitted as evidence for this core competence.

Assess and plan

Stages 3 and 4 of the care management process are concerned with **assessing need** and **care planning** (see Figure 7.1).

At this stage of the process, the student, as key worker, will have distributed the assessment pro formas to the various disciplines. As an integral task of care management, comprehensive assessment seeks to provide a **holistic view** of the person's physical, social and emotional needs in which a range of other professionals are involved. Within the ethos of a needs-led approach, assessment should be seen as a self-contained process which is carried out independently of the allocation of services (Orme and Glastonbury 1993). In this sense care management differs from traditional service responses in that it seeks to tailor services to identified and unmet needs instead of fitting clients' needs into existing services (SSI/SWSG 1991). By promoting the **exchange** model of assessment (Smale *et al.* 1993), the student's aim should be to empower the patient and carers by enabling them to voice their particular needs and wishes. The student social worker in the Brown case has already begun to gather and analyse information obtained from the primary carers. She has developed an early working relationship with the relatives and is gradually building a picture of their perceived needs, strengths and potential resources. The student has, therefore, worked in an empowering way with Mrs Brown and her daughter by keeping them central to the decision making process.

In taking this process forward, it is now necessary for the student to facilitate the patient and his family in articulating their needs about the type of health and social care 'package' that would enable them to live as normal a home life as possible (Smale *et al.* 1993).

Assessment of Mr Brown

In undertaking assessment of stroke patients, the student should remain sensitive to the patient's needs and wishes and work at their pace. The assessment and care management process has by now been explained to Mr Brown and he is aware that other disciplines will also be contributing to the assessment. Through a number of phased and time-limited sessions, the student has enabled Mr Brown to identify his perceived needs and has sensitively encouraged him to be as specific as possible. The following are the needs identified by Mr Brown:

(1) Remain at home.

(2) Help for his wife at home – breakfast/lighting the fire/ shopping/ cleaning/laundry.

(3) Move bed downstairs – neighbour to assist.

(4) Commode – toilet upstairs.

(5) Help with getting in/out of bed and toilet and wash.

(6) Companionship – possibly Day Centre (undecided).

The student records Mr Brown's identified needs and provides him with a copy. It is agreed that the student should meet with all family members to build on this initial assessment.

Meeting with Mr Brown, Mrs Brown and Mrs Smith

The joint meeting with the family serves as a forum for sharing Mr Brown's identified needs and exploring additional needs identified by Mrs Brown and Mrs Smith. The student reviews the earlier concerns, and assists the family in exploring their preferred package of domiciliary support. Mrs Smith identifies two additional needs:

(1) Her own need to attend AA meetings three times a week (Mon/Thur/Fri).

(2) Respite care for Mr Brown in the future.

Risk factors associated with Mr Brown's return home are thoroughly discussed and a financial assessment is undertaken. The student records and evaluates the information obtained from the meetings with the family and completes her social enquiry report for the care manager.

Regular liaison with the multi-disciplinary team is maintained by the student and potential risk factors for the patient and carers have been discussed and analysed. A detailed assessment of Mr Brown's self-care abilities has been carried out by the occupational therapist.

Assessment case conference

Following the completion of the multi-disciplinary assessments, a case conference is held in the hospital to share assessment outcomes. It is chaired by the care manager. The family attend the meeting and receive a copy of the final assessment. The range of needs and objectives identified by the various assessments are shared and the Brown family's preferences are comprehensively analysed and agreed. Timescales for the delivery of aids and appliances (e.g. commode, aids for daily living) are established and will form part of the agreed **individual action plan**. The occupational therapist agreed to undertake her initial assessment for housing adaptations within one week of discharge.

Table 7.3 Current Care Package Timetable
Client: Mr Brown

Agency	Tasks	Mon.	Tue.	Wed.	Thur.	Fri.	Sat.	Sun.
Home Care Organiser	Breakfast fire shopping cleaning laundry	8.30 a.m.–9.30 a.m	8.30 a.m.–9.30 a.m.	8.30 a.m.–9.30 a.m.	8.30 a.m.–9.00 a.m.	8.30 a.m.–10.0 a.m.	8.30 a.m.–9.00 a.m.	8.30 a.m.–9.00 a.m.
District Nurse	To get Mr Brown up, attend to personal hygiene	12 noon–1.00 p.m.	12 noon–1.00 p.m.	12 noon–1.00 p.m.	12 noon–1.00 p.m.	12 noon–1.00 p.m.	12 noon–1.00 p.m.	12 noon–1.00 p.m.
Crossroads Care Attendant Scheme	To enable Mrs Smith attend AA meetings			8.30 p.m.–10.30 p.m.	2.00 p.m.–5.00 p.m.	8.30 p.m.–10.30 p.m.		
Crossroads Attendant Scheme	Make supper, attend to toilet, wash, assist to bed	9.30 p.m.–10.30 p.m.	9.30 p.m.–10.30 p.m.	9.30 p.m.–10.30 p.m.	9.30 p.m.–10.30 p.m.	9.30 p.m.–10.30 p.m.	9.30 p.m.–10.30 p.m.	9.30 p.m.–10.30 p.m.

Care planning

Based on the identified needs and objectives of the **comprehensive assess-ment**, the care manager will be responsible for costing and eventual commis-sioning of services drawn from the mixed economy of welfare. The student will be responsible for **monitoring** and **reviewing** the care plan and **liaising** with the care manager concerning any necessary alterations (SSI/SWSG 1991). She will also act as an **advocate** for the patient *vis-à-vis* the care manager. During the remainder of Mr Brown's stay in hospital, the student continued to support and counsel Mr Brown and his family and assisted them in discharge planning. Regular contact has also been maintained with the care manager in monitoring developments in the care package and feeding this information back to the patient and relatives.

Pre-discharge planning meeting

The meeting is held three days before Mr Brown is discharged home and is chaired by the care manager. The care plan is discussed at length with all the service providers and the family is centrally involved throughout. A copy of the final care plan is given to the family and the community based service providers. Objectives of service inputs, monitoring and review arrangements are agreed and recorded. The student will monitor the case for six weeks, at which time the Brown's situation will be formally reviewed. (See Table 7.3 for details of the care plan.)

   Throughout this phase of intervention, the student has demonstrated her ability to work in partnership with Mr Brown and his family as part of the comprehensive assessment and has maintained effective links with the multi-disciplinary team. Competence has also been demonstrated in her organisa-tional ability of collating assessments from the various disciplines and contributing to the final care plan. Recorded details of involvement in the assessment and planning process (e.g. Individual Care Plan, Table 7.3) can serve as evidence of competence and be included in a portfolio of evidence.

Intervene and Provide Services

Implementation of the care plan, monitoring and reviewing represent stages 5, 6 and 7 of the care management process (see Figure 7.1). The role of the student social worker in the post-discharge period will be to support and sustain the Brown family through the process of change and to monitor and review the provision of care. Maintaining established working relationships with the family will require skilled use of self and the ability to pace work effectively. According to Badawi and Biamonti (1990, p.55): 'Discharge from hospital represents not the start of a return to normality but of discovering limitations which will probably increase with time'. During this period of personal and social transition, effective inter-personal and organisational skills will be necessary.

Prior to the patient's discharge, the student has explained that she would continue to be involved in the case for the next six weeks, after which time the case will be transferred to another worker. It will be important for the student to continue to address 'endings' sensitively with the family at appropriate stages, and to be aware that eventual disengagement can represent a loss for those with whom a relationship has been established (Coulshed 1991).

The student has been informed by the care manager that the care plan has now been implemented following Mr Brown's discharge.

Monitoring

Monitoring involves checking that agreed objectives are being achieved and are actually beneficial to the individuals concerned (Payne 1995); and addresses both the quality of care provided and the efficiency and effectiveness of overall management arrangements (SSI/SWSG 1991). Over the first week of discharge, the student has maintained regular contact with the family to monitor developments in the case. The carers have agreed to record points of note in a **daily log**. This form of involvement enables carers to take a more active part in the on-going monitoring process (Raiff and Shore 1993). A planned home visit in **week 2** enabled the student to monitor and evaluate the following areas:

- patient and carers' evaluation of care plan
- usefulness of daily log
- family forum: counselling to address tensions and strains.

Weeks 4–6

During this period the student's monitoring and evaluation focused on the following areas:

- liaison with service providers
- Mr Brown's attendance at Day Hospital
- carers' attendance at carers' support group
- attendance allowance applied for
- user and carer satisfaction questionnaire.

The student has maintained regular contact with the care manager about developments and has made detailed records of her monitoring involvement.

Review Meeting

Formal review of the care plan is a central feature of the care management process (Orme and Glastonbury 1993; Payne 1995). Its purpose is to identify changing needs and modify the care plan accordingly while maintaining a needs-led focus (SSI/SWSG 1991, p.83). During the course of the meeting held in the family home, feedback from all the relevant professionals was generally positive with all the objectives having been achieved. Several adjustments to the care plan were, however, agreed:

(1) Mr Brown to attend local Day Centre (10.00 a.m. – 3.00 p.m.). Timescale: 1 month.

(2) Domiciliary cover at weekends withdrawn – Mrs Smith to attend to meals, etc. Timescale: 1 week.

(3) Occupational therapist to arrange an assessment for doors to be widened and ramp built to accommodate wheelchair. Timescale: 2 weeks.

(4) Intermittent respite care scheme to be arranged. (eg '2–6'scheme). Timescale: 1 month

Unmet need identified

(1) Chair lift. To be reported to service planning system. Action: care manager

Subsequent to the meeting, a copy of the **review report** was sent to the family and service providers. The next review meeting is agreed for four months' time, or sooner if necessary.

Students involved as key worker in 'care managed' cases will find it necessary to consider and carefully plan **disengaging from their relationship** with the family. It will also be necessary to negotiate with the practice teacher and care manager the **transfer of the case** to another worker and to introduce the worker to the family. Careful preparation and planning for these with the practice teacher can help ensure that the emotional and organisational demands of the process are satisfactorily handled.

A practice example such as the **outline summary of involvement in the monitoring and review process** (see Table 7.4) may be included in a portfolio to demonstrate evidence of this core competence.

Table 7.4 Monitoring and review: Outline summary

Process	Tasks	Skills
Hospital (pre-discharge)	Explain monitoring and review process and case transfer plans	*Communication *Counselling/engaging *Emotional support: patient and carers
Week 1	Regular telephone contact	*Communication *Monitoring/evaluation: Care plan *Planning/organisation *Enabling skills: 'daily log'
Week 2	Home visit	*Negotiation/interviewing skills: feedback on care plan *Monitoring/evaluation: Quality/effectiveness of services Feelings, perception of patient and carers *Counselling and emotional support: Mr Brown *Enabling/summarising: 'Family forum'
Weeks 4–6	Regular telephone contact Home visits	*Monitoring/evaluation: care manager *Liaison/collaboration: Service providers Day hospital Attendance Allowance Carers Group *Planning: Questionnaire Review meeting Disengagement/case transfer *Communication: Review meeting

Conclusion

Hospital placements present students with a range of personal, professional, organisational and inter-professional challenges, as well as confronting them with the distressing consequences of illness and disability. On one level, social work practice in this setting is about managing 'systems' in a competent manner. On another level, skilled professional practice is concerned with responding to human need and vulnerability in a sensitive and compassionate way. Effectively integrating these dimensions is the challenge facing the social work student. The student in the Brown case has responded to a range of challenges at each stage of the care management process and has turned these into opportunities for demonstrating competent practice. Supervision sessions have also enabled her to evaluate critically her work in a challenging yet 'permissive' and supportive environment. Table 7.5 contains a summary of the practice requirements and evidence indicators relevant to the Brown case. Exemplars of evidence are also referenced. Although other core competences have not been referred to in the Brown case (i.e. development of professional competence, working in organisations), involvement in 'care managed' cases in hospital affords the student ample opportunity to provide evidence of competence in these two areas.

It may prove instructive for students to recognise that 'competent practice' is indicated only when practice requirements are consistently demonstrated throughout the placement. Professional development is a continuous and cumulative process and competence therefore should not be seen as being 'achieved' at any one point in time; or even over a series of assessment events during placement. Competence 'achieved' is not an absolute indication of ability or 'know how' but should be viewed rather as a new milestone in the overall process of consolidation and professional development. Students committed to undertaking the necessary practice preparations and integrating professional knowledge, skills and values in a reflective way, can greatly enhance their potential in demonstrating and maintaining competent social work practice in the health care field.

Table 7.5 Summary of Practice Requirements and Evidence Indicators

Core Competence	Practice Requirements	Evidence Indicators	Evidence Exemplar
COMMUNICATE AND ENGAGE	*Form and develop working relationship with Mr and Mrs Brown and daughter	1. Establish initial contacts	Written plan for first meeting
		2. Communicate effectively	
	*Network and form effective working relationships with other professionals	3. Identify shared and differing perspectives values and aims	(Table 7.1)
		4. Develop working relationships with adults and carers	
		5. Establish contact and communicate effectively with multi-disciplinary team	
		6. Develop and sustain networking relationships with other professionals	

Table 7.5 (Cont.)

Core Competence	Practice Requirements	Evidence Indicators	Evidence Exemplar
PROMOTE AND ENABLE	* Work with Mrs Brown and Mrs Smith to enable them to use their own strengths to meet responsibilities and achieve change	1. Assist family in expressing needs and concerns	Summary Analysis of interview with relatives
		2. Assist relatives to clarify goals, objectives resources and potential obstacles	(Table 7.2)
	* Provide information and advice to individuals, families, carers	3. Areas of strengths and weaknesses identified	
	* Promote and enable the family to participate	4. Provide details of care management process	
		5. Provide information on community support agencies	
		6. Assist relatives to participate in decision-making	

Table 7.5 (Cont.)

Core Competence	Practice Requirements	Evidence Indicators	Evidence Exemplar
ASSESS AND PLAN	* Work in partnership with patient and relatives to assess needs, risks, responsibilities, strengths and resources	1. Gather, record and evaluate information to make and assessment	Individual care plan
	* Work in partnership with multi-disciplinary team to identify and analyse risk of harm	2. Work with patient, family and multi-disciplinary team to evaluate actual and potential needs, strengths, responsibilities and resources	(Table 7.3)
	* Work in partnership to develop packages of care and support	3. Collate information form multi-disciplinary team on potential risk and harm for patient and carers	
		4. Select and combine sources of care from mixed economy of welfare	
		5. Negotiate and confirm with patient/family/multi-disciplinary team agreed care package and monitoring arrangements	

Table 7.5 (Cont.)

Core Competence	Practice Requirements	Evidence Indicators	Evidence Exemplar
INTERVENE AND PROVIDE SERVICES	* Contribute to the management of package of care	1. Monitor and evaluate provision of care	Outline summary of involvement in monitoring and review process patient
	* Support and sustain Mr and Mrs Brown and Mrs Smith through the process of change the process of change	2. Provide emotional support to sustain and carers	(Table 7.4)
		3. Regularly review changing perspectives priorities and effectiveness of arrangements with patient and relatives	
		4. Disengage from relationship with family	

References

Anderson, R. (1992) *The Aftermath of Stroke.* Cambridge: CUP.

Badawi, M. and Biamonti, B. (1990) *Social Work Practice in Health Care.* Cambridge: Woodhead-Faulkner.

Ball, C., Roberts, G., Trench, S., and Vernon, S. (1991) *Teaching, Learning and Assessing Social Work Law: Report of the Law Improvement Project Group,* Improving Social Work Education in Training Seven. London: CCETSW.

Bergman, A.S. (1976) 'Emergency room: a role for social workers.' *Health and Social Work 1* (Feb 1976) 32–44.

Blumenfield, S. (1986) 'Discharge planning: changes for hospital social work in a new health care climate.' *Quality Review Bulletin 1,* 51–55.

CCETSW (1995) *Rules and Requirements for the Diploma in Social Work* CCETSW Paper 30 (Revised Edition) Working Copy.

Connor, A. and Tibbitt, J. (1988) *Social Workers and Health Care in Hospitals.* Edinburgh: HMSO.

Coulshed, V. (1991) *Social Work Practice: An Introduction, Second Edition.* London: Macmillan.

DoH (1989) *Caring for People: Community care in the Next Decade and Beyond.* Cmnd 849. London: HMSO.

DoH (1990) *Community Care in the Next Decade and Beyond.* Department of Health, London: Price Waterhouse, HMSO.

DoH (1994) *Stroke: An Epidemiological Overview.* London: HMSO.

Ebrahim, S.B.J. (1990) *The Clinical Epidemiology of Stroke.* Buckingham: Open University Press

Getzel, G.S. (1982) 'Helping elderly couples in crisis.' *Social Casework 63* (Nov.1982), 515–521.

Hewer, R. and Wade, G. (1988) *Strokes: A Practical Guide Towards Recovery.* London: Dunitz.

King, P. (1990) *Living with Stroke.* Manchester: Manchester University Press.

Laidler, P. (1994) *Stroke Rehabilitation: Structure and Strategies.* London: Chapman and Hall.

Mulley, G.P. (1985) *Practical Management of Stroke.* Beckenham: Croom Helm Ltd.

Oliver, M. (1983) *Social Work with Disabled People.* London: Macmillan.

Orme, J. and Glastonbury, B. (1993) *Care Management.* London: Macmillan.

Parker, R. (1990) 'Elderly people and community care: The policy background.' In I. Sinclair, R Parker, D. Leat and J. Williams. *The Kaleidoscope of Care: A Review of Research on Welfare Provision for Elderly People.* London: HMSO.

Payne, M. (1995) *Social Work and Community Care.* London: Macmillan.

Raiff, N.R. and Shore, B.K. (1993) 'Advanced care management: New strategies for the nineties.' In M. Payne (1995) *op. cit.*

Smale, G., Tuson, G., Biehal, N. and Marsh, P. (1993) *Empowerment, Assessment, Care Management and the Skilled Worker*. London: HMSO.

Spano, R.M. and Lund, S.H. (1986) 'Productivity and performance: Keys to survival for a hospital-based social work department.' *Social Work in Health Care 11*, 25–39.

SSI/SWSG (1991) *Care Management and Assessment: Practitioner's Guide*. London: DoH SSI/SWSG.

Stevenson, O. and Parsloe, P. (1993) *Community Care and Empowerment*. York: Joseph Rowntree Foundation.

Swain, J. Finkelstein, V., French, S. and Oliver, M. (eds) (1993) *Disabling Barriers – Enabling Environments*. London: Sage/Open University Press.

Taylor, B. and Devine, T. (1993) *Assessing Needs and Planning Care in Social Work*. Aldershot: Arena.

Wade, D.T. (1985) *Stroke: A Critical Approach to Diagnosis, Treatment and Rehabilitation*. Cambridge: Cambridge University Press.

Youngson, R. (1992) *Stroke: A Self-help Manual for Stroke Suffers and their Relatives*. Exeter: David and Charles.

CHAPTER 8

Competence in Criminal Justice

Gerry Heery

Introduction

Can social work training provide an appropriate basis for students wishing to work within the criminal justice sector? How relevant is such training in preparing workers to 'assess and assist some of the most disturbed, anti-social, deprived, alienated and demoralized members of society' (Clarke 1994)? Traditionally, probation social work training has tended to stress 'a combination of humane concern for individuals and social reformisn' (Harris 1992, p.7). How does this fit with the current underlying objective of probation work which prioritises the reduction of offending behaviour. The goal is not to offer a social work service. Rather it is to offer an agreed programme which seeks to reduce and curtail a person's criminal behaviour. This distinction is crucial. It has major implications, not only in deciding on the underpinning Values, Knowledge and Skills which are most relevant to reducing crime, but in formulating what exactly is competent practice.

The role of punishment

There has always been and continues to be tension and argument as to how to balance the interests of the offender with those of their potential victims. Indeed, 'variations of this 'punishment versus welfare' debate have been a feature which has long dogged the development of effective approaches within the Probation Service' (Macdonald 1994, p.406). Tension between 'help' and 'surveillance' have been brought into sharper focus by the 'revival of an unashamedly punitive rhetoric, and a practice to match' (Feaver and Smith 1994, p.383). The current punishment in the community approach contains a punitive and negative value base which presents serious difficulties for social work trained proponents of a criminal justice service.

What works with people who offend?

There is no research which 'would unequivocally support a purely correctional and controlling approach to offenders who are being supervised in the community' (Gelesthorpe 1994, p.5). The need for supervision and monitoring may well be relevant; however, an exclusive focus on control without attention to offenders' needs and the availability of resources to address these needs can, in fact, often be counter-productive. Detailed analyses of the characteristics of successful work have identified key elements such as a focus on offending behaviour and related problems, a cognitive approach which encourages active participation by clients, and community reintegration (Gendreau and Ross 1983). Further elements, such as, targeting of more serious and persistent offenders, the quality of the relationship between the worker and the person who has offended, the provision of concrete services addressing clients' needs, and working on interpersonal life skills and social skills, have also been identified (Smith 1994). The emergence of this body of research-based information has largely undermined the previously held view that nothing works with offenders. It also provides a strong argument for the continuing role of social work within the world of criminal justice.

Social work training and criminal justice

It is critical that social work opens itself to this new knowledge and the demands it makes on practice. It needs to continue to strive to widen its knowledge and skills bases, and to seek to offer imaginative and effective interventions, in responding to offending behaviour. In particular, it needs to overcome its tendency to associate prioritising the reduction of offending behaviour with controlling and punishing people. As such it needs to continue to strive to develop a more appropriate value base which is both about seeking to empower people but also about requiring them to take responsibility for their offending behaviour. The reluctant and belated response to such challenges has not helped social work maintain a meaningful and credible place within the criminal justice system. Indeed that place is now under threat as a recent government report is proposing to remove the requirement that those working within the probation service need to have a social work qualification (Dews and Watts 1995).

This chapter will respond to the challenge of these developments. It presents a case study in which a social work student demonstrates competent practice in work carried out with a person who has committed criminal offences. The work will centre on the preparation of a pre-sentence report (social enquiry report) and will seek to illustrate the significant knowledge, skills and values demonstrated by the student in the work undertaken, and how these have been integrated into the Core Competences of Social Work.

The Case

Mr Sean Moore, a 23-year-old white man has just been sentenced to six months' imprisonment at a magistrates court in respect of several offences of theft. He has entered an appeal against the sentence imposed by the court, has been given bail and is due to appear at the appeal court in five weeks time.

Mr Moore lives with his partner and their two young children in a two-bedroomed rented accommodation in a deprived inner city area. He has a history of displaying unreasonable and violent behaviour within the family unit, directed at his partner. Although there have been settled spells in the relationship, such a negative pattern has been present for several years.

Social indicators such as levels of unemployment, housing conditions, levels of income, health problems, truancy rates, and crime levels all consistently point to a disadvantaged and difficult community situation.

Mr Moore has experienced a difficult early family life, being removed from his family at 12 years of age into residential care because of concerns about aspects of his behaviour; particularly truancy and glue sniffing. His teenage years were unstable: he regularly ran away from care, there were difficulties within his family, increasing dependence on solvents and alcohol, and involvement in criminal behaviour mainly car crime and city centre thefts.

The formation of a relationship with his current partner and birth of his children failed to have a significant positive impact on his lifestyle. Mr Moore has developed a pattern of regularly withdrawing from the family home and subsequently involving himself in street drinking and glue sniffing binges, usually accompanied by further more sustained bouts of offending. Such behaviour, which by its nature is very noticeable, has tended to isolate and alienate Mr Moore from his own community.

At this point, Mr Moore feels pessimistic about his future. He is bitter about the treatment he has received from members of his family, community and the police. He feels that he does not have access to legitimate ways of achieving a reasonable lifestyle. He feels there is little he can do about his problems and needs to 'escape' regularly into solvents and alcohol. He finds it hard to control his anger, and hasn't given much thought to the consequences of some of his behaviours both for himself and for others.

Competence in report writing

The successful completion of a court report for Mr Moore will require the student to demonstrate the following Core Competences:

- **to communicate and engage with him,** providing him with detailed information about the report and obtaining his consent for the work

- **to then seek to promote and enable** Mr Moore fully to avail himself of and participate in the service on offer.

- **the ability to assess and plan** with Mr Moore a realistic response to his offending and its causes within the context of a court appearance (this will comprise the major portion of the work)

- there will be only limited opportunity for the student to **intervene and provide services** although one significant piece of work will be outlined.

- the student's work will take place within the context of a statutory agency and will involve adherence to legal requirements and also various agency procedures and guidelines. In doing this, **the ability to work in organisations** will be demonstrated.

- the difficult nature of the piece of work will require the student to reflect on and **develop professional competence** across a range of areas.

Knowledge Skills and Values

What is the critical knowledge required in trying to understand why and how some people become and persist as offenders? What knowledge and skills are necessary to respond effectively to offending behaviour? What is the value base upon which such knowledge and skills should rest? Here are some of the elements within each of these three central pillars in social work training.

Knowledge

- theories explaining crime and its causes
- sentencing patterns
- statutory responsibilities and agency requirements in writing reports
- range of community resources available
- effectiveness and impact of custodial and community disposals
- theories and models for work with offenders (what works)
- understanding people and the impact of change
- theories and methods of motivation
- assessment of risk of reoffending
- aims, methods and theories of intervention
- discrimination and the criminal justice system.

Skills

- interviewing (motivational interviewing)
- interpersonal and communication skills
- information gathering
- assessment and risk analysis
- networking
- advocating
- report writing.

Values

- offering the best possible service
- treating people fairly, openly and with respect
- challenging attitudes and behaviours which have resulted in crime and caused distress to others
- affirming and bringing out positives
- reconciling the person with their community whilst recognising the obligations on both.

In the ensuing pages, the efforts of a student (a 24-year-old white woman) to apply some of these elements of knowledge, values and skills will be described. She will have to relate these to Mr Moore's own situation and the local context in which his offending has taken place. Her ability to demonstrate core competences will ultimately depend on her acquisition and application of the relevant elements of knowledge, values and skills.

Communicating and engaging

The student quickly identified potential blocks to effective communication and engagement with Mr Moore. She was concerned, both about the extent of the violence in his criminal record and previous difficulties he had had in complying with a community service order. In addition she was also frustrated by Mr Moore's failure to attend for an interview which she had offered him by letter. given that there were just five weeks until court. Through gathering relevant information from previous reports and contacting other sources in the office and local community the student was able to increase her knowledge about Mr Moore and his situation. Through this process she was able to make a judgement that an unannounced brief home visit was safe. She also concluded that this would ensure that Mr Moore was at least aware of the service being offered to him. The student felt that this value based decision to visit and establish an initial contact would be significant in helping her to begin *to form and develop a working relationship with Mr Moore.*

When the student called, Mr Moore was at home with his partner and some friends. She was able to speak to him for a few minutes on their own. She adopted a warm and friendly tone, stressing that she was not there to put pressure on him rather she wanted to make sure that he knew that a report was on offer to him and that her agency was keen to work with him and offer him this service. Given that the court date was so near, she wanted him to have this information now, to give enough time to do a report should he want one done. She suggested that if he wanted to consider it further that they meet together as soon as possible. Mr Moore appeared to be pleased at being contacted at home and agreed to meet the next morning in the probation office.

The student had three tasks she wished to achieve during her first formal meeting with Mr Moore:

(1) To explain her status as a student and obtain Mr Moore's agreement to work with her and her practice teacher

(2) To explain in detail the process involved and implications in having a court report and obtain Mr Moore's informed consent to have one written

(3) To begin the process of assisting Mr Moore to begin to explore and reflect on his current situation.

The above tasks required the student to use some of the knowledge, skills and values identified above: knowledge of agency requirements as to writing reports, a range of inter-personal and communication skills aimed at encouraging Mr Moore's involvement in the process and a value base aimed at offering him the best possible service. These are all necessary in the continuous task of initiating and developing a working relationship with Mr Moore.

Promoting and enabling
In carrying out the tasks identified for their meeting the student sought to ensure that Mr Moore's *rights were promoted and he was empowered to take decisions where appropriate.* She recognised his right to know about her role as someone being trained, and whether or not he wanted to work with the student and her practice teacher. The student also ensured that *she provided information and advice to* Mr Moore about a court report. She outlined in plain language the legal basis of the court report and how it was to be used. She told Mr Moore the type of information that would go into the report; about his offending and why it is taking place, about his personal circumstances and how some of these may be related to him offending, and about looking at a range of ways that could be offered to the court for dealing with the offending. The student was careful not

to rush through this part of the interview. She regularly asked for Mr Moore's opinion of what she was telling him. She explained that she was working for an agency who wanted to work with people as much as possible in their own community and not have them sent to prison. However, she stressed that this did not mean that offending behaviour was not taken seriously and that the report was not about trying to 'get people off'. She made sure that Mr Moore was aware that if he agreed to have a report done, it would involve looking closely at his offending behaviour. This would involve, among other things, contacting the police officer in charge of the case, and looking at Mr Moore's previous convictions and previous probation reports and files. She also informed Mr Moore as to limits of confidentiality in that if he told her about further offending behaviour then she may have to share such information with the police.

As well as demonstrating her ability and statutory to *work in accordance with legal requirements*, the student also stressed the more positive co-operative nature of the enterprise. She explained to Mr Moore that the report was a way for him to try to find a means of avoiding further offences, if this was what he wanted, and offering it to a court as an alternative to imprisonment. Mr Moore had had previous reports and agreed to have one done although he did say that he 'didn't see the point of having a report in this case as he was going to jail anyway'. He also didn't agree to the student contacting the police officer in charge of the case to talk about the offences as he 'didn't trust him'. Nevertheless he accepted that this was required and he gave his consent to the report.

The student now moved into her third task in which she sought to encourage Mr Moore to explore further and reflect on his current situation with regard to the court case. To achieve this, she introduced knowledge of motivational interviewing and theories of change into her interaction with Mr Moore. Despite his apathy, she recognised that a court appearance was a time of crisis for him. From her knowledge of theories of change, she recognised that for someone facing the unpleasant consequence of imprisonment, there was a possibility that they 'may well for a short period of time have considerable energy available to make limited changes in particular areas of concern' (Marshall, Weaver and Loewenstien 1992, p.9). Her goal was to seek to enable him to stop, take stock of his situation, examine his offending and 'the possible reasons behind it, and explore the possibilities for things being different in the future' (Powell 1985, p.84).

Motivational theory also told her that there was little point in trying to force or cajole Mr Moore into certain courses of action simply to avoid the unpleasant prospect of jail. Mr Moore needed to see the necessity for change himself and make his own decisions. Again, the student's knowledge of motivational theory informed her that this vital first stage was often overlooked (McDougal 1992). Table 8.1 outlines how she used the skills of motivational interviewing and personal construct theory and applied them in a structured way in trying *to enable Mr Moore to use his own strengths and expertise in trying to meet his responsibilities.* She started from where he was at, and sought to begin the process of facilitating him to take as much responsibility as possible for dealing with the situation he was in.

Table 8.1 Helping Client Make a Decision about Court Case

Stage 1 Engaging Interest and Participation

Objectives	*Methods*
(i) To obtain client's perception of sentence and situation	(i) Conversational
	(ii) Using affirmation
(ii) To begin to identify issues which reinforce discomfort in client's thinking about situation	(iii) Using empathy
	(iv) Reflecting back to client issues raised

Stage 2 Generating Information and Empowering to Make Decision

Objectives	*Methods*
(i) To reflect as objectively and empathetically as possible an assessment of risk of custody for client	(i) Avoid labelling
	(ii) Avoid judging
(ii) To explore with client what he needs to deal with risk	(iii) Avoid threatening
	(iv) Seeking to reinforce responsibility on client to respond to current situation
(iii) Get a clear idea in client's language of what he would do to avoid custody	
	(v) Reinforce self motivational statements

Stage 3 Enabling choice

Objectives	*Methods*
(i) Provide information and allow client to explore various options	(i) Allowing sufficient time and continuing with strategies outlined above
(ii) Help client choose	

So for the remainder of the first interview, the student focused on engaging Mr Moore's interest and participation in exploring his own view of the situation. She resisted the temptation to jump straight into asking direct and probing questions about his offending behaviour. She consciously worked hard at following her framework; slowing things down, giving Mr Moore the opportunity to look at his current situation from his perspective and to explore his feelings about it.

The student strived to use some of the key skills of motivational interviewing; asking open ended questions, listening, affirming, reflecting back and generally facilitating Mr Moore to explore and think about his situation. Through this process, Mr Moore began to experience some unease and discomfort. For example, after being able freely to explore his aversion to prison, he then began to consider some of the reasons why he was regularly ending up there. As he did this, he began to recognise the discrepancy between some of his current behaviours and his objective to avoid regular periods in prison. By reflecting back some of these issues to Mr Moore the student increased the amount of discomfort that he was experiencing in his thinking. She recognised that motivation for change is created when the person perceives a discrepancy between their present behaviour and important personal goals (Miller and Rollnick 1991).

As the session continued, the student used further strategies of this approach. Primarily she was able to elicit from Mr Moore his own motivational statements about things he could do in reducing or changing some of the behaviour patterns which kept leading him to custody. He was able to begin to identify himself some of his behaviours that he should think about changing. For example 'I'm going to have to cut down on the glue'; 'I'll have to stop spending so much time with some people'; 'I'd love to have the chance of some sort of job' etc. The student sought to amplify and reinforce such positive statements. Through this process she was able to facilitate Mr Moore to begin to use his own strengths and expertise in meeting some of his responsibilities.

Assessing and planning

Moving into stage 2 of her framework (Table 8.1), the student now sought to begin the process of linking Mr Moore's newly emerging goals with regard to his lifestyle, with the reality of his current situation. This required that she re-introduce his offending behaviour into their discussion. She reminded him of the requirement on her to analyse his offending behaviour, and 'to make a provisional assessment of the seriousness of the offence in order to properly focus the report' (Gillyeat 1994, p.vi). Given the relationship that she had already succeeded in forming with Mr Moore, the student was able to sensitively and directly address his offending behaviour. She worked in accordance with statutory and agency requirements in exploring a range of issues with him. These included: his particular role in the offences; the value of the property taken; his level of personal gain; and his attitudes towards such behaviour. She also consulted with the police officer in charge of the case who provided her with further information on the offence which she was able to discuss with Mr Moore. Finally, and as required by the agency, the student also completed a Reconviction Indicator with Mr Moore.

Using the non-confrontational interpersonal skills listed in Table 8.1, and a knowledge of offending behaviour, the student and client reached agreement on the analysis of his own behaviour. Through a consideration of the circumstances of his current offences the student was able to identify mitigating and aggravating factors (see Table 8.2). This was important and relevant in seeking to make judgements as to the seriousness of Mr Moore's offending (Raynor, Smith and Vanstone 1994).

Table 8.2 Working on Seriousness of Mr Moore's Offending

What makes the Court see my offending as more serious	*What makes the Court see my offending as less serious*
(1) Planned and organised city centre shoplifting	(1) Related to my problems with glue and alcohol
(2) Large amount stolen	(2) Part of a group, not the leader
(3) Certain shops targeted	(3) Nobody hurt
(4) Some personal gain	
(5) Long record of similar offences	

The student worked in partnership with Mr Moore in identifying and analysing the risk of harm he presented in the community. The information in Table 8.2 with regard to the seriousness of the offences, the police and prosecution view, the high risk of reconviction score, plus the significant fact that he had already been sentenced to custody at the lower court, all highlighted the seriousness of Mr Moore's offending and the reasons for the likelihood of custody. The student reflected as objectively as possible these reasons to Mr Moore and encouraged him to take responsibility for the next phase of their work in thinking about the sort of commitment he would be prepared to make in avoiding such a possibility.

The student was aware from her knowledge of various criminological theories and also longitudinal research on people who had become persistent offenders, of the wide range of factors which appeared to have a correlation with criminal behaviour (Farrington and West 1990; Farrington 1991). She now sought to use this material in her work with Mr Moore, and identified with him a range of such factors which were present in his situation and were possibly relevant to his offending (see Table 8.3). Several of these factors had

Table 8.3 Factors in Mr Moore's offending

Social	o history of unemployment
	o lack of vocational opportunities
	o limited income
	o part of alienated group within own community
Behavioral	
1. Defects	o educational underachievement
	o lack of occupational skills
	o lack of self control
2. Excesses	o solvent abuse
	o aggressive and violent behaviour
Cognitive problems	o blaming others for circumstances
	o seeing his behaviour as being beyond his control

already been identified by Mr Moore and he was already motivated to try to deal with them, for example his abuse of solvents and his lack of employment skills.

The student used her knowledge of the relevance of cognitive problems in explaining why certain people offend (Ross 1992). As Table 8.3 indicates, she raised the issue of some of Mr Moore's thinking with regard to his offending behaviour. For example, how he tended to rush into offences without stopping to think, how he failed to weigh up gains and losses from offending over the longer term, and how he thought of offending as a way of gaining esteem and meeting expectations of his male friends. Mr Moore was intrigued by the student's identification of these issues, but appeared resistant to taking them any further. He felt that there was nothing he could do about the way he thought about various issues in his life. The student, recognising the relevance of motivational interviewing skills, explored this potential block with Mr Moore. She acknowledged the difficulty inherent in doing such work, and that it was intended to be challenging. She also made Mr Moore aware of the possible consequences for himself if he agreed to involve himself in such work and subsequently changed his mind, thereby putting himself in breach of a court order.

At the probation centre, the student sought to move Mr Moore into the final stage of their work and to continue *to work in partnership to negotiate and plan responses to his assessed needs.* She provided him with information and the chance to talk about various courses which took place in the centre. (She demonstrated her knowledge of the range of relevant programmes available to Mr Moore which would enable him to stop and look at the thinking processes around his offending and to begin to make positive changes. To varying degrees they would target the social, behavioural and cognitive factors which the student had tentatively identified with Mr Moore as being relevant to his offending.) In doing this, the student was able to maximise his choice 'with due regard to function of the agency and the development of imaginative community sentences' (Raynor and Vanstone 1994, p.398).

The student now sought to use her writing skills to put her and Mr Moore's assessment into a format which met the standards expected of her agency and the court. She was able to edit, organise, and refine the information she had gathered. As she read in a circular; 'The essence of a good report is that anybody should be able to read it and make sense of it. Secondly, it should be selective: it should contain relevant facts about the offenders attitude to their crime but not an entire case history. Thirdly, having read the report, the conclusion should be obvious and inevitable' (Home Office 1993). Eventually, with some trial and error, she completed the work. As the client remarked, 'I think its fair enough, it's the way it is for me, there's no point in trying to hide it'.

The student's report outlined and analysed the offences which the Court had to deal with, and his offending history. It examined Mr Moore's attitudes towards his offending and identified some of the factors referred to earlier and which appeared to be relevant. It also provided the court with limited relevant personal information and attempted to bring out some of the potentially positive elements therein. It looked at the range of sentences already used with Mr Moore and particularly examined the limited impact of custody. Finally, it provided the court with a range of possible non-custodial options. These included community service as a direct alternative to custody as well as probation orders with additional requirements, related to the programmes already referred to.

Intervening and providing services

In this chapter, it will not be possible to follow through the work with Mr Moore after the completion of the court report. (In fact, he was placed on probation and work already carried out by the student proved to be a very solid base upon which to seek to deliver a challenging programme of supervision.) However, before the court appearance the student did take the opportunity to intervene and provide a particularly relevant service in Mr Moore's life. She was aware of research linking unemployment and deprivation to offending. (Farrington et al. 1986). She was able to help Mr Moore to explore this area and begin to identify ways of moving it forward. Whilst acknowledging the difficulties he would face in adjusting to the routine and monotony of the world of work, and in accepting the low levels of pay, Mr Moore himself also identified his need to get the chance to work. To this end, and following negotiation within her team, the student was able to refer him to a probation funded local employment project. Fortuitously, he was offered a one year position to start two weeks after the court case. Not only had *she been able to contribute to the direct provision of a service* for Mr Moore; an important positive element for inclusion in the court report had also been created.

Working in organisations

In carrying out the work which has been described in this chapter, the student has had to act *as an accountable and effective member of a particular probation team.* Throughout the period of her work with Mr Moore she remained aware of and was also able to respond to the relevant statutory and agency guidelines, priorities and standards. For example, her decision to do a home visit to Mr Moore after he had missed his first interview reflected her knowledge of an agency objective to increase the number of reports prepared on people appearing at the appeal court. Her decision stemmed from awareness of an appeal court judge's positive feedback on the quality of the reports of the agency; the judge indicated a desire to consider community disposals if he felt them to be at all appropriate.

In actually constructing the report, the student was also conscious of the need to produce a document for the court which as well as being relevant to Mr Moore also maintained the credibility of the agency she was representing. She succeeded in producing a report which adhered to agency guidelines and standards.

Finally, with regard to her decision to seek to offer Mr Moore a place on the employment project, the student was able *to contribute to the planning, monitoring and control of one of the team's resources.* Fully aware of the resource implications of such a decision she discussed and negotiated Mr Moore's referral to the project within the team. She was able to demonstrate that, given the seriousness of his offending, the risk of custody and his level of motivation, that he met the criteria for referral to a resource which was much in demand.

Developing professional competence

From the start of her involvement in this case the student sought to critically evaluate and develop her own professional practice, knowledge and values. She took a range of issues into supervision and was able to demonstrate her ability to use this process positively. For example, upon first receiving the referral, the student immediately recognised that her own background was of a different religious and political identity from her prospective client. She recognized how, at one level, she was almost relieved that Mr Moore did not attend for interview. Indeed she had to force herself to ensure that she sought to deliver as full a service as possible to him. When she visited Mr Moore's home she was surprised by the friendly welcome, the openness, the quality of the living conditions. The home was much better maintained and 'cleaner' than she expected and the atmosphere was much less aggressive She reflected on her still limited knowledge of the community in which she was on placement and the extent of her own preconceptions and prejudices.

The student was able to develop such feelings in supervision with her practice teacher and also begin to explore wider issues. For example, Mr Moore came from a community which had experienced a range of discrimination and had serious concerns as to the fairness of the criminal justice system. She needed to be sensitive to such issues in her work with Mr Moore. The student also reflected on what her practice would be like in an inner city area in England with a large Black community. She recognized the importance for her in looking more closely at the extent of her knowledge and some of her attitudes with regard to people from different ethnic groups and their position within the criminal justice system.

On another level, and further on in her work with Mr Moore, the student was able to reflect on the difficulties she had experienced on the placement in discussing and analysing offending behaviour. On the one hand, she felt awkward about pressurising people to talk about their offences. She was very aware of the potential power inherent in her role as report writer, and the danger of dominating and imposing a 'solution' on the subject. 'Reports can become part of the process of humiliation that courts use to emphasise their power. Being discussed, being evaluated, being judged, can be an uncomfortable experience at the best of times' (Powell 1985, p.29). However, as the placement progressed and she reflected more, the student came increasingly to recognize 'the tightrope that has to be walked between offering a non-judgemental respect for clients as people, empathising with their pains, whilst not colluding with their offending and its perceived impact' (Marshall, Weaver, and Lowwenstein 1991, p.42). In developing her skills in using motivational interviewing techniques the student felt she had achieved a critical stage in her learning with regard to the whole issue of how to raise and explore with a person their offending behaviour.

Report writing was another area in which the student developed her practice in working with Mr Moore. During the placement she had struggled with gathering too much information for her reports. Indeed, after her second interview with Mr Moore, the student had already amassed a considerable amount of information. Much of this, as has been shown, was obviously and immediately relevant to the production of the Court report. However her practice teacher indicated that her first draft was much too long. It contained too much irrelevant personal information on the client. She needed to focus in on the range of relevant factors – individual, inter-personal, social – which were operating in this man's life and which were implicated in his offending behaviour.

However, in refining her report-writing skills the student had to face and begin to resolve the professional dilemma as to what she should do with other information of which she was now also aware. This included Mr Moore's unfortunate personal history and his deep feelings of frustration and bitterness in respect of some of his experiences. She was also conscious of his negative attitudes towards his partner (and women in general) and his aggressive and violent behaviour to her. On another level she was also aware of a man with a sense of humour, and with a strong interest in music and also in reading about the history of his own community.

The student could see that the above areas could well become significant areas for attention in on going work with Mr Moore. However, at this stage, she realised that she could not, nor was it appropriate for her to provide a detailed and comprehensive assessment of this man's situation. Nevertheless, at their meeting at the probation centre, the student did spend some time with Mr Moore looking at some of his attitudes and behaviours towards women. She shared with him the expectations that all people in the centre were to be treated as adults and with respect, and there was a requirement that he should treat other persons similarly irrespective of their gender, religion, race or sexual orientation.

Finally, the student also experienced another fundamental professional dilemma with regard to her work with Mr Moore. This concerned the seriousness of his position, and the unpredictability of what would happen at court. Was she being in some way dishonest in facilitating and empowering Mr Moore to take as much responsibility for making decisions about changes in his life but which the court may not sanction? Through their interaction, she had sought to ensure that with his motivational levels increasing, this uncomfortable reality was not lost. Nevertheless, she had a niggling worry that all the work she was doing with Mr Moore, and the foundation he was building to try to make positive changes in his life, would be for nothing. Indeed there remained a small possibility that his prison sentence would be increased! As it turned out, the work was vindicated by the court, but it did help the student realise that, especially in working with more serious and persistent offenders, such results would not always be forthcoming.

Evidence of competent practice

The work carried out by the student on the court report for Mr Moore demonstrated her ability across the different core competences. Paper 30 requires students to produce evidence of their competent practice while on placement. Below are listed the ways in which the student produced the actual evidence of competence for her portfolio.

(1) The student and her practice teacher co-worked the first formal
     interview in which Mr Moore's consent to working with a student
     and having a report prepared were discussed. This allowed the
     practice teacher to observe live the student's inter-personal skills and
     her ability to provide detailed information about the report.

(2) The student obtained Mr Moore's consent to tape one of their
     meetings and she was able to use brief extracts from their interaction
     to demonstrate various inter-personal skills and her knowledge of
     agency procedures.

(3) The student simulated with the practice teacher part of the session in
     which she intended to explore and explain Mr Moore's offending
     behaviour. Not only did this help prepare her for a particular piece
     of work, it also served as a further source of evidence of her
     professional development.

(4) The student did brief analyses of key stages of the work for
     supervision. For example, in one exercise she reflected on and
     developed the knowledge, skills and values she used in coming to a
     decision with Mr Moore as to what type of programmes to offer the
     court. She also completed an exercise in which she explored her own
     prejudices and her lack of knowledge of Mr Moore's religious
     background. She was then able to examine such issues and the
     implications for her practice in seeking to offer such a service to a
     person from a different ethnic background.

(5) After the court case, the practice teacher obtained direct feedback
     from Mr Moore as to how he felt about the service he had received
     from the student.

(6) Finally, the actual report, along with feedback from the sentencer and
     barrister also provided a degree of evidence of the student's
     competence.

(It is clear that the writing of court reports will provide students with a wide
range of opportunities to demonstrate competence. These are usually possible
to negotiate and plan between the client, student and practice teacher.)

Conclusion

Writing reports on people who have committed offences is a complex business.
My own practice in this area has evolved over several years and is still
developing. The need to produce reports of an acceptable standard for court
and within a tight deadline can place students under considerable pressure and,
in fact, block the learning opportunities available in such work. The importance
of being sensitive to the stage a student is at, not setting too high expectations,

and providing appropriate support can not be overstated. All students will not be in a position to cover all the areas demonstrated in this example. Nevertheless, through co-working arrangements a range of learning opportunities can be negotiated with clients and provided for students.

The co-operation and involvement of clients is obviously important in providing meaningful learning experiences for students. Care needs to be taken in ensuring that clients are not seen as a means to an end. There is a real danger that the necessity to demonstrate competence may be perceived as more important than the client or service user. By being aware of this, the student ensured that her work with Mr Moore was not impeded by her need to acquire evidence of competence.

In her work the student has demonstrated her ability across the range of the six Core Competences of Social Work Practice. She acquired and used a body of knowledge, applied a range of interpersonal and assessment skills, and integrated a clear and consistent value base. Through this process, she has shown that she is equipped to begin practice and to move forward to meet the Core Competences for Probation Officers (Home Office 1994).

Offending is a complex phenomenon, to which there are no easy answers. Further knowledge is still required as to how and why some people start to offend, why they continue and how their offending may decline (Burnett 1994). Much of the work is with people who are apathetic, unmotivated, who feel they have no stake in society, who have been subject to discrimination and who sometimes behave inappropriately. Punishment on its own will not ensure that such people make sufficient changes in their lifestyle to reduce their dependence on offending behaviour. Effectiveness is still determined in large measure by the extent of the worker's personal skills (CCETSW 1995). A range of imaginative, flexible, challenging and relevant responses are also required. It remains my view that social work still has much to offer to the knowledge base, the range of skills, and the values which are required for competent practice within the criminal justice system.

References

Burnett, R. (1994) The Odds of Going Straight: Offenders' Own Predictions. Paper presented to 10th Annual Research and Information Conference. Midlands Probation Training Consortium.

CCETSW (1995) Rules and Requirements for the Diploma in Social Work: Paper 30 (Revised Edition).

Clarke, C. (1994) Probation Qualifying Training: Can the Dip SW Deliver. NAPO Journal 41, 3, 152–154.

Dews, V. and Watts, J. (1994) Review of Probation Officer Recruitment and Qualifying Training. London: Home Office.

Farrington, D.P., Gallagher, B., Morley, L., St Ledger, R.J. and West, D.J. (1986) 'Unemployment, school leaving and crime.' *British Journal of Criminology 26*, 335–56.

Farrington D.D. (1991) 'Explaining the beginning, progress and ending of anti-social behaviour from birth to adulthood.' In J. McCann (ed) *Advances in Criminological Theory.* Vol 3. New Brunswick: Transaction.

Farrington, D.D. and West, D.J. (1990) 'The Cambridge study in delinquent development: A long term follow-up of 411 London males.' In H.J. Kerner and G. Kaiser (eds) *Criminality: Personality, Behaviour and Life History.* Berlin:Springer-Verlag.

Feaver, N, and Smith, D. (1994) Editorial in *British Journal of Social Work 24*, 4, 380–386.

Gendreau, P. and Ross, R. (1983) 'Success in corrections: programs and principles.' In R. Corrado (ed) *Current Issues in Juvenile Justice.* London: Butterworth.

Gelesthorpe, L. (1994) Editorial in *British Society of Criminology Newsletter* 20, 1–7.

Gillyeat, D. (1994) *A Companion Guide to Offence Seriousness.* Yorkshire: Owen Wells.

Harris, R. (1992) Probation in the UK Today. Paper Delivered at Conference Permante Europeanne de la Probation. Newcastle, Northern Ireland.

Home Office (1993) *Facing up to Crime: The Changing World of Probation Work.* London: Home Office.

Home Office (1994) *Core Competences for Probation Officers.* London: Home Office.

Jones, A., Kroll, B., Pitts, J., Smith, P. and Weise, J. (1992) *The Probation Handbook.* London: Longman.

Macdonald, G. (1994) 'Developing empirically based practice in probation.' *British Journal of Social Work 24*, 4, 405–455.

Marshall, K., Weaver, P. and Lowenstien, P. (1991) *Targets for Change.* Nottinghamshire Probation Service.

Miller, W.R. (1983) 'Motivational interviewing with problem drinkers.' *Behavioural Psychotherapy 11*, 147–172.

Miller, W.R. and Rollnick, S. (1991) *Motivational Interviewing: Preparing People to Change Addictive Behaviours.* New York: Guilford Publishers.

McDougal, C. (1992) 'Changing behaviour and attitudes of imprisoned offenders.' In *What Works: Effective Methods to Reduce Re-offending.* Conference Proceedings, Manchester.

Powell, M. (1985) 'Court work.' In H. Walker and B. Beaumont (eds) *Working with Offenders.* Basingstoke: Macmillan.

Prochaska, J.V. and Di Clemente, C. (1984) *The Trans-theoretical Approach: Crossing Traditional Boundaries of Therapies.* Illinois: Dow Jones Irwin.

Raynor, P., Smith, D. and Vanstone, M. (1994) *Effective Probation Practice.* Basingstoke: Macmillan.

Raynor, P. and Vanstone, M. (1994) 'Probation practice, effectiveness and the non-treatment paradigm.' *British Journal of Social Work 24*, 4, 387–404.

Ross, R.R. (1992) 'Reasoning and rehabilitation of offenders.' Paper presented at What Works: Effective Methods to Reduce Re-offending. Manchester.

Smith, G. (1994) 'Intervention supervision – what works?' Paper delivered at Permute Europeanne de le Probation. Oslo, Norway.

CHAPTER 9

Competence in Respite Care for Learning Disability

Clare Waring

Introduction

Competence in social work practice with any client group necessitates familiarity with changing perceptions and evolving services. This is particularly important in mental health generally, where descriptive terms and definitions have undergone significant change, and service provision increasingly concentrates upon maintaining the client or clients within their family and/or community. For example, the term 'mental handicap' has made way for terms such as 'learning difficulty' or 'learning disability' or 'intellectual disability', though 'mental handicap' is still widely used in medical orientated texts and journals (Clarke 1989; Fraser, MacGillivray and Green 1991).

Respite (or short-term) care has proved immensely valuable for numerous categories of problems experienced by people with learning disability, and their families. Respite care is the principal focus of this chapter. It begins by looking at the general social work task in providing for people with learning disability. It discusses the long-term nature of the work, and provides some understanding of the family's perspective. Second, it presents one particular case: a child with learning disabilities whose parents are facing the prospect of ill-health. A student social worker is given some responsibility for working with the parents with the aim of helping them decide in the interests of the child and the family as a whole. Numerous competences are required, narrowly focused though the work is. The chapter will explore the knowledge, values and skills underpinning the competences required. These competences will be demonstrated in practice, and identified in accordance with the practice requirements and evidence indicators of Paper 30 (CCETSW 1995).

The Social Work Task

The duties and responsibilities of social workers working with people with learning disabilities have increased significantly in recent years. The main reason for this is legislation, primarily the Children Act, 1989, with its emphasis on the duty of local authorities to provide adequate resources and support for the families of disabled children. The Disabled Persons Act (1991) extends the duty and responsibility beyond the school life of the individual client (whatever their disability); support and help for client and family may have to be a life-time commitment. The principle of partnership now enshrined in most welfare legislation is of crucial significance in intervention plans: consumers, be they individuals in need or their carers, have to be fully consulted in assessment, and their wishes and concerns addressed in strategy. Partnership does not only embrace agency and client(s), but many other agencies as well; thus the necessity of developing links with numerous service providers (i.e. working within organisations). In summary, a student social worker today, embarking upon working with people with learning disabilities, will quickly note (1) the long-term nature of the work (as opposed to brief, crisis laden work); (2) the stringent legal and ethical imperatives within which the work is carried out; and (3) the complexity of responding to differing and sometimes competing demands within families. They will also learn that the investment of time, energy and commitment by them and their agency colleagues, most often reaps a rich reward in the enhancement of the quality of life for both client and family. Table 9.1 gives some indication of the dimensions of such cases, in terms of possible impact upon individual family members and of the demands made of numerous specialist agencies.

The challenge in training

Students in placements providing services to people with learning disabilities face many challenges. These challenges may be located within the family, community, or within the students themselves (Glendinning 1983). Students must rigorously explore, with the help of their practice teacher, the personal impact of working with this particular client group. They must be able to confront any negative perceptions and feelings which they have brought to the placement. In addition, learning disability may create enormous strains within families. The nature of the problem may be determined by the class and economic status of the family. A fragmented, poverty-stricken lone parent family may easily be overwhelmed by the challenges posed by a family member with learning disability. A stable, affluent, basically confident and competent family may find it difficult to acknowledge problems in coping; yet they may resent and resist agencies that seek to help them cope. Crises can easily be generated in both of these contrasting scenarios. The student may be perplexed, or unprepared, or even frightened by such developments.

The focus of intervention depends upon the age and stage of development of the client, their carers, and their support systems. For example, a parent or parents of a child with learning disabilities may become dependant upon their own parents (the child's grandparents) to help in maintaining a satisfactory level

Table 9.1 Impact of Learning Disability

Mother	Father	Siblings	Extended family	Medical services	Community	Education	Respite resources
Grief, loss, sense of failure, guilt. Usually main responsibility for caring; usually the one most often in contact with professionals; usually the one carrying responsibility for appointments, enrolments etc.	Sense of failure and guilt. Massive impact upon self-perception with marital and social life, and, in employment	Impact on siblings needs to be continuously assessed, and *vice versa*, i.e. how siblings impact upon child. Strong possibility of siblings being marginalised with adverse consequences	May be an enormous sense of support and encouragement; may have felt stigmatised and avoided	Frequent appointments with medical personnel, often necessary, i.e. GP, paediatrician, HV, speech therapist, dentist	Different communities: different impacts, for good or ill. Community context must be addressed, including cultural and religious factors pertinent to life of family	Important choices and decisions to be made. Family participation crucial	May or may not be required, dependent upon community/family context. A vital resource nevertheless, for many families

of care and balance within the family as a whole. As the grandparents get older, however, their physical and mental health may deteriorate, and they may have to relinquish some of the responsibilities they have carried in respect of the family. That situation needs reassessment. Similarly, the needs of a family suddenly decimated by bereavement (death of a parent/wage-earner, or sibling, or significant other) will have to be carefully reassessed over a long period of time. A sense of loss, grief, and additional caring demands can impact upon all aspects of family life (Lonsdale, Elger, and Ballard 1979). Parents may find it difficult to acknowledge the impact of any unforeseen eventualities or may deny stress and feel guilt (Davis 1993). Yet the impact of having a child with learning difficulties may be enormous, drastically altering lifestyles and increasing responsibilities, ensuring frequent contact with, and monitoring and reviewing by numerous agencies. Many families succeed in making the necessary adaptations. The lives of carers and cared-for are enhanced. We can imagine such a family in the following case; it is quite obvious that the parents have succeeded magnificently in caring for their child, in maintaining their own social and professional lives, and in avoiding over-involvement by welfare agencies. But like any other family, they cannot predict the future; nor can they easily adapt to misfortune that will inevitably impact upon their proven capacity to care.

Case Study

Susan is a four-year-old Down's Syndrome with severe learning disabilities. She is the younger of two children and lives with her parents, Mr and Mrs White, and her six-year-old brother, Jason. The family live in a comfortable house in a pleasant suburban avenue. Mr White is a lecturer at a College of Further Education; Mrs White is a librarian. She has recently opted to job share as she was finding full time employment difficult. Susan has a history of short-term admissions to hospital. Mr White has been very supportive, but he has recently been diagnosed as suffering from acute rheumatoid arthritis, and he has found it difficult to manage everyday tasks at home and at work. The family have no extended family support network. Mr White is an only child and his parents are deceased. Mrs White's family do not live locally. The family had been referred to social services shortly after Susan's birth. Susan had suffered from recurrent chest infections, and was diagnosed as asthmatic; her mother spent many days and nights with her at the hospital. Mr White cares for Jason. In addition to Susan's health problems, she was a very slow feeder and poor sleeper, and had a global learning disability. Her family found the services of the physiotherapist and speech therapist helpful; she also benefited from attending a Down's Syndrome Association Support Group. A social worker remained in contact with the family and referred them to the local Mencap nursery. Susan attended for three days per week. This was the family's first opportunity to recognise Susan's needs for 'specialist provision'. Mrs White was almost overwhelmed by the range of disabilities of the children attending; Mr White found it stigmatising.

The social worker supported the couple during this period. She prepared them for the process of statementing, i. e., Susan's educational needs in accordance with the 1991 Education Act. Susan was severely impaired in terms of developmental milestones, and and parents and professionals gave careful consideration to how best her needs would be met. They discussed issues of inclusion, i.e., the possibility of mainstream schooling, aided by a personal assistant. They considered application to a number of 'special' schools. This was a difficult period for the parents. They shared in the assessment process, but they often expressed a sense of powerlessness. They visited several schools and talked to other parents and professionals. They decided that Susan's needs were best met attending a special school; they accepted the same recommendation from the education authority. Susan began attending and settled in her new school. Her parents became involved in the Parents/Teacher's association.

Later however, Mr White's health declined. Mrs White asked about practical support for the family. A social worker tentatively discussed respite care with her. Mrs White felt that respite, as she understood it then, was too extreme a measure, and that Mr White would never agree to it. Mr White's health continued to deteriorate. The question of support arose again. Another social worker had taken over the case. The social worker believed that Mr and Mrs White would at least be more receptive to the mention of respite care. She suggested to them that her student discuss respite facilities with them. They agreed. The social worker (the student's practice teacher) would retain overall responsibility for the case, and for the provision of, and integration of additional services to the family.

Comment

This is in many ways a typical case in the context of services for families of children with learning disabilities. The practice teacher has considered it appropriate to allocate some responsibility for the case to a student. The core task is highly focused and unambiguous: to explore the possibility of respite care for a family that until now was coping relatively well, and to enable the parents to see that respite care may, at some time, be in Susan's, their own, and the family's interests as a whole, Other tasks and challenges may arise in the course of the student's work, but at the outset, she will concentrate on meeting and establishing a relationship and trust with the parents.

The practice teacher and student discuss the case. They both seek to ensure that any work by the student is based on adequate knowledge, values and skills.

Knowledge

The knowledge base for this *category* of case has numerous strands:

(1) Reputable and tested general textbooks informative about many aspects of learning disability, e.g., origins and development; significant stages; impact upon all family members, and carers, public perceptions; case histories (these may include some of the excellent fictionised cases in recent novels, drama, and films).

(2) Knowledge of theory on family functioning, particularly on families coping with disability and/or illness.

(3) Literature and/or research on the concept and development of respite care.

(4) Legislation pertaining to learning disabilities, in particular, the Children Act, 1989, Regulations of that Act, and Disabled Person's Act.

(5) Agency procedures and process in respect of this category of case.

(6) Available resources for respite care: key locations, personnel, expertise and experience.

(7) Self-knowledge.

(8) Information about the prognosis of Mr White's condition.

The social work course which the student was completing, her previous placement, and her longstanding interest in learning disability, ensured that she was adequately knowledgeable in respect of most of these strands. She had read standard texts, literature, and research (e.g., Aldgate 1993; Cunningham 1990; Clarke 1989; Fraser, MacGillivray and Green 1991; Sutcliffe 1992). She found Oswin (1994) particularly helpful. Oswin explores the initial trepidation of parents, their sense of failure in needing respite care; and her view that respite care arrangements were often made without sufficient awareness of the dilemma they posed for parents. The student had already undergone much critical self-analysis on her own perceptions and feelings about learning disability. She and her practice teacher therefore agreed on the need to concentrate on learning about the agency's response to this type of referral, and about the existing quality respite services and personnel available in the area.

Values

The issue of values has immense significance in a case like this. It is fraught with the prospect of trauma, conflict, loss of self-esteem and independence, and, the conscious or unwitting abuse of power (by agencies and their personnel). The Value requirements of the revised Paper 30 are very pertinent in this case; in particular, the need on the part of the student constantly to question her own value system and prejudices: **to promote family members' rights to choice, privacy, confidentiality and protection, while recognising and addressing the complexities of competing rights and demands; to assist people to increase control of and improve the quality of their lives; and, to practice in a manner that does not stigmatise or disadvantage either individuals, groups or communities.**

Skills

Some of the core competences themselves constitute skills which are of fundamental importance in this case: **communicate and engage, enable, intervene effectively; place and assess.** More specifically, the focus of the work, i.e., on the parents of a child with learning disabilities, necessitate a considerable repertoire of skills, many of them derived from and transferable across social practice as a whole. The skills which enable one to gain the trust of parents in crisis are a priority (Glendinning 1983, 1986): listening, pacing, conveying sincerity and empathy, knowledge and authority (no one expects a student to be an authority *per se*, but all students should seek to gain an authoritative grasp of numerous aspects of the case; for example, even having mastered the history of the case, and/or the legislative context, constitutes an authority which parents will appreciate; as is a knowledge of the disability, available resources and limitations on resources). The skill lies not, of course, in the authority, but in the tone and manner of its conveyance, and its effectiveness is determined primarily by the degree to which it reassures, supports, and encourages the parents. Advocacy skills are important too; the student often has to represent the interests of the family in communication with other specialist agencies and departments, and with the community as a whole.

Initial strategy

The student obtained details of the current provision of respite services by both voluntary and statutory agencies. She visited hospitals and residential respite units, and met with the coordinators of a family based respite and domiciliary care service. The student's strategy at this point was merely to equip herself in terms of knowledge and confidence in preparation for her first visit to the family. This visit would primarily be exploratory, though it should provide the opportunity to communicate and engage with the family. The student assured her practice teacher that she would not fall into the common trap of ingratiating herself with the parents by unjustifiably raising their expectations, exaggerating the availability of services that may fulfil their needs. Nor would she be unaware of the sensitivity required to explore the family's situation without triggering off powerful emotions and conflict amongst family members, or between parents and herself.

Demonstrating Competence

First visit and introduction

The practice teacher accompanied the student on her first visit, and introduced her to the parents. The visit was arranged when Susan and Jason were at school. The student had agreed with the practice teacher that the introduction and the task relating to respite care were formidable enough without the near over-whelming task of being introduced to, and having to communicate with a whole family. The practice teacher observed the following interactions between the student and the parents.

The student enquired about Susan and Jason. Her interest seemed genuine, and the parents responded freely and enthusiastically. Mr White in particularly welcomed the opportunity to talk about Jason's swimming achievements. This contrasted sharply with Mr White's initial tension and reluctance to talk.

The student later said she understood they would be interested in hearing about 'respite' and respite services that might be available for Susan. She wondered, before she tells them anything, what they knew and thought about 'respite'. Mrs White responded immediately by saying other parents of pupils in Susan's school recommended respite care... said it was a great help.

There was a risk here of the student being too appreciative and enthusiastic of Mrs White's response, and marginalising or alienating Mr White by a reciprocal enthusiasm. But she avoided this risk by maintaining her objectivity, and asking Mr White what he thought about respite care. He replied:

> 'I wouldn't want her going into a hospital; she's had enough of hospitals when she's ill... many times.'

> 'Well that's a very good reason for making sure we don't offer you a hospital-based respite care; maybe I could talk a while about other kinds of respite care... would that be okay?'

Both parents agreed.

The student gave a brief history of respite care. She relied heavily upon Aldgate's (1993) paper and on The Children Act 1989 Guidance and Regulations, Vol. 2 (Family Support...) and Vol 3. (Family Placements). The student spoke of the government's and local authority's emphasis upon the need to provide respite facilities for the parents of children with disabilities. She referred indirectly to a number of passages from the Children Act, 1989, in particular, to Schedule 2, Sections 17, 23, and 29: Local Authority Support for Children and Families. She emphasised that the development of respite care for many differing groups of people and their carers came about largely because parents like themselves, facing similar difficulties, had little or no resources or support. Very often, in the past, without respite facilities, families ended up in crisis, and social services often had to intervene. There was plenty of research to prove now – exactly the point that Mrs White's friends at Susan's school seemed to be making – how valuable respite care was in enabling families to cope without too much involvement by social services (Aldgate 1993).

The student then spoke about respite facilities in the area (she was very much aware that the location of the service is a crucial point). She had brought a collection of brochures and departmental policy statements on respite care. There were different kinds of respite. ('We know the one Mr White isn't too keen on!'); differences in locations, personnel, and time spans. For example, parents could periodically place their child for short periods – a weekend say – in a residential purpose-built home that provides for children with learning disabilities on a daily basis. Or they could periodically place Susan with a family, a family with much experience in this particular area, and/or a family already caring for a Down's Syndrome child of their own. Another type of service was that of experienced 'visitors', actually helping parents in their own home, for much briefer periods, of course. The student emphasised, however, that there was no guarantee that every service was available at any time. Sometimes the demands for particular services was very high.

MRS WHITE SPOKE:	'I think Susan would benefit from getting to know another family.'
	The student looked at Mr White, giving him a very clear message that she was interested in his view and feelings.
MR WHITE REPLIED:	'But how are these people vetted? How would we know if she was going to be looked after?'
STUDENT:	'We have a coordinator for this respite scheme, Mr White. It's her responsibility to ensure that anyone we may use for the scheme is carefully vetted and trained. She does that not just because it's good professional practice, but because The Children Act has very stringent assessment conditions that have to be met before anyone is approved for providing this kind of service. We have a Panel which finally decides whether or not someone is approved.'

Mr White nodded his head approvingly. The student looked at both parents and added: 'Parents have the final say.'

The student invites both parents to say what they think Susan may feel about these various types of respite care. This opens up a considerable dialogue in which they enlighten the student a good deal about Susan. The student speaks generally about children with learning disabilities, emphasising that what's she's hearing about Susan vindicates much of what she's read in books and learnt from more experienced colleagues. This dialogue is very informative, but it is also full of humour and rich anecdotes. At the end of the interview, the student invites them to reflect on the various possibilities. She leaves them with the assurance that respite care, in their situation, is introduced very carefully and methodically, with parents fully involved.

Commentary

There is evidence here of the student's use and integration of knowledge, values and skills. She displays knowledge and awareness of family dynamics in her sensitivity to Mr White. She realises and she can sense the potential for conflict in whatever contribution she herself attempts to make. She has also researched well on the legislative context and on the available respite sources. Her visits to these resources enables her to speak about them with confidence. Her strong value base influences her response to Mr White; she knows that in many ways he is vulnerable, and that an inappropriate word, gesture, or suggestion may exacerbate his position. She has deliberately chosen not to explore his illness and its impact at this time. She exercises considerable skill in responding to his uncertainties, his doubt, and above all, his pride. She has the skill of adaptability, enabling her to respond appropriately to the mood of the moment, empathising with whichever parent is addressing her. Her expressed interest and curiosity about the whole family was appreciated by the parents.

Preparation for second visit

The student continues strengthening her knowledge base for this particular case. She finds Baker's (1991) paper on parental perspectives illuminating and Clarke's (1991) section on mental health and the family constructive. She begins to draw on her course work on the family and family work, and increasingly views this family from a systems theory perspective, relying in particular upon the work of Coulshed (1991) and Davies (1981). She realises the this family system is undergoing fundamental change with the onset and deterioration of Mr White's condition. Mr White was, in systems terms, a very powerful subsystem within a family system which, previously, was functioning successfully; his relationship with each other family member (subsystems) will also undergo significant change in the months ahead. She discussed the case at length with the respite coordinator. She was disappointed to learn that at this particular time 'family' respite resources were stretched; if the parents decided they wanted this type of respite, they may have to wait (the student's placement period in the agency was limited). But this preliminary meeting with the coordinator was nevertheless valuable, and the latter was able to focus the student's mind on the task of making a referral for this kind of service; she had much to learn about such referrals, and about the comprehensive profile of the child and family which all referrals must contain. She examined many of these in respect of current and past cases.

The student visited Mr and Mrs White (again when the children were not there). After some informal chat, she enquired about their consideration of respite. Mrs White answered immediately and uncomfortably, saying that she thought another family would be ideal for Susan. There was an awkward pause then, and she looked at her husband in such a way that it was obvious he had serious reservations. The student realised immediately that Mr White would feel under pressure to respond, to explain, to justify his stance. She said:

> 'I get the impression that both of you have very much shared bringing up the children?'
>
> 'Oh yes' Mrs White said; 'in fact I'd say that Gerry had more of a share than me many a time.' Her husband smiled and nodded. 'It can't be easy then, if you think you're being asked to hand over even a tiny bit of that responsibility to someone else.'
>
> 'But there's good reason for it...' Mrs White said. The student looked at her husband. 'Do you think so Mr White?'
>
> 'Of course.' There was an ever so slight cynicism in his tone. He was silent then for a few seconds; but it was obvious he needed to say more, which he did: 'and there'll be better reason for it soon'.
>
> The student felt secure and confident enough to test out the implication of what he had said: 'You mean... your own health?'
>
> 'What else?'

The student very sensitively began exploring Mr White's and Mrs White's perception of his condition and of its impact within the family; they talked quite freely about this, Mr White candidly admitting his awareness of its impact not just within the family, but in his work, play, and life in general. The student later directed the focus of the discussion onto the impact of his illness upon his relationship with, and his care of Susan. She asked:

> 'What is the thing you think you would most regret in perhaps not being able to care for Susan, or in not being so active with her?'
>
> 'I don't know... maybe the thought that somebody else is doing it for me.'
>
> The student pondered a moment. Mrs White spoke: 'We're conscious of what we read... about social services getting a foothold...'

The student realised the trend of their thoughts: Mr White's illness gets worse, and more and more burdensome for his wife; social services get more and more involved, increasing the parent's dependency. There was a powerful logic in the couple's shared perception – though the student was pleased that it was being shared and that even Mrs White had some doubts about the long-term implication of respite. The logic was this: respite was based upon 'the idea of prevention and partnership with families' (Aldgate 1993). Partnership implied equality of input. But here, she was sensing that the parents were aware of becoming less and less equal to social services as Mr White's condition deteriorated, and also, an apprehension, that respite care may become something else.

The student reassured the couple. She emphasised that respite care for children with disability is governed by the Children Act 1989. It was precisely this apprehension she was sensing that led to the conditions in Regulation 13. These conditions are specifically meant to prevent a drift into the over-involvement by social services, and over-dependency on the part of families. Respite had to be carefully planned in partnership with the parents, and strictly controlled in terms of frequency, duration and continuity. Should the situation of the family alter in the future, and the original plan found to be unsuitable, then parents would remain crucial and central to whatever decision or plan replaces it.

> 'What do you think would be the most important thing for Susan, if she was being looked after by someone for brief periods?'

> The couple looked at each other, and smiled. Mrs White said: 'I don't know... she's very adaptable I think.'

> Mr White nodded in agreement.

> 'Perhaps you and Mr White could think more about that.'

Commentary

The student exercises sensitivity and skill in this second interview. In the brief extract above, she treads the potentially risky arena of Mr White's impending loss of mobility and independence, and its impact upon his position and function within the family, particularly in respect of Susan. The student is not attempting to provide a counselling service for respite – that is far beyond her brief and her ability; she is well aware that other more experienced and specialised personnel may have to provide such a service in the future. But what the student has done here is to enable the parents, particularly Mr White, to begin to unlock some of the hitherto concealed baggage of obstacles which may have been preventing him from making the right decision for Susan. The student is applying knowledge about the impact of illness upon family functioning in general, and about the psychology of loss experienced by the individual in particular. She is aware of the development of respite care and of the detail of its legislative context. Her value base is particularly marked in this second interview. Whilst she explores the issues with the utmost sensitivity towards Mr White, she nevertheless holds onto, and eventually brings to the fore the issue of what is in the child Susan's best interests. It is at this crucial point that she leaves them in the privacy of their own home, to decide for themselves.

Decision and preparation

A few days later, Mr White phoned from his office in work and told the student he and his wife had decided to seek family respite care. The student thanked him for communicating this to her. She said that she would deliver an application form to them, and requested that she call when both parents and children were home. In the meanwhile she would inform the respite coordinator of their decision, and discuss when the latter may visit the family too.

The student discussed developments with her practice teacher. Having established a good relationship with both parents, and helped them reach a decision on requesting the support of respite care, it was now time to concentrate her efforts on meeting the children, observing them, separately and individually, observing them in interaction with their parents, their school and social environments. Over the next two weeks, the student visited the children at home on three occasions, and with the permission of the parents, also visited Susan's school and consulted with her teachers. She also had discussions with professionals previously involved with the family, and she carefully read the voluminous file pertaining to Susan's statementing by the education authority. The student easily persuaded the parents of the wisdom of constructing this comprehensive profile of Susan, but emphasised that the most important aspect of it would be the their own contribution, obviously the most up-to-date assessment based upon their daily observations, and upon their intimate knowledge of her. The student's visits gave her additional insight which reaffirmed the wisdom of the original suggestion to the family by her practice teacher, that the family should seek some form of support. She observed:

(1) A child with learning disabilities loved and respected by each family member.

(2) Susan's ceaseless demands for engagement by each family member.

(3) Her demand for physical affection and her demanding expressions of physical affection.

(4) A particularly marked bond between Susan and her father.

(5) Mr White's attempts (sometimes visibly painful) to respond physically, verbally and emotionally to Susan's expectations.

(6) That the parents in their patience and love for both children, actually provided the role model for Jason in his relationship with Susan, who was, on so many occasions, very demanding of his own tolerance level (the student's reading of Siegel and Silverstein (1994) had given her much insight into the experience of siblings of

children with disability; the absence of many of the complications she had read about however, was a reflection on the success of the parents in providing for both of their children, and upon their acute awareness of the potential difficulty for Jason in particular).

During these visits, the student consolidated much of what she had learnt, and developed good relationships with Jason and Susan. She frequently asked the parents about many of the observations she was making about their children. She made the point that it was vital for them to share their experience and knowledge of Susan with whoever may provide the respite care they received. Mr and Mrs White were reassured that they would have ample opportunity to meet and maintain contact with the carer(s).

Evidence of Competence

Although this chapter has concentrated upon a relatively confined objective, the work nevertheless contains varying degrees of evidence of all the core competences, and, of the knowledge, values and skills underpinning them. We will address each of the competences separately.

Communicate and engage

The principal practice requirement for this competence is to **form and develop working relationships with children, adults, families etc.** Some of the evidence indicators are: **establishing initial contact and reason for contact... communicate effectively... identify shared and differing perspectives, values and aims...**

Effective communication depends upon (1) sincerity: the communicator should sound and feel sincere in communicating; (2) knowledge of and sensitivity to the way a particular communication may be received and/or interpreted; (3) the content of the communication should be of relevance and importance for the receiver. We have clearly seen sincerity and relevance in the student's initial contact. She very quickly engages the parents on the topic of their children, a subject they can talk about freely and proudly. Later she acknowledges, and by implication, agrees with Mr White's resistance to hospital-based respite care; she is in effect, **sharing his perspective**. She **makes the purpose of her visit clear** to both parents, and ensures that they are willing to accept her, and to listen to what she may say: she wishes to explore this issue of respite care with them, and they will begin that enquiry with a look at different types of respite care. At all times she demonstrates acute sensitivity to the one she regards as most vulnerable, Mr White, and she enlists her **knowledge of law and agency procedure** to reassure him on the question of how respite carers are selected. The student can quote from numerous other knowledge sources, i.e., texts and research findings, which also positively influence the way she conducts herself in these interviews.

The student makes a firm beginning in fulfilling another practice requirement: **communicating and engaging…to seek to minimize factors which cause risk and need**. The student's goal is to avoid the risk of likely consequences if Mr White becomes increasingly incapacitated: these are: he becomes more frustrated and despairing as a result of not being able to provide for and respond to Susan and Jason as he has done throughout their lives; the children sense his frustration and despair but are helpless in dealing with it; Mrs White's burdens of responsibility are dramatically increased and the quality of care she can provide is diminished. The student's careful emphasis on the **role, responsibility, policy and potential contribution** of agency/respite care coordinator is crucial in fulfilling this practice requirement, and is in itself an important evidence indicator.

Promote and enable

CCETSW's definition of this competence: '**promoting opportunities for people to use their own strengths and expertise to enable them to meet responsibilities, secure rights and achieve change…**' helps to pinpoint precisely where it is manifest in the student's work. This case is to some extent about diminishing strength and capacity, but the student's strategy revolves around her projection of the parent's knowledge and expertise as fundamental to the assessment process and the provision of any service they may be offered. She worked with both parents, a formidable competence for any worker, let alone a student. She was in effect, their advocate, once their decision had been made.

The first practice requirement: **promote the rights of children and adults at risk or in need in the community**, is fulfilled to some extent. The student directly and indirectly conveys to the parents that it is as reasonable for them to have some assistance in caring for Susan as it is for Susan to have a similar quality of care to which she has become dependant. A good beginning is made on the second practice requirement: **provide information and advice…**; first and second interviews contain the evidence indicators for this requirement: **directly provide information… and: facilitate… to other sources of information**. A third practice requirement is to: **provide opportunities for learning and development to enable children… to function and participate**. Susan's mother strongly favoured another family environment in which additional learning and development could take place. The student had agreed with this aim and succeeded in enabling Mr White to overcome his resistance to it.

Assess and plan

This core competence is evidenced in the student's ability to **(1) work with service users...(in all three extracts from interviews); (2) establish rights, statutory requirements, and organizational responsibilities and priorities (begun before meeting parents, and manifest throughout interviews); (3) identify available resources within her organization, other agencies and support networks** (begun before interview, and shared with parents during interviews). These three evidence indicators fulfil the first practice requirement of this competence: **work in partnership to assess people's needs**.

Another practice requirement is: Work in accordance with statutory and legal requirements, for which the evidence indicators include: **adhere to statutory and legal requirements, and agency policies and procedures relating to them**. Virtually all of the words and actions of the student constitute such evidence indicators.

Intervene and provide services

This chapter is predominantly about a student's successful attempt to intervene in a deteriorating situation, and to provide the service necessary to prevent further deterioration. A fundamental practice requirement for this competence (not incidentally, recognised in the CCETSW paper) is to help cultivate the relationship and create the atmosphere most conducive to intervening and providing services. There is ample evidence of the student fulfilling this requirement in each of the interview extracts. The practice requirement most pertinent to her task is: **support and sustain children... and adults through the process of change**. The parents are inevitably being subjected to painful change. Each parent looks at the change differently, and their feelings are different too. There is the potential for conflict, exacerbating their difficulties in confronting and accepting change. The student in the first and second interviews displays an empathy with Mr White, which is crucial in enabling him to move towards the more pragmatic position of his wife, and the requirements of his daughter. There are two evidence indicators in these extracts: **assist... adults to express their emotional needs through the process of change; facilitate effective communication between service users, their families, carers and the community**. Also, the student was very conscious of the need to monitor and evaluate whatever service was provided, and of the likely need for a more specialised support and counselling for Mr White.

Working in organisations

The student has made a sound beginning to fulfilling the main practice requirement for this competence: **demonstrate capacity to work as an**

accountable and effective member of the organization in which she is placed. The student continuously strives to learn about her organisation, its policies and procedures, and, its statutory obligations within current legislation. A number of evidence indicators arise from the extracts; for example, the student throughout has been **accountable for her own behaviour and practice, and has worked within agency policies and procedures**, and, she has **contributed to the establishment of and maintainence of effective communication between the agency and service users**. The student also indirectly, and probably not intentionally (like many students learning about resource distribution) moves towards fulfilling the practice requirement: **contribute to the planning, monitoring and control of resources**. She is made aware of the finite nature of resources, yet holds onto the ethical and statutory imperative of being responsible to help families in need. She shared her concern about unavailability of resources at the team meeting and in supervision. Here are some of the evidence indicators for that requirement regarding resources: **find out about funding available… and commitments, priorities, criteria, and procedures for its dispersal** (this the student certainly did in supervision and in consultation with the respite coordinator); **plan for the use of available resources** (virtually all actions of the student make some contribution to planning for the use of resources).

Develop professional competence

The student fulfilled the main requirement for this competence within the narrow confines of the case. The requirement is: **use supervision effectively, agree priorities and manage own work schedule**. The evidence indicators include: **prepare for and use supervision effectively, and, act in accordance with role and responsibilities**. The student did use her supervisor and supervision in planning for the interviews, sharing her concern, and prioritising. Her words and actions during the interviews are characterised by the sensitivity and care derived from careful preparation, including knowledge of that type of case gained from substantial reading.

The student continuously made progress in fulfilling another practice requirement: **exchange, process, and report information**. Her work produced ample evidence of this in **her contribution to meetings, group discussions, and decision making**; She was able to **record, evaluate and store information in accordance with agency procedures, and, provide reports for colleagues** (e.g., her practice teacher, respite coordinator) **other professionals and organisations**.

Perhaps the most significant practice requirement for this competence is: **contribute to the resolution of professional dilemmas and conflicts, balancing rights, needs, and perspectives**. The most relevant evidence indicator is: **identify and analyse the nature and complexity of potential and actual dilemmas and conflicts**. As with all students, she became fully aware of the professional and ethical dilemma arising from the finite nature of resources, and the inability of the agency to provide immediately and adequately. She constructively put her case, and its legal, ethical and professional implications, to the team of' which she was a member.

Summary and Conclusion

This chapter clearly does not set out to cover comprehensively working with disability; nor, even, to provide an in-depth study of working with the parents of children with learning disability. Its focus has been much narrower than that: it has been restricted to a relatively minor piece of work, with a particular couple, at a particular moment of crisis in their lives. But the opportunity for learning and development of competence has been enormous; the challenges for the student have been varied and formidable; the potential for exacerbating problems, unlimited. This student took advantage of the learning opportunities. The focus of face-to-face work was indeed narrow, but success depended as much upon the student's knowledge of, and contact with numerous individuals within her own agency and agencies beyond, and upon a knowledge of the legislative context in which the service was being provided. The case thereby offered ample opportunity to fulfil many of the practice requirements and pinpoint many of the evidence indicators of Paper 30. Her work in this case would easily take its place in any practice portfolio. More important, perhaps, the knowledge values and skills which she demonstrated, and her proven competence in many instances, would be as applicable and as effective in numerous other fields of social work practice, as they were in this particular case.

References

Aldgate, J. (1993) 'Respite care: an old remedy in a new package.' In P. Marsh and J. Triseliotis (eds) *Prevention and Re-unification in Childcare.* London: Batsford.

Baker, P. (1991) 'Parents – problems and perspectives.' In W.I. Fraser, R.C. MacGillivray and A.M. Green (eds) *Hallas's Caring for People with Mental Handicaps.* Oxford: Butterworth Heinemann

Clarke, D. (1989) *Mentally Handicapped People: Living and Learning 4th edition.* London: Balliere Tindall.

Coulshed, V. (1991) *Social Work Practice: An Introduction.* London: Macmillan.

Cunningham, C. (1990) *Down's Syndrome – An Introduction for Parents.* London Souvenir Press.

Davies, M. (1981) *The Essential Social Worker (A Guide to Positive Practice).* London: Heinnemann.

Davis, H. (1993) *Counselling Parents of Children with Chronic Illness or Disability.* London: BPS Books.

Fraser, W.I., MacGillivray, R.C. and Green, A. M. (1991) *Hallas' Caring for People With Mental Handicaps 8th edition.* London: Butterworth Heinemann.

Glendinning, C. (1983) *A Single Door; Social Work with Families of Disabled Children.* London: Allen and Unwin.

Glendinning, C. (1986) *Unshared Care: Parents and their Disabled Children.* London: Routledge and Kegan Paul.

HMSO (1991) *The Children Act 1989 Guidance and Regulations, Vol 2. Family Support, Day Care and Educational Provision for Young Children.* London: HMSO.

HMSO (1991) *The Children Act 1989 Guidance and regulations. Vol 3. Family Placements.* London: HMSO.

Lonsdale, G., Elfer, P. and Ballard, R. (1979) *Children, Grief, and Social Work.* Oxford: Blackwell.

Oswin, M. (1994) *They Keep Going Away.* Suffolk: Hollen Street Press.

Seigel, B. and Silverstein, S. (1994) *'What About Me?' – Growing up with a Developmentally Disabled Sibling.* Plenum Press: New York.

Sutcliffe, J. (1992) *Adults With Learning Difficulties.* Leicester: National Institute of Adult Education, and Buckingham: Open University Press.

White, R., Carr, P. and Lowe, N. (1991) *A Guide to the Children Act 1989.* London: Butterworths.

Worthington, A. (1992) *Coming to Terms with Mental Handicap.* Huddersfield: Helena Press.

CHAPTER 10

Competence in Working with Families

Dorota Iwaniec

Introduction

The CCETSW Revised Paper 30 (1995) puts forward requirements for necessary competences to be achieved by students during their professional training. A qualified social worker who undertakes work with families should be able to:

(1) communicate and engage

(2) promote and enable

(3) assess and plan

(4) intervene

(5) work in organisations

(6) develop professional competence.

In working with families, these core competences are compatible with the philosophy and principles of the Children Act (1989). It emphasises that children are generally best looked after within the family, with both parents exercising responsibility, and neither having recourse to legal proceedings (HMSO 1989). That belief is reflected in:

(1) the new concept of parental responsibility

(2) local authorities' duty to give support for children and families in difficulties

(3) working with families in need on a multi-disciplinary basis

(4) local authorities' duty to return a child to the family, unless this is against the child's interests.

Working with families in need of various types of help, support, and protection is a complex task, embracing a wide range of problems and difficulties. The purpose of social work involvement is to assist families, to assess their dilemmas, and to provide necessary and skilful help as well as protection. All these tasks require attaining those core competences that will determine the quality of intervention and subsequent outcomes. But, in order to be competent in practice, a social worker must acquire knowledge about families and children, methods and techniques of intervention, and sufficient understanding of *what* is happening and *why*. Skills have to be learnt, enhanced by repetition of tasks, and their effectiveness assessed by rigorous and objective evaluation. Knowledge and skills need to be applied in a sensitive manner which will strongly reflect social work values and practice ethics. Competent practice can only derive from sound knowledge, informed skills, and values that guard and promote the rights and dignities of families.

This chapter will concentrate on working with families. More specifically, it will discuss the requirements of core competences in the assessment phase of a failure-to-thrive child. In addition, the knowledge skills and values underpinning these competences will be explored. This chapter does not attempt to provide various assessment models based on different theoretical perspectives (there is no scope for it), but rather will describe the content and processes required for competence-led assessment of a specific case as an illustration of working with families with child-care problems. The case will be presented briefly from the referral point and taken through the stages of assessment, analysis of information gathered, and formulation of the problems.

Case Illustration

Susan, aged four years, is a middle child of a family of three children: Mark, aged seven, and Peter, aged two, respectively. She was referred by the consultant paediatrician to a student social worker during her second placement in hospital. Susan was admitted to hospital for the second time within one year for failure to thrive. The GP and health visitor became concerned when Susan stopped taking food, became lethargic and withdrawn, lost some hair, and generally looked ill. She looked small for her age and was extremely thin. Her weight and height were well below the third percentile for some time, and she showed developmental delays in language, social, emotional, and cognitive areas. The parents complained that her behaviour was difficult to manage, and that they were at their wits' end, not knowing what to do. There was concern about the quality of emotional care available for Susan, and about questionable child-rearing methods and attitudes: Susan was showing signs of being emotionally neglected, apparently due to maternal depression and ill-informed child-rearing methods. Mother–child interaction, as noted by the paediatrician, was at best confusing to the child, and at worst damaging. Medical investigation did not show any organic reason for her poor growth, development, and disturbed behaviour, so the case was referred for full psycho-social assessment to the social worker.

Knowledge

The nature of referral usually indicates what kind of knowledge is required to carry out well-informed and accurate assessment. First, the social worker must be familiar with the law, know about agency policies and procedures, be aware of the availability of local resources, and have sufficient understanding of his or her role when working with parents and children. Second, the worker needs sound knowledge about family structure, dynamics, functioning, family relationships and interactions, and awareness of *what* can go wrong and *why*. The *what* and *why* questions enable a practitioner to make sense of behaviour, emotions, thinking, reactions, and the circumstances of the families in question. Third, the social worker should possess the ability to link past events and difficulties to current family problems. Social work with families is dominated by concerns about children's welfare, rights, protection, and well-being. Knowledge about developmental needs, and parental awareness as how to facilitate those needs, are vital. In order to assess a child's developmental attainment at different developmental stages, the worker has to be well-informed about developmental norms and deviations.

Furthermore, he/she has to be aware of what stands in the way of optimal development generally and specifically in any given case. A child might be under-stimulated, or his/her physical and emotional needs uncatered for: whatever the reasons, we need to take them into consideration for intervention purposes. For example, a child might be developmentally delayed because of its mother's depression which will diminish her energy and drive to interact with and care for the child. In another case it could be parental unawareness of a child's needs, unwittingly impairing the child's potential. But it also might be deliberate neglect, due to rejection.

Parents are often unsure of what is regarded as appropriate behaviour for a child's age. Some have unrealistic expectations, either expecting too much or too little: their child-rearing methods might be too restrictive or intimidating, and consequently damaging to a child's self-esteem and confidence in acquiring new life-skills. Some are overprotective and therefore inhibit a child's ability to become independent. As we can see, although the child's developmental outcomes can be problematic, the reasons for the delays might be different, and need to be identified during the assessment stage. Interpretation of a child's behaviour, appearance, and emotional expression is extremely important to arrive at an appropriate conclusion. For example, in order to understand why some children fail to grow in spite of good physical health (as in the case of Susan), knowledge of emotional neglect and abuse, non-organic-failure-to-thrive, psycho-social dwarfism, attachment and bonding and child-development theories are essential to put the presenting problems into a theoretical context. Research findings in these areas are quite substantial (Ainsworth 1962, 1980; Baily and Baily 1996; Iwaniec 1985, 1995; O'Hagan 1993; Skuse 1985), and familiarity with empirical research provides a good basis for well-informed practice.

The child, when being assessed, has to be seen in the family context. A family does not operate in a vacuum; it belongs to a certain community, culture, and social structure that influences behaviour, attitudes, customs, and beliefs. Recent studies emphasise the necessity to adopt broad ecological perspectives when examining neglect and unmet needs of children. Belsky and Vondra (1989) and Dubowitz (1993) postulate that if the family and societal systems are deficient in promoting sensitive and adequate nurturing, then the child is exposed to hardship and maltreatment. It would seem that responsibility for the child's welfare and well-being lies not only with parents and families, but also with the communities in which they live and with society at large. Ecological perspectives are in tune with the philosophy of the Children Act (1989) and with the principles of knowledge, skills, and values underpinning social work practice in the CCETSW revised Paper 30.

Skills

Skills and information (if they are to be of value to the service user) have to be operationalised and applied in practice, and practice requires many skills. The social worker, therefore, has to be skilful and competent in communicating, interviewing, collaborating, negotiating, assessing, working out care plans, writing reports, collecting and presenting evidence, and intervening, by using methods and techniques appropriate to the case.

A social worker starting his or her career in working with children and families must learn to work directly with children using different means of communication and intervention – play, play-therapy, drawings, projective techniques, reinforcement methods (to mention a few) to engage fully with the child at his or her developmental level. Skills in how to measure and interpret developmental attainment by using developmental charts and scales are essential for comprehensive assessment, as is the ability to observe and analyse the behaviour of the child and of the parents. There are various developmental charts available which are helpful to assess child motor development, language, play, and social behaviour. Often used are charts devised by Sheridan's *Child Developmental Progress* (1973), Frankenburg's *Denver Developmental Screening Test* (1992), and Bellman and Cash's *Developmental Scales of the National Foundation of Educational Research* (1988). Using charts without sound knowledge about child development would be meaningless, if not dangerous. Advice and guidance are needed, especially for students and newly-qualified workers.

Values

CCETSW's revised paper puts a strong emphasis on value-based social-work practice. It states that it is necessary to:

(1) **promote rights to choice, privacy, confidentiality, and protection, while recognising and addressing the complexities of competing rights and demands** (these are particularly important to keep in mind when carrying out an assessment)

(2) **assist people to increase control of and improve the quality of their lives, while recognising that control of behaviour is needed at times in order to protect children and adults from harm**

(3) **identify, analyse, and take action to counter discrimination, racism, inequality, and injustice**

(4) **practise in a manner that does not stigmatise or disadvantage people**.

During the assessment stage the student must balance the needs and predicaments of both parents and children, but has to be constantly aware that the welfare of the child is paramount and that advocacy on behalf of the child is part of the protection and ethics of social work practice. Judgment about families should be based on evidence and not on personal prejudices, preferences, or impressions. Listening to what parents are saying, acknowledging and recognising their difficulties, and respecting their point of view and their choices are parts of mutual problem-solving. One of the most important aspects of the assessment interviews is to allow parents to express their worries, difficulties, and concerns, and give their explanations without rushing them or making judgments.

The worker should follow the parental 'agenda', encouraging, listening, and creating an atmosphere free of anxiety and fear. The manner and content of early assessment sessions with the families are of vital importance if the assessor wants to form a collaborative partnership with the parents. The worker must strive to promote parental rights as well as responsibilities and to demonstrate that parental participation is going to be of vital importance and value during the process of assessment, decision-making, planning, implementing, and evaluating the intervention. Establishing a trustworthy and respectful working relationship with all the family is a key factor for the appropriate outcome, even if the child has to be removed from home. In some instances parental attitudes and beliefs have to be challenged and properly addressed, but in a way which will facilitate positive change, as happened in Susan's case.

Susan's mother would not allow her children to play outside, to prevent them mixing with black children, as she believed the latter would have a bad influence on her children's behaviour. She herself would not talk or form neighbourly relationships with black families, out of sheer prejudice and distorted beliefs. Apart from that, she expressed unjustified and negative attitudes; she disadvantaged her children and herself by creating social isolation, and limited opportunities for the children to develop proper interpersonal relationships with adults and their peer-group. These issues are difficult to deal with, and an inexperienced social worker might need some help and advice from a colleague or a supervisor on how to approach this subject and how to deal with it.

Parents also have to be seen as *people* experiencing some dilemmas regarding child rearing, and not as wicked and deliberately cruel. In the majority of cases the problems may lie in child-rearing and child-care deficits rather than in mental disturbance or in acute character disorders. Naturally, there are those who inflict pain and are aware of their damaging action towards their children, and they need to be dealt with according to the statute and agency procedures in order to protect children who may be at risk. But this is what assessment is all about: to find out what is going on and then to act on available information.

The table below gives some indication what knowledge, skills, and values are likely to be needed when working with families who are experiencing child-rearing problems leading to failure to thrive.

Table 10.1 Necessary Knowledge, Values and Skills

Knowledge	Skills	Values
understanding of what constitutes emotional abuse and neglect	to engage and make initial contact	showing of respect and concern for parents in difficulties
how abuse and neglect affects a child's physical growth and psychosocial development	to communicate with parents and children	being honest and open with parents and children
non-organic failure to thrive	to listen, hear, and encourage	avoidance of being judgmental
psychosocial dwarfism	to observe and to make judgments	involvement of parents in the process of assessment, decision-making, and working out a care-plan
child's development and developmental needs	to interview and to assess	promotion and respecting choices of required intervention

Table 10.1 Necessary Knowledge, Values and Skills(Cont.)

Knowledge	Skills	Values
risk factors	to form positive working relationships	identifying strengths and build on them
relationships with the family	to identify problems and difficulties and to analyse	teaching and encouragement of appropriate child-care skills in a manner which does not denigrate and humiliate parents
attachment and bonding	to work in partnership with parents	challenging racial, cultural, and religious prejudices and helping parents to change attitudes
child-rearing attitudes and practices	to work with other professionals and to establish good contact and communication	acknowledging limitations, seeking advice, and consulting colleagues and supervisors
child's individual characteristics and behaviour	to write clear reports and provide process-recording	
parental characteristics and background histories	to use relevant research findings to inform practice	
family functioning	to negotiate compromise, and to agree and challenge	
social and economic factors	to use supervision constructively and to seek advice	
discrimination and its influence on children and families (culture, race, religion, disability, single parents)	to co-ordinate work across agencies	
child-care legislation, agency policies, procedures	to work out a realistic care-plan and to implement it	
availability of resources and support-systems	to work directly with children and to communicate	
methods of intervention and treatment	to use different methods of intervention to evaluate work	

Case Assessment

Assess and plan

The core competence 'Assess and Plan' is described in CCETSW's revised Paper 30 as:

- **work in partnership to assess and review people's circumstances and plan responses to need and risk.**

Two significant practice requirements for assessment and planning intervention are as follows:

- **work in partnership to assess and review peoples needs, rights, risks, strengths, responsibilities, and resources, and**
- **to identify and analyse risk of harm, abuse, or failure to protect.**

Methods, content and process of assessment

Assessment is usually based on semi-structured interviews with parents and older children, direct observation of parents and children and their living conditions, examination of existing files and recordings, and gathering information from other professionals and agencies involved in the case. Comprehensive assessment requires a few sessions which should be well planned and thought through, therefore preparation for assessment is as important as its content. This is a skill on its own to prepare all tools and get acquainted with the necessary knowledge to do the job effectively.

The worker must focus on the problems referred for assessment and follow them through. Interviews might not be easy, as parental fear of being judged as bad and incompetent might be expressed by apprehension, reluctance to talk, aggression, and refusal to get engaged with the assessor in a constructive and helpful way. However, it is well known that when skills, concerns, respect, and objectivity are shown, parents tend to relax, to warm up, and to become more co-operative. Changes of parental moods indicate that a positive working relationship has emerged.

The social worker's task during the assessment is not only to identify parental and family strengths and limitations, but capacity, willingness, and ability to work towards identified goals. Resources and support-systems need to be specified and included in the assessment report. Honesty, openness, and jargon-free communication, as well as the full engagement of parents in the assessment process, will help to elicit relevant information about the child's dilemma and the parents' predicament.

Preparation for the initial home visit

Referrals of Susan's kind will need some preparation before an initial visit is made. Discussing such a referral with the supervisor will help to clarify some of the procedures and issues related to the child at risk, as well as the process and content of assessment. It will be necessary to do some reading about emotional abuse and neglect and more specifically about failure to thrive. Further information regarding Susan and the family needs to be gathered by talking to nurses, the paediatrician, the GP, and the health visitor. Good preparation for assessment speeds up the process, is more accurate, and generally makes tasks easier.

Competences required during an initial stage of assessment
COMMUNICATE, ENGAGE, PROMOTE AND ENABLE

During an initial visit, the student explains to the parents why assessment is taking place, how the referral came about, how an assessment will be conducted, what information will be required, how this information is going to be obtained, and what is going to happen at the end of this process. The manner of conducting the first interview in particular should be anxiety free and honest, promoting mutual goals to problem-solving. The interview may be started by saying:

> 'Doctor Green, the paediatrician, asked me to see you about Susan. He thought you might benefit from some advice and help. I understand you have some problems with Susan's eating, sleeping, and generally difficult behaviour. He was particularly concerned that Susan and you do not get on very well and that Susan needs a bit of catching up with her speech, toileting, and playing, as well as growing and putting on weight. Before we can do anything to help you I need to see you two or three times to find out more what these problems are, and then discuss with you what will be the best way of helping Susan and you as well. There might be other difficulties that you might want to tell me about so that we can provide some assistance to help you.'

The student should ask to be introduced to the children, have a chat with them,. and have a general conversation with the parents for a few minutes to break the ice, then should ask the parents what are their major worries and concerns, encouraging them to express themselves in their own way. It is appropriate to make a list of these problems and issues, prioritising them according to parental perceptions as to what are the most difficult areas with which to cope. Listed problems should be stated, defined, and clarified at this stage. Since the referral is about Susan's welfare and both parents are anxious to talk about it, an initial interview should focus on her. The following list of Susan's problems was made by the student and the parents:

- acute eating problems since her birth, involving eating too much or nothing at all, faddiness, refusal to eat, throwing food, at times, and (more recently) gorging and vomiting

- defiance – lack of response to requests, either ignoring them or doing the opposite to what she was asked to do

- sleeping problems – wandering around the house at night, coming down after being put to bed, refusal to stay in bed, coming to the parents' bed during the night

- toileting problems – refusal to use potty or toilet, soiling and wetting herself

- frequently looking withdrawn and apathetic and not wanting to do anything

- setting fire to, burning things, and obsessions with fire

- stubbornness and irritability.

Eating problems were identified as the most worrying, since they associated them with Susan's poor growth, but it will be necessary for the student to explore all these issues in detail in the context of parent/child interaction.

The following check-list can shed some light on the child's feeding/eating behaviour and parental management of this:

(1) is the child regularly fed?

(2) is the child given enough food?

(3) is the child given appropriate food?

(4) is the child handled patiently during feeding/eating?

(5) is the child encouraged to eat?

(6) is there reasonable flexibility in feeding/eating routine?

(7) is there evidence of anger, frustration, and force-feeding during the feeding/eating period?

(8) is the child punished for not eating?

(9) is there awareness that the child is too thin?

(10) is there concern about the child's well-being?

(11) is there evidence of seeking help and advice?

(12) is there evidence of responding to help and advice?

An initial interview might end at this stage, the student subsequently writing up its substance and discussing the latest findings with the supervisor.

Table 10.2 Practice Requirements and Evidence Indicators

Practice Requirements	Evidence Indicators
planning assessment based on information available	preparation of an assessment schedule and issues to be assessed. Checking of agency assessment procedures and discussion processes, and contact with the supervisor
communication with agencies and professionals to whom the family is known	getting in touch with the consultant paediatrician, nurses, GP, and health visitor to obtain further information about Susan's case
making of initial contacts with the family and establishment of a working relationship	making of necessary arrangements with parents to see them at homeand making the first visit to set up an agenda with them as to how an assessment is going to be carried out
effective communication regarding reasons for and purposes of the worker's involvement with the family	communication with both parents to establish clearly and openly why social-work involvement is necessary and what the aims are in order to find out why Susan is failing to grow and develop, and what can be done to help
engagement of parents as partners in the assessment process	involvement of parents in defining problems, and prioritising the latter as mutual tasks and responsibilities
sharing with parents what the process and content of assessment is going to be	discussions with parents as to how an assessment is going to be carried out, what information will be required, and for what purpose
listening to take on board parental concerns and difficulties	listening to parental statements of their difficulties with Susan, prioritising problems as they perceive them, and setting up an agenda for further assessment
acquisition of necessary knowledge about the manifestation, identification, and assessment of emotional failure to grow	reading several research papers and discussing them with the supervisor
making use of supervision to enhance professional development	discussion of issues and working plan with the supervisor, checking agency procedures and assessing availability of resources

Practice requirements and evidence indicators during the initial stage of assessment
During the preparation and the initial engagement with the family, competences
to **communicate, engage, promote, enable, plan, work in organisation,
and enhance professional development** were demonstrated and evidenced
by the accomplished tasks.

Further assessment
Further assessment was based on the list of questions on Iwaniec (1995),
assessment proforma to elicit information in the following areas:

(1) child-rearing attitudes and methods

(2) parent/child relationship in interaction

(3) attachment and bonding

(4) child's behaviour and individual characteristics

(5) child's growth and development

(6) family functioning and unity

(7) parent's backgrounds and experiences as children

(8) physical and emotional state of parents

(9) parental strength and limitations

(10) environmental and economic factors

(11) support and help available to the family

(12) help and resources required for the family and child to secure an
appropriate care-plan.

List of questions

(1) What kind of problems do you have with Susan? Can you describe
each of them?

(2) How do you handle these behaviours? Can you give me an example of
how, for instance, you deal with Susan's defiance?

(3) How do you discipline Susan?

(4) Can you describe the rules and routines in your family?

(5) How do you correct and teach her to behave well?

(6) How do you teach her to learn different life tasks and skills, such as
eating, dressing, toilet training, playing, and so on?

(7) Do you praise Susan and show pleasure in her achievements?

(8) How much time do you spend with her and what do you do when you are together?

(9) Do you cuddle, hug, kiss, and smile at Susan?

(10) Do you play with her and do you enjoy doing it?

(11) How often do you speak with Susan and do things with her?

(12) Do you enjoy Susan's company?

(13) What do you like about Susan? Please describe these likeable qualities to me.

(14) What are your expectations of Susan?

(15) What do other members of the family think about her?

(16) Can you describe how you get on together?

(17) How does she get on with her brothers and other children?

(18) How does she get on with other adults when she is in their company?

(19) Did you want to have Susan? Was she a planned child?

(20) What was your life like when you were expecting her and when she was a baby?

(21) What kind of pregnancy, labour, and birth did you have with Susan?

(22) What was she like as a baby in terms of feeding, sleeping, contentment, responsiveness, and health?

(23) What were the major difficulties experienced when she was a baby?

(24) Did you feel close to her when she was a baby and how do you feel now?

(25) Can you tell me when she sat, crawled, walked, and said her first words and sentences?

(26) How would you like to change the present situation so you and Susan are happier together?

(27) What assistance and help do you need to make things work for Susan and the family?

(28) Would you be prepared to work with us so that we can improve the present situation?

The analysis of the answers to the above questions revealed the following issues:

(1) The mother's handling of Susan's behaviour was inconsistent and confusing for the child.

(2) There were no coherent or set limits regarding discipline, and the mother and father had different attitudes to and methods of dealing with child-rearing, the father having a more constructive approach.

(3) There was little stimulation or teaching of basic skills.

(4) Physical and emotional contacts between mother and child were limited, but were more developed between father and child.

(5) The mother found it difficult to enjoy Susan's company and could not find much in her about which to be positive.

(6) There was a destructive and unhelpful relationship between Susan and her siblings, and the child did not get on well with other people, due to her lack of social skills.

(7) Susan's development was retarded in all areas.

(8) The mother expressed a desire to improve things but had insufficient skills herself to respond to the child's needs.

Parent–child interaction

Data on parent–child interaction was obtained by direct observation during home visits, and was supplemented by information provided by hospital staff and by the health visitor, all of whom had the opportunity to observe the parents and Susan. There are various check-lists that can be used to measure the nature and quality of interactions (Iwaniec 1995):

Table 10.3 Observation Checklist

Visit No_____	Assessor_____	Name of client_____		
Child's Reactive and Proactive Behaviour		*Often*	*Seldom*	*Almost Never*
1.	playing freely			
2.	laughing/smiling			
3.	running			
4.	talking freely			
5.	coming for help			
6.	coming for comfort			
7.	cuddling up to parents			
8.	responding to affection			
9.	responding to attention			
10.	at ease when parents are near the child			
11.	joining in activities with other children			
12.	not frightened when approached by parents or corrected			

Table 10.3 Observation Checklist (Cont)

Father's/Mother's Reactive and Proactive Behaviour	*Often*	*Seldom*	*Almost Never*
1. talking to the child			
2. looking at the child			
3. smiling at the child			
4. making eye contact (loving)			
5. touching (gently)			
6. holding (closely, lovingly)			
7. playing			
8. cuddling			
9. kissing			
10. sitting the child on the lap			
11. handling the child in a gentle way			
12. giving requests (as opposed to commands)			
13. helping the child if it is in difficulties			
14. encouraging the child to participate in play and other activities			
15. being concerned about the child			
16. picking the child up when it cries or when it is hurt			
17. answering the child's questions			
18. not ignoring the child's presence			
19. emotionally treating the child the same as other children			
20. handling children consistently			
Siblings' Reactive and Proactive Behaviour	*Often*	*Seldom*	*Almost Never*
1. playing with the child			
2. talking to the child			
3. participating in activities			
4. accepting the child			
5. treating the child well			
6. pushing the child away and rejecting it			
7. blaming the child for everything that happens			
8. protecting the child			
9. helping the child when in difficulties or in trouble			
10. scapegoating the child			

The analysis of the data obtained on parent/child interaction indicated that:

(1) Mother–child interaction was limited and of poor quality, due to maternal depression, and a lack of understanding of Susan's developmental and emotional needs.

(2) Father–child interaction showed warmth, affection, and better provision of stimulation and responsiveness to Susan's needs.

(3) Sibling–Susan interaction was either hostile or non-existent because of the mother's confused messages to the children.

(4) Physical care of Susan was good.

(5) Although provision of food was adequate, the handling of the child during the feeding process was anxious and fear-provoking. It was clear that there was an element of manipulation of the mother by Susan if she wanted to get her own way, resulting in frequent confrontations.

Parental history

Childhood experiences of parents are often reflected in their child-rearing practices. This case revealed that the mother had herself suffered from a very deprived childhood, spending part of it in care, being rejected by both her parents, and exhibiting extremely disturbed behaviour. Susan's father, on the other hand, referred to his childhood as pleasant and happy, with the usual ups and downs. His parents were caring and loving, and he maintained close contact with his parents and with his three brothers.

As can be seen from the background histories of Susan's parents, the way each of them responded to Susan's needs was a mirror of the way they themselves once were treated, and what they learned as children clearly affected them in the evolution of their attitudes and parental skills. The father's relationship with Susan was always much more caring, and his child-rearing methods more constructive. The mother, although wanting to be better than her own mother (and having vaguely good intentions), did not know how to provide emotional care or how to apply appropriate child-rearing methods, to promote a healthy and happy development as well as well-being in her child. Susan's mother's relationship with her two sons was more positive (as was the case with her own mother's relationship with *her* sons). Remembering her unhappiness (partly caused by parental rejection and cruel treatment at the hands of her parents), she allowed Susan to do whatever she wanted, but at the same time felt resentful of Susan's behaviour, and her interaction with Susan was often stormy. There were quarrels and disputes between the parents as to how to handle the child. Thus background histories of parents may have major relevance to the ways in which parents respond to their children.

Recommendations

The case of Susan represents a child whose poor growth and development appears to be the result of inappropriate and ill-informed child-rearing practices. Her acute feeding difficulties over a long period led to a distortion of the mother–child interaction and, consequently, of the relationship, inhibiting the child's development and well-being. Differing child-rearing attitudes between the parents led to the development of manipulative behaviour and confused responses. Constant battles between mother and child led to mutually antagonistic interaction and a sense of helplessness in the mother. Susan's difficult temperament made caring for her more challenging than was the case with her two brothers. Distorted perceptions and prejudices of the parents regarding black families living in the neighbourhood presented the development of inter-personal relationships with peers, thus putting severe limitations on Susan's social learning.

The problems discussed above indicate parental (and especially maternal) deficits in child-rearing, but these can be corrected and resolved if appropriate parent-training is provided, either on an individual or group-work basis. Susan's delayed development can be dealt with by an early start of infant schooling, or by provision of day-care (attendance at a Family Centre or a Day-Nursery), while developmental counselling can be provided for the parents. Prejudiced and distorted beliefs about black people may best be tackled using cognitive re-structuring in order to change inappropriate attributions and attitudes. Susan's growth and development should be monitored by the GP and by the health-visitor. Since there are considerable strengths in this family (the mother's desire to help Susan; her concern for her child, the father's good relationship with, or protection of, Susan; the affection of the parents for each other; and evidence of reasonable care given to Susan's brothers), the prognosis (if resources and help are provided) is favourable. The case should be closely monitored and active therapeutic work needs to be provided and evaluated. The

Table 10.4: Practice Requirements and Evidence Indicators During Further Assessment

Practice Requirements	*Evidence Indicators*
identification of issues required for emotional abuse and neglect assessment	preparation of questions and check-lists to elicit information on: parent–child, and sibling–child interaction; quality of physical care and nutrition; and parental backgrounds
analysis and interpretation of data based on direct observations and interviews	analysis made and based on relevant knowledge and understanding of the presenting problems

Table 10.4: Practice Requirements and Evidence Indicators During Further Assessment (Cont.)

Practice Requirements	Evidence Indicators
writing of assessment report based on evidence	comprehensive assessment conducted and written up
findings of the assessment to be shared with the parents	sharing and exploring assessment findings, seeking personal views as to the accuracy of the analysis and conclusions
findings of the assessment to be submitted with the supervisor	writing report and discussing it with the supervisor
working out of care plan in view of available resources and agency	negotiation of care plan with the parents, procedures seeking their agreement and commitment

measure of change is indicated by the child's improved weight, height, development, and behaviour, and noticeable carer-child relationship.

Conclusion

As has been demonstrated in this chapter, the competences led assessment is firmly based on knowledge, skills, and values and evidenced by the accomplished tasks (Tables 10.2 and 10.4). Assessment has to be considered as a most important aspect of social work intervention because its outcomes determine action for good or ill for the child and family as a whole. A step-by-step approach to the process and content of data collection, the use and interpretation of observations, information from interviews and various check-lists, as well as skills in communicating with adults and children, are essential to arrive at appropriate conclusions.

References

Ainsworth, M.D.S. (1962) 'The effects of maternal deprivation.' *Deprivation of Maternal Care*, Public Health papers No. 14, 97–165. Geneva: World Health Organization.

Ainsworth, M.D.S. (1980) 'Attachment and child abuse.' In G. Gerbner, C.J. Ross and E. Zigler (eds) *Child Abuse: An Agenda for Action* (pp.35–47). New York: Oxford University Press.

Baily, T.F. and Baily, W.H. (1986) *Operational Definitions of Child Emotional Maltreatment: Final Report.* National Centre on Child Abuse and Neglect (DHSS90-CA-0956). Washington DC: US Government Printing Office.

Bellman, M. and Cash, Y. (1988) *Schedule of Growing Skills (Development Screening Procedure)*. Windsor: NFER-Nelson.

Belsky, J. and Vondra, J. (1989) 'Lessons from child abuse: the determinants of parenting.' In D. Cicchetti and V. Carlson (eds) *Child Maltreatment: Theory and Research on the Causes and Consequences of Child Abuse and Neglect.* Cambridge: Cambridge University Press.

CCETSW (1995) Paper 30 (revised edition), DipSW Rules and Requirements for the Diploma in Social Work. London: CCETSW.

Dubowitz, A. (1993) 'A conceptual definition of child neglect.' *Criminal Justice and Behaviour 20*, 1, 8–26.

Frankenburg, W.K. (1992) The Denver II. A Major Revision and Restandardization of the Denver Development Screening Test. *Paediatrics 89*, 91–97.

HMSO/Department of Health and Society Security and the Welsh Office. (1988) *Working Together: A Guide to the Arrangements for Inter-agency Cooperation for the Protection of Children.* London: HMSO.

HMSO (1989) *An Introduction to the Children Act, 1989.* London: HMSO.

Iwaniec, D., Herbert, M. and McNeish, A.S. (1985) 'Social work with failure-to-thrive children and their families – Part I: Psychosocial factors.' *British Journal of Social Work 15*, 243–259.

Iwaniec, D. (1995) *The Emotionally Abused and Neglected Child: Identification, Assessment and Intervention.* Chichester: John Wiley.

O'Hagan, K. (1993) *Emotional and Psychological Abuse of Children.* Buckingham: Open University Press.

Sheridan, M. (1973) *From Birth to Five Years: Children's Developmental Progress.* Windsor: NFER-Nelson.

Skuse, D. (1985) 'Non-organic failure-to-thrive: A reappraisal.' *Archives of Disease of Childhood 60*, 173–178.

CHAPTER 11

Competence and the Children Act

John Pinkerton and Stan Houston

Introduction

Fulfilling the practice requirements and providing the evidence indicators of core competences in CCETSW's revised Paper 30 necessitates adherence to a number of key principles of the Children Act. Contemporary debate about the Children Act is primarily concerned about how to turn the widely endorsed principles of the legislation into practical realities for child welfare service users and providers. Much of this debate has rightly focused on lack of resources necessary to ensure services expressing the principles of the Act. However, too little attention has been given to the equally crucial question of how to ensure the matching of child welfare workers' knowledge, skills and values to the requirements of the Act.

The Children Act holds out a radical challenge to the way that practice has developed over the last two decades. During the 1970s and 1980s the main preoccupation of child care workers became how to effectively manage child protection systems. It is important that the Act's challenge to social work practice is met as early as possible in social work training. The aim of this chapter is to demonstrate that the challenge to social work practice from the Children Act can be tackled during qualifying training because there is a congruence between the principles of the Children Act and the Diploma in Social Work's (DipSW) new competence statements. The chapter starts by making some general points about the context that gave rise to the Children Act. It then goes on to show how a fictional student might go about demonstrating CCETSW Core Competences in a way that addresses key principles of the Children Act. To do this the student uses final placement practice material drawn from involvement in a local authority consultation day with a group of parents with children in care.

The Children Act 1989

The tremendous significance of the Children Act for children and young people and for their carers, whether parents or professionals, is well expressed in Lord

Mackay's often quoted description of the Act during its passage through Parliament: 'The most comprehensive and far reaching reform of child care law in living memory'. The Act represents a watershed in British child care. It holds out the prospect of radical change in the relationship between children and young people, their carers and the State. The Act came at a time when such change was clearly needed to respond to the increasing complexity of child care needs, and to overcome the gaps and shortcomings in services which had become a matter of widespread public concern.

The death of Maria Colwell in 1973 precipitated a 'moral panic' in child welfare that was to dictate the direction of developments for the next two decades (Frost and Stein 1989; Parton 1985). The response to the crisis in professional confidence that ensued took the form of extending centralisation, regulation and procedures. Yet, as research findings on children's care careers during the 1980s showed, this was no answer. Taken together the research painted a dismal picture of compulsion, drift, severance of contact and the eventual pathos of young people ejected from the care system without adequate after care (DHSS 1985). Child care workers, particularly social workers, were just not getting it right. As early as 1984 a parliamentary committee chaired by Renee Short had recognised the extent of the problem. This recognition was further reflected in the influential 'Review of Child Care Law' in 1987. The impact of the events in Cleveland the same year served further to reinforce the messages that child protection had gone awry by divorcing itself from a broad child welfare system based on coherent legal and professional principles and practice.

It is worth noting that whilst these formative events were shaping the thinking behind the new legislation for England and Wales, the other two jurisdictions in the UK, Scotland and Northern Ireland, were also moving in the same direction. The imposition of Direct Rule (1973) in Northern Ireland strengthened legislative 'parity' with Great Britain leading to a Children (Northern Ireland) Order 1995 which closely mirrors the Children Act. In Scotland, where much greater freedom exists for developing it own legislation, the end result seems likely to be further endorsement of the same basic principles on which the Children Act is based (Scottish Children's Bill). Thus not only was the Children Act an attempt to ensure extensive change but also to change in a direction that was welcomed by a broad, UK-wide constituency – not least within social work. As Fox Harding has argued (1991), the Children Act can be seen as an attempt to harmonise a number of competing value perspectives in child care policy and law. Children's rights, child rescue and support for a kinship model, have been interwoven by the architects of the Act in an attempt to achieve a new consensus. Whether this has been fully achieved is debatable; particularly as these elements might equally be seen to represent a set of conflicting ideologies (Frost and Stein 1989). Nevertheless, the main principles of the Act (the five 'P's of paramountcy, partnership, parental responsibility, prevention and protection) have won widespread support.

Finding Practice on Placement to Explore Children Act Principles

Social work training is essentially about providing students with the learning opportunities for finding, in an informed fashion, a place for themselves within the profession. Successful practice teaching involves exploring that search in a way that both clarifies and develops students' values, knowledge and skills. Competency-led training provides a focused agenda for that exploration. Demonstration of competences must be as much about individual students and the support they receive from their practice teachers as about the general knowledge, values and skills framework identified by CCETSW in Paper 30. Accordingly, to develop our argument we need to introduce our fictitious student, Geoff, and his practice teacher, Jenny.

Geoff is on his final placement in a family and child care team with Jenny, the team leader, as his practice teacher. Geoff's experience of his Diploma in Social Work course has been a bit mixed but, compared to when he started the course, he can see that he has developed as a social worker. He now has a fund of knowledge that provides him with a much more accurate picture of what is expected of social workers by their employers and of the types of problems people bring to social workers. Through social skills training he is clearer about his own basic communication skills. The methods teaching had to cover too much but was interesting and he was particularly taken with the social action group work model that had been discussed during one class. The course had also helped him to spell out his basic values and reinforce them – in particular through the teaching and reading he had done on the UN Convention on the Rights of the Child and on the Children Act as part of his specialist option in child care. It is in that area of practice that he hopes to work on qualifying.

On placement Geoff is being encouraged by Jenny, his practice teacher, to review constantly what he was getting from his DipSW course and from the placement. Jenny provides Geoff with plenty of opportunities to talk about how he sees himself developing and fitting into social work. Geoff is keen to take these opportunities; not least because the placement seems to him to show child care social work to be more about monitoring and managing families in which there is a possible risk of 'significant harm' than about resourcing families 'in need'. He feels uncomfortable with this because it is not how he perceived childcare work, and he believes it is not wholly compatible with the requirements of the Children Act.

Jenny accepts Geoff's description of the work he is doing – monitoring and managing families under stress in a way that does not seem to connect with the Children Act principles. In her view the widespread support for the Act's main principles is in part an expression of the frustration felt by many practitioners.

They came into the work wanting to practice in a child- and family-centred fashion but feel unable to achieve this in a system so heavily dominated by administrative child protection. For them, the Act holds out the possibility of changing this and allowing them to practice the type of child care they believe in. So Jenny is not surprised that this frustration is shared by Geoff. To help him work on what to do about this issue she wants to find a piece of practice that very clearly expresses at least some of the principles of the Act.

Jenny believes that if Geoff can be involved in such work he will gain a firm grasp of what the Children's Act principles mean in practice for his own knowledge, values and skills. He will then be able to develop the necessary connections between these and the monitoring and managing of families under stress. Jenny believes such practice is likely to continue to dominate child care for some time, but that it is possible to infuse such practice with the principles of the Act. In making this assessment of Geoff's learning needs Jenny is carrying out her role as practice teacher in the way that is vital if students are to be able to address in their own specific way and within their own placement circumstances the general agenda set for them by CCETSW Paper 30.

The opportunity for involving Geoff in practice which clearly expresses Children Act principles comes when Jenny hears about plans by social services to run a consultation day with Family Links, a local mutual support group for parents and families of children in the care system. She speaks to Naseem, a senior social worker from another family and child care team who is taking the lead for social services in setting up and running the consultation day, and gets her agreement that Geoff can help her work with Family Links on organising the day. Geoff and Jenny agree that the consultation day as a group experience would not only help him explore in practice the principles of the Children Act but also give some consideration to self-directed group work.

The consultation day

At their first meeting Naseem explains to Geoff that the idea for a consultation day has come from the Family Links group following an article in the local newspaper about social services' commitment to listening to service users. On being approached by Family Links, social services management agreed to facilitate a one day event to hear parents' and families' views on the Children Act. At a meeting between Naseem, Geoff and two members of Family Links it is agreed that social services organise the actual consultation day and Family Links notify their members and other relevant organisations such as Gingerbread, Women's Aid and the local multi-cultural resource centre. Geoff offers to organise an appropriate venue in the University. After two or three weeks and half a dozen phone calls, Naseem decides that the out-of-date mailing list of Family Links group members and inconsistent efforts by the group to follow through on plans, means they will never get the invitations delivered. She and

Geoff take over organising the whole day. Geoff feels uneasy about this but takes responsibility for drafting the letter of invitation.

On the day about 25 people turn up. They include couples, grandparents, single mothers, a local councillor, a social worker, and a law centre solicitor. Naseem welcomes them and explains the purpose of the day. She invites everyone to share their reasons for coming by way of mutual introductions. It becomes clear that most people are there because they have had 'bad' experiences of 'bad' law and 'bad' social workers. Naseem does not dispute these bad experiences but stresses that the purpose of the day is not to look at individual circumstances. It is to produce a written comment for the local authority on what they as users think of the Children Act. She had engaged in similar exercises with various groups of service providers and is comfortable in giving leadership in this task.

In Geoff's view Naseem misses an opportunity to explore whether other goals and other forms of communicating user views to management might be more appropriate. One father had suggested the aim of the meeting could be to organise a march. Geoff thinks fuller discussion of that might not only have led to a more forceful presentation of user views but might also be a useful way of exploring what the users themselves wanted from the day. This would also have been in line with the practice principles of Self Directed Groupwork (Mullander and Ward 1991). In the event, however, everyone, including Geoff, agrees with Naseem that the goal of the day is to produce something in writing for social services management giving a user view on the Children Act.

Naseem gives the planned presentation on the Children Act. She explains social services approach to implementing it, and the range of relevant local services. She uses handouts and overheads which she and Geoff had prepared together. A general discussion then takes place and key comments are noted on a flipchart. Four topics are agreed for discussion in small groups after lunch; 'Support Services', 'Protection/Investigation', 'In Court' and 'In Care'.

Geoff notes that over lunch in a nearby cafe, paid for by social services, much was made of the fact that it was being provided free. This simple gesture of respect is clearly appreciated. Several people also comment on the location of the meeting; it is the first time they have ever been in a university. They seem to experience this as both intimidating and exciting.

On return from lunch each of the groups discuss its topic in the light of what they had heard about the Children Act and related local services. Membership of each group is self-selected and each agree a volunteer to act as recorder. The main points from these discussions are then shared as part of a final discussion in the full group. At the end of that discussion two things are decided. First that a record of the day's discussion should be sent to the Director of Social Services. This is to be done by Naseem. When she asks how people think this might be done the man who at the start of the day had suggested the march replies – 'You wanted the report so that's your problem!'. Geoff can hear some anger behind the joking way this is said.

Using the flip chart record of the large group discussion and the notes made by the recorders in each of the small groups, the changes that the meeting most wanted to see are set out by Naseem and Geoff as lists under the four headings 'Support Services' 'Protection/Investigation', 'In Court' and 'In Care'. The meeting also want it clearly stated that the Children Act requires changes in the way social workers, solicitors and magistrates work, and that this requires special training and new support services. Accordingly there are a number of central questions that need to be answered – is the money being made available? Will new services be provided? Will social workers and the other occupations change their attitudes and ways of working? Naseem agrees to make sure that both the general points and the four lists of specific points are typed up and submitted to social services management. She ends off the day by asking all the participants to complete an evaluation form which Geoff has drawn up and by thanking them all for coming and taking part.

Linking Placement Practice to Core Competences

In order to link any placement practice to CCETSW's six core competences there are five steps that need to be taken:

(1) Clarify what 'competence' means and how it combines knowledge, values and skills.

(2) Choose which of the six 'core competences' are relevant to the placement practice under consideration.

(3) Identify the 'practice requirements' relevant to the chosen core competence(s), taking into account the particular placement practice under consideration.

(4) Choose the 'evidence indicators' linked to the identified practice requirements, again taking into account the particular placement practice under consideration.

(5) Select from the placement practice 'evidence' appropriate to the evidence indicators that have been picked.

These five steps ensure that a link is made between placement, the core competences, practice requirements and evidence indicators. They also ensure that the student's learning needs and his practice remain the principle focus. It is a student's competence and the underpinning knowledge, values and skills, which are the issue, not, how successful or otherwise overall outcome might be.

Step one

In answer to the question about the nature of competence posed at step one, it is crucial to recognise the combination of knowledge, skills and values. The revised Paper 30 clearly spells this out:

> 'It is only practice which is founded on values, carried out in a skilled manner and informed by knowledge, critical analysis and reflection which is competent practice.' (CCETSW 1995, p.3)

Accordingly, if Geoff is to address the competence agenda set by CCETSW, he needs to make explicit his values, the skills he used to pursue these, and the knowledge base he drew on. In making these three components of his competence explicit he takes the first step towards critical analysis and reflection.

Step two

The student and the practice teacher identify three core competences most applicable to his efforts within the users' group: **Communicate and Engage, Promote and Enable**, and **Develop Professional Competence**. Other competences may also be relevant to some degree but the three identified would best allow Geoff to focus on the issue of how to relate his practice to the principles of the Children Act.

Steps three and four

To illustrate the third and fourth of the five steps necessary for linking placement practice to the core competences, we will focus on **Promote and Enable**. Revised Paper 30 sets out this competence as meaning

> 'promote opportunities for people to use their own strengths and expertise to enable them to meet responsibilities, secure rights and achieve change.' (CCETSW 1995, p.13)

Four practice requirements are attached to this competence along with twelve evidence indicators. Three of these practice requirements and six of the evidence indicators are relevant to Geoff and his Family Links work. These are set out in Table 11.1.

Having made his selection of competences, practice requirements and evidence indicators, the final step for Geoff is to select matching material from his placement practice which expresses the appropriate knowledge, values and skills.

*Step five – **knowledge***

The Practice Requirement **(Provide information and advice to individuals, families, carers and groups)**, and its Evidence Indicator **(Directly provide**

Table 11.1: Selected Core Competence, Practice Requirements and Evidence Indicators

Core Competence – Promote and Enable

Practice Requirement 1

Promote the rights of children and adults at risk or in need in the community

Evidence Indicator

- Assist children and adults to represent their own interests and rights.

Practice Requirement 2

Provide information and advice to individuals, families, carers and groups

Evidence Indicators

- Directly provide information and advice to individuals, families, carer and groups.
- Facilitate access for individuals, families, carers and groups to other sources of information and advice.

Practice Requirement 3

Provide opportunities for learning and development to enable children and adults to function and participate.

Evidence Indicator

- Access or provide opportunities for learning and development to meet identified needs.

Practice Requirement 4

Enable people to use their own strengths and expertise to meet responsibilities, secure rights and achieve change.

Evidence Indicators

- Assist people to express their own strengths, abilities, needs and perspectives.
- Assist people to clarify goals, objectives, resources and potential obstacles to meeting responsibilities and achieving change.
- Assist people to choose an option which will help them meet responsibilities and achieve change.

information and advice to individuals, families, carers and groups) (Table 11.1), both contain numerous tasks which arose during preparation and presentation. Such tasks necessitated a working knowledge of the Act. The most useful texts were: *Making Sense of the Children Act* (Allen 1992) and *The Children Act – Putting it into Practice* (Ryan 1994). The Act itself of course, was crucial. Such texts provided important social policy and childcare research which examined the concept of user participation influenced the emergence of new legislation. The voice of the user is an increasingly important aspect of social work in the family and child care field:

> 'What was appreciated most was honesty, naturalness and reliability along with an ability to listen. Clients appreciated being kept informed, having their feelings understood, having the stress of parenthood accepted and getting practical help as well as moral support. The social workers whose assistance was valued had a capacity to help parents retain their role as responsible, authority figures in relation to their children.' (DHSS 1985, p.20)

Appropriate knowledge would also include an understanding of the aims and principles of the Act and the main messages it gives for practice. The student needs to know the basic layout of the Act (108 sections in twelve Parts) and the meaning of its various key terms, such as 'significant harm' and 'in need'. Evidence that Geoff did know could be provided in the form of photocopies of the overheads he prepared for use on the day (Table 11.2) and also written

Table 11.2: Evidence of Knowledge – Presentation Overheads

Aims of the Act

1. To simplify the law and make it easier to use.

2. To set new balances between:
   - state's duty to safeguard the welfare of children
   - parents' rights and responsibilities of parents
   - children's own view of their needs and how these can be met.

A child IN NEED is a child who:
   - without help from the local authority
     - is unlikely to achieve or maintain a reasonable standard of health or development, or the opportunity to do so
     - is likely to have health or development significantly or further impaired
   - is disabled

comment by the practice teacher, and Nadeem, the social worker, on his grasp of the Act as demonstrated in his verifying of competence.

In addition, Geoff could submit extracts from his self-evaluation notes on his involvement with the consultation day produced for use in supervision with Janet, his practice teacher. Appropriate sections would be those clearly showing that his understanding of the purpose and process of the day was underpinned by the commitment to partnership promoted by the Act. Evidence would also be available from Geoff's involvement in the process of organising and running the day. Appropriate knowledge refers not only to the substantive content of the presentation made to the group, but also to a knowledge of social work theory; particularly theory underpinning the work facilitating group discussion. Here Geoff could draw on his use of Self Directed Groupwork. It provides an appropriate model of practice based on 'concepts of empowerment, advocacy and human and civil rights' which are required by Paper 30 (p.6) as part of the knowledge base for the core competency Promote and Enable.

Mullander and Ward (1991) provide a practice model based upon three fundamental value statements:

- everyone has skills, understanding and ability
- structural oppression may underlie client problems
- collective action generates power.

From these value positions Mullander and Ward draw out two practice imperatives:

- service users must decide whether or not to be involved and when involved must define the issues to be acted on and the action to be taken
- workers must use their knowledge and skills to facilitate group members to understand and challenge oppression.

In order to pursue these imperatives Mullander and Ward suggest twelve steps making up the five stages of self directed group work (Table 11.3). This model provides a conceptual framework which Geoff can use to describe and critically evaluate his involvement in the process of organising and running the day.

As a knowledge base in relation to service users' and carers' perspectives, Geoff could also draw on lecture and seminar notes, on the child care research reviews, such as 'Social Work Decisions in Child Care' (DHSS 1985), 'Patterns and Outcomes in Child Placement' (DoH 1992), 'Child Protection: Messages From Research' (DoH 1995), and on a child care practice text such as *Child Placement: Principles and Practice* (Thoburn 1994). Evidence of Geoff's knowledge of these sources could be demonstrated in a variety of ways. He could submit an outline account of the work according to the five stages of Self-Di-

Table 11.3: Stages and Steps of Self Directed Groupwork

STAGE A. Workers Take Stock

    Step 1. Assembling a compatible co-worker team

    Step 2. Establishing appropriate consultancy support

    Step 3. Agreeing empowering principles for the work

STAGE B. Group Takes Off

    Step 4. Open planning

STAGE C. Group Prepares to Take Action

    Step 5. Asking the question 'What'?

    Step 6. Asking the question 'Why'?

    Step 7. Asking the question 'How'?

STAGE D. Group Takes Action

    Step 8. Participants carry out agreed actions

STAGE E. Group Takes Over

    Step 9. Group reviews achievement

    Step 10. Reformulating 'What'?

    Step 11. Reformulating 'Why'?

    Step 12. Reformulating 'How'?

---

rected Groupwork showing both the match (the open and inclusive way in which the day had in the main been organised and run) and the mismatch (the way in which organisation had been taken out of the users' hands and the missed opportunity to fully explore the 'Why' of the users' experience). He could also present the plan for the day drawn up with Naseem and the Family Link representatives. Further evidence could be found in extracts from his self-evaluation notes for supervision focusing on his contributions to both the content and the process of the day. Verification of his contribution and the knowledge he brought to this could be provided by Naseem.

Step five – values

As for the values component of this competence, Geoff's practice teacher had already got him to do an 'I believe…' exercise as a means of identifying the values and prejudices he was bringing to the placement (Table 11.4). This is a useful means of preparing to demonstrate the first of the value requirements set out in Paper 30: 'Identify and question… own values and prejudices, and their implications for practice' (CCETSW 1995, p.4).

Table 11.4: Values Exercise

I believe:

- any child's welfare is of paramount importance
- children should be listened to and respected
- every child is a unique individual
- parents are individuals with their own needs
- parents have rights as well as responsibilities
- children should be raised in families
- child care services should be an expression of social justice and must be anti-discriminatory
- child care workers are individuals who have rights and feelings.

In discussing these values with his practice teacher Geoff had become aware of how particular values he held could come into conflict with one another when applied in specific situations. He had also become aware that to resolve such conflicts he was having to make judgements about the relevance and relative weighting to give to each value and that this could change according to the specifics of the situation being dealt with. In the case of his Family Links work the key values were: parents are individuals with their own needs; parents have rights as well as responsibilities; child care services are an expression of social justice and must be anti-discriminatory.

These are in accord with the value requirements set out in Paper 30 (CCETSW 1995, p.4).

- Respect and value uniqueness and diversity, and recognise and build on strengths.
- Assist people to increase control of and improve the quality of their lives, while recognising that control of behaviour will be required at times in order to protect children and adults from harm.

- Identify, analyse and take action to counter discrimination, racism disadvantage, inequality and injustice, using strategies appropriate to role and context.

- Practice in a manner that does not stigmatise or disadvantage either individuals, groups or communities.

These values are compatible with both Mullander and Ward's model and the approach to child care advocated by Thoburn (1994). They are also in line with the key principles of partnership and prevention within the Children Act.

Step six — *skills*

The types of skill required to put into operation the values and knowledge identified as relevant to this practice requirement are skills in enabling straight-forward and effective communication using a range of techniques; skills in facilitating clear and honest communication even where there are significant differences in opinion; skills in encouraging users to build on their own strengths and resources. This involves using a range of modes of communication, such as talk, writing and body language, in order to ensure effective building and maintaining relationships, attending and listening and sharing information. Geoff would be able to articulate these skills through the vocabulary and understanding gained from his social skills training and a text such as *Communication in Social Work* (Lishman 1995), in addition to the self-directed group work and child care methods texts already mentioned.

Again, extracts from Geoff's self-assessment notes done for supervision with his practice teacher could be drawn on to provide evidence of these skills being used. These could include process records of particular points in the process of planning and running the day where a skilful response was required to ensure partnership working was achieved. For example, the way in which information about the Act and Social Services was shared would have to have been clear but not patronising. Recording of the group discussions had to be done in a coherent and organised fashion and yet retain something of the raw emotion and spontaneity of the discussion. The letter he drafted inviting people to the consultation day would provide evidence of his written communication skills.

Geoff could also use the evaluation forms filled out by those attending the consultation day to measure the effectiveness of his communication skills. In addition, he could list those skills he thought he was using, such as empathy, reflection, clarification, information giving and summarising, and ask Naseem and the two Family Links members who had helped organise the day to mark him on a 0–5 scale on each of them.

Conclusion

Geoff's involvement in the Family Links consultation day has enabled him to fulfill relevant practice requirements, and, to provide evidence, in seeking to achieve core competences. In so doing, he has adhered to some key principles of the Children Act. His placement (at first sight limited) has in fact proven to be a rich source of potential for achieving competence. This task began long before the consultation day; in fact, his discomfort, based upon a perception that the principles of the Act were not being adhered to by the placement agency, can be seen to as a positive development. The tasks implicit in the organisation of and involvement in the consultation day necessitated substantial knowledge, a sound value base, and a repertoire of skills. The knowledge base included social policy, sociology, social work theory and, of course, the Children Act itself. Geoff was provided with an excellent opportunity to witness (and feel) the tensions which may arise whenever one is attempting to adhere to and promote a new and challenging set of legal principles within an agency. Many of the detailed practice requirements and evidence indicators in CCETSW's revised Paper provide useful reference points which will contribute to a consolidation of the Act in childcare practice.

References

Allen, N. (1992) *Making Sense of the Children Act.* Essex: Longman.

CCETSW (1995) *Rules and Requirements for the Diploma in Social Work.* London: CCETSW.

DHSS (1985) *Social Work Decisions In Child Care.* London: HMSO.

DoH (1992) *Patterns and Outcomes in Child Placement.* London: HMSO.

DoH (1995) *Child Protection: Messages From Research.* London: HMSO.

Fox Harding, L. (1991) *Perspectives in Child Care Policy.* London: Longman.

Frost, N. and Stein, M. (1989) *The Politics of Child Welfare.* London: Harvester/Wheatsheaf.

HMSO (1987) The Law Relating to Child Care and Family Services. White Paper Cmnd. 62. London: HMSO.

Lishman, J. (1995) *Communication in Social Work.* London: Macmillan.

Mullander, A. and Ward, D. (1991) *Self Directed Groupwork.* London: Whiting and Birch.

Parton, N. (1985) *The Politics of Child Abuse.* London: Macmillan.

Ryan, M. (1994) *The Children Act 1989 – Putting it into Practice.* London: Macmillan.

Thoburn, J. (1994) *Child Placement: Principles and Practice.* Aldershot: Arena.

The Contributors

Jim Campbell is a lecturer in social work at the The Queen's University Belfast. He is a former approved social worker (mental health), and worked for many years in a psychiatric hospital as a member of a community mental health social work team. He has published widely in the subjects of mental health social work, the role of the approved social worker and the impact of sectarianism on social work services in Northern Ireland. He is involved in the planning and training of ASWs, and is currently collaborating on a cross-European project on the concept of citizenship.

Margaret Fawcett is a lecturer in social work and coordinator on the MSW/Diploma course at The Queen's University Belfast. She is also a practising mediation counsellor for RELATE, in Northern Ireland. She has been practising and researching in mediation work over many years. She is presently engaged in government-funded research into the impact of separation and divorce upon adolescents. Before joining Queen's, she was a residential social worker in Barnardos. She has contributed papers to many national training conferences on these subject areas.

Johnnie Gibson is Officer in Charge in a children's home, and has had fourteen years' experience in team leadership in adolescent group care settings. He is a qualified social worker, and is also qualified in youth and community work. He is an accredited trainer with Cornell University, and has organised courses for qualified residential staff. He contributes to social work training at The Queen's University, Belfast, and at the University of Ulster. He is an active researcher in numerous aspects of residential childcare.

Gerry Heery is employed by the Northern Ireland Probation Service. He has been a practice teacher in the probation service for ten years, committed to the application of motivation and learning theory in work with offenders. He is a longstanding member of the planning group for the Northern Ireland Practice Teacher Award programme, and is particularly interested in combating discriminatory practices within the criminal justice system. He provides regular input into the Master's/Diploma course at Queen's.

Stan Houston is Principal Social Worker with responsibility for commissioning children's services, Eastern Health and Social Services Board. He was previously a trainer, and team leader, specializing in services for child protection

219

and children with learning difficulties. He was a joint coordinator of the post qualifying course in child protection, and is a regular contributor to the Master's/Diploma course at Queen's.

Dorota Iwaniec is Professor of Social Work at The Queen's University, Belfast. She is also Director of the Centre for Child Care Research at Queen's and head of the department of social work. She was previously based in Leicester where she engaged in childcare research and practice, particularly in the area of failure-to-thrive children. She is the author of numerous papers on this subject, and has recently published a book on emotional abuse and failure to thrive. She is the founder and editor of *Child Care in Practice*.

Greg Kelly is a senior lecturer in social work and programme director for the Master/Diploma in social work course at The Queen's University Belfast. He also has major responsibility for the development of post qualifying courses in childcare. He was previously head of the department of social work at Queen's, and coordinator of the department's submission to HEFCE for assessment of quality of education. His previous research and publications have focused upon foster care.

Kate Lewis is the Head of Professional Services of RELATE, the Northern Ireland counselling and mediation services. Formerly, she was a qualified social worker and social work team leader in Belfast, concentrating on family and childcare, fostering provision and inter-disciplinary working.

John McLaughlin is a lecturer in social work and coordinator on the Master's/Diploma in social work course at the Queen's University, Belfast. He teaches and researches on the subjects of health and disability, and, ethics in social work practice. Before joining Queen's, he was a team leader in health care, and a staff development and training officer with social services in Belfast. He is a supervisor and trainer for CRUSE and Bereavement Care (NI) and a tutor in Social Sciences with the Open University.

Kieran O'Hagan is an established writer and social work practitioner. He is currently lecturing at The Queen's University, Belfast. He worked in UK social work departments for nearly twenty years, completed social work placements in Calcutta and Los Angeles, and lectured in Victoria, Australia. He was a principal case worker (child abuse) in Leeds between 1987 and 1991. He has published many books and papers on social work topics, particularly family and childcare, crisis intervention and child protection. His work has been translated and published abroad. He is the author of *Emotional and Psychological Abuse of Children*, and a freelance consultant on issues revolving around emotional and psychological abuse.

John Pinkerton is Senior Research Fellow at the Centre for Child Care Research at Queen's. His principal interest is community-based work with children and families. He has recently completed a major research project monitoring children discharged from the care of local authorities. He is a committee member of the Northern Ireland-based Parents' Aid. He is a regular contributor to childcare and social work journals in Ireland and the UK.

John Turtle is a residential social worker and practice teacher in a children's home. After initially qualifying in social work, he joined a residential unit for adolescents. He later left this post and took up an appointment in South America, where he had responsibility for a number of developmental projects, aimed towards enabling and empowering local communities. He later returned to Belfast to work with adolescents in the voluntary sector. He is particularly interested in training residential workers for crisis intervention in residential settings.

Clare Waring is a qualified social worker and practice teacher based in a community mental health team (learning disability) in South Belfast. She established and coordinates a Respite care scheme for children and young people with disabilities. Previous to this appointment, she was a family and childcare social worker in Barnardos.

Subject Index

Author
Index